"Only once or twice a year does a book come along that makes me set aside priorities and stay up late into the night reading it in one sitting. I could not put this book down. I give it my highest recommendation and know it will be a runaway best seller!"—*Sheri Stevenson, Pasadena, CA*

"A beautiful spiritual journey of two women whose lives ran parallel but on opposite sides of the world and how love can reach the farthest side of the universe."
—*5 stars, Goodreads review*

"One of the most powerful books I have ever read! It is haunting, and the message never leaves you after you read it!"—*Betty Lee Hunter, Milwaukee, WI*

"It is a book that has something for everyone's soul, whether man or woman, son or daughter, or mother or father. Best seller for sure!"—*Paul Murry, La Canada Flintridge, CA*

"From the first page to the last, this is an utterly engaging and beautifully crafted story. Each character is complex but sympathetically drawn. Each main character has his or her own journey and character progression, with its serious tragedies and crises and its moments of joy. Following these smaller narrative arcs within the larger arc of the boy's life makes the reading experience compelling.

"I was asked to proofread this project, but the story so engaged me from the first page that I worked on it without pausing, even to eat. Based on my years of experience as an editor and a proofreader, I feel that this will be a best seller.

"Beautifully done on all fronts. I highly recommend *Dreams of my Mothers* to anyone looking for a quality read." —*Ulrike Guthrie, Bangor, ME*

"Author Joel Peterson has written a gripping book that sheds extraordinary new insights into the American dream as well as themes common to all human beings."—*Herb Chilstrom, St. Peter, MN, Presiding Bishop Emeritus of the Evangelical Lutheran Church in America*

"Soul-searing, but ultimately amazingly uplifting and heartwarming! I am definitely recommending this book to my book club. Here is a book that will deeply touch your heart on so many levels while providing insight and lessons that apply to us all.

"Lovingly, yet powerfully and beautifully written and filled with life lessons and anecdotes you'll want to write down and keep forever. This book, its characters, and their stories engrossed me and affected me as few I've ever read. It is a must read for anyone who believes that dreams, hope, and the human heart can change the world."—*Karen Guzzetta Mathison, Bigfork, MT*

"First-time author, Joel L. A. Peterson, has written a surprising, masterful, and beautiful story based on true events from his life that ranks it among the very best works of this type that I have ever read.

"If a pure fiction novelist wrote this story, it would likely be ridiculed as being too over the top—the story too unlikely and fantastical to be believed. But this is not the case with *Dreams of My Mothers,* because Peterson actually witnessed and experienced most of the events that form the basis for the story and set the stage for the book's characters. Adding to this, Peterson's narrative and exquisite prose is absolutely enthralling and instinctively believable and powerfully real.

"This story will pierce your heart a thousand times on its way to reaching the pinnacle of inspiration. Before you start this book, allot plenty of time—you just may not be able to set it aside. And even when you are finished, it will stay with you."—*Daryal Gant, former Director, Business Operations and Executive Council Member Jet Propulsion Laboratory/NASA, La Crescenta, CA*

Dreams of
My Mothers

Dreams of My Mothers

A Story of Love Transcendent

Joel L. A. Peterson

HPA | HUFF PUBLISHING ASSOCIATES

MINNEAPOLIS

Publisher: Huff Publishing Associates, LLC, Minneapolis
www.huffpublishing.com

Cover design by Printefex, www.printefex.com
Interior design by Dorie McClelland, www.springbookdesign.com
Manufactured in the United States of America

Quote from Luther's Large Catechism on page 71 is from *Book of Concord*,
p. 383, © Fortress Press, 2000.
"To the Little Boy in Korea Who Will Be Our Son" by Julie Ann Stine on
page 323 is from *Scope Magazine*, May 1970. Used with permission of the
Women of the ELCA.

Library of Congress Control Number: 2014951755

ISBN: 978-0-9908073-0-8

To Darleen—you are beyond all my dreams.

Contents

In the blood of the dying sun
I heard the screams of the mists of day
Floating in the ether of eternity.
And I saw the stellar tears of black night run
Through the dreams of my mothers to pool away
In the halls of heaven to christen their maternity.

As the crickets sang the chance song that is life
My soul ran red in the heat of the dark
And generations marched before my eyes.
For what is love but the Holy Strife
The cry of my soul but the flightless lark
And life the sound of starlight's whispered sighs.

Prologue

JUNE 1957, MINNEAPOLIS

Elmore Lindquist was driving way past the speed limit as he revved his two-year-old Chevy Bel Air through the streets of Minneapolis.

"There's something WRONG! There's something WRONG!"

Elmore's wife, Ellen, was screaming. She was sitting in the passenger seat, gripping the car door handle with one hand while pushing hard against the glove compartment cover in front of her. Her body was rigid and locked in pain and fear, her belly huge and bulging with an eight-month-old baby. And she was bleeding on a towel she had placed on the car seat, and the flow had increased alarmingly in just the last five minutes. As a trained nurse, she knew that there could be only a couple of causes for her bleeding. And neither was good, and both were very, very serious. She knew that her life and the life of her unborn baby were in real and immediate danger. She needed to see a doctor. Now.

Chapter 1

Noah

H i, Mr. Lindquist. I'm Jackie, your driver. Here, let me take that."

With those words she reached down and grabbed the roller bag's handle out of Noah's hand, started walking to the SUV, and opened the passenger-side, rear door when she reached the vehicle. She noted that the man was only slightly taller than herself.

"Thanks, Jackie, but why don't I get in front. People around here don't usually have drivers, and it'll look odd for me to be in the back seat."

Noah opened the front passenger door and got in. It was about a fifteen-minute drive along County Road 22 from the private airfield to the small, rural Minnesota town of St. Peter through gently rolling farmland with swaying stalks of corn that stretched from horizon to horizon.

This landscape was very familiar to Noah. The land and its people and their values had left their mark on his identity, outlook, and the values cherished in his soul. They were his mother's values after all. Noah knew how fortunate he was and how unlikely his journey had been. With a certain sense of loss, he knew how distant he now was from the small town to which he was headed. And he thought of how even more distant he was from another smaller village he'd left much longer ago.

He knew there was a woman waiting for him at the end of this short ride through stretching farmland. He was on his way to see one of the two women who had made his improbable journey possible, whose sufferings, dreams, beliefs, and whose different but equally unshakable senses of duty had led to his first airplane ride, so many years ago, even as they had ultimately led to his airplane ride today.

Jackie tried to make some polite conversation, inquiring about the flight. It was unheard of for a sleek corporate jet to come into Mankato Regional Airport, and she was beyond curious. But his short responses and outward gaze across the waving fields signaled her to let Noah be alone with his thoughts.

She wasn't sure who her passenger was, but she had never seen someone so seamlessly polished and put together in a perfectly tailored, dark blue suit and perfectly creased trousers that set off the man's trim figure. His starched white shirt and tightly knotted light blue tie and gleaming black leather shoes expertly completed the polished look.

Hmmmm . . . coming in on his high-class private jet . . . must be some kind of major bigwig . . . but at least he's not too stuck-up to ride up front with me.

He exuded an executive presence, an aura; it spoke of refinement, worldliness, power, and wealth. He had the most striking green eyes and his face had an exotic blend of features that seemed at odds with the name on her manifest: Mr. Noah Lindquist.

But she sensed a humanness and normalcy—touched with a settled sadness—in him as she stole a glance to her right, before turning back to the winding two-lane county road. Normally, she was put off by and felt a deep divide between herself and people who seemed to have it all. She saw herself as part of the hardworking middle class, and usually she resented those who had too much and had never had to scramble the way she did daily. But this guy strangely didn't.

That's really odd . . .

The Citation V private jet was the sleekest, most high-end airplane that she had ever seen at Mankato Regional. This man sitting in her livery SUV was clearly from a world very different than hers.

There had been quite a buzz and much speculation among the ground crew as she had waited for the private jet's arrival. The only information they had was that the flight originated from a private runway near Atlanta. Jackie was booked to drive this man back to Mankato Regional tomorrow, early afternoon.

Who is this guy? Why would he come to St. Peter, Minnesota? And who is he visiting in a small condo complex in a town like St. Peter?

Damn! He looks so freaking rich! . . . must be nice to be born lucky

Chapter 2

Hee Ae

She swallowed from the bottle again, and her body shuddered. She hated her poverty that made her cheap. It was 1967 in the underdeveloped, third world country of South Korea. Poverty and poorly educated women like her were all too plentiful and all too cheap. In her hate and growing numbness, she didn't notice she was crying.

She felt so dirty.

She hated herself for how unclean she felt.

She hated the world for making her hate herself.

Her skin crawled, even as it grew numb from the alcohol. She hated the smell of sex still on her body.

It was a cold morning, even for a fall day. The sun threw off little warmth as it clawed its wan, remote way up the morning sky and had not yet chased the frost from the brown, autumn-scorched land. Yet its light devoid of warmth spread a golden haze through the ice crystals in the upper reaches of the sky and flung tiny rainbows that sparkled among the grass blades and spider webs.

It was midmorning as she shivered and gazed at the twinkling tiny rainbows and raised the bottle to her lips. Her swallows were visible in the movement of her neck muscles—long, slow gulps as the liquid tortured its way down her throat. Her body shuddered involuntarily from the assault of the alcohol as she lowered the bottle and let it hang heavy and dead from her hand.

Lee Hee Ae stood from her leaning stance against the mud wall of the old farmhouse where her one rented room was home to her and her son. Her body's convulsion seemed to have spread the warmth of the alcohol to her limbs and face. She stumbled and clung to the wall and drunkenly returned to her room. And her prison. She looked at the prison that trapped her in a life sold for a few dollars. For her, prison was her four-year-old son. And in her drunken pain, she hated the memories before the betrayal and everything that he represented and implied. She held a switch in her hand.

Lee Young Nam stared at his mother through eyes that were startlingly green. She exuded the stench of alcohol and morning halitosis, assaulting him with each rasp of her labored breathing. She swayed in the doorway, the look of pain and drunken belligerence twisted and blatant on her face. Somehow out of place, tears were running their trails down her high-cheeked, Asian face. Her hand gripped and tightened on the switch in short spasms. She took a step, staggered and fell sprawling on her face. The bottle from her other hand went spinning across the room to thump against the one, small, black lacquered chest.

"You piece of shit! You fucking little bastard! On top of everything! See what you've made me do now!"

The words were barely intelligible in her drunken and enraged slurring. The words roared from her contorted face as she pushed herself up from her headlong sprawl. She pitched and swayed her way to her feet and took another step.

"I'll whip you for what you've made me do to my life."

She hissed the words and spittle hit the little boy's face. He pushed himself, pumping his tiny legs and scooting rearward, until his back hit the room's corner. Trapped. The stench and the hate and the words kept coming. Young Nam started to cry and whimper.

"No Mommy! Please, noooo! I'm sorry! I'm sorry! PLEASE DON'T HURT ME, MOMMY!"

He whimpered in little sobs, fear making his green eyes into globes too big for his face.

"Shut the fuck up! You bastard piece of crap!"

She screamed as she stood and swayed and stenched in front of the cowering little boy.

"Because of you, my life is shit. Because of you, I beg and whore myself to feed your filthy bastard American face."

The boy screamed silently, his mouth forming into a little thespian's mask of horror, mute and gagging, as the hand rose at the end of his mother's arm.

A flash and a blur. Air was cut in two with a whispered, sinister protest that was quiet, but unmistakably clear through the guttural, drunken rantings. The branch was supple, not yet dried in the kilns of autumn, still green in the center. It whip-whished through air and slashed across the tiny boy's face. The branch left a line of red, perfectly surrounded by an outline of white, shocked, and disbelieving skin. Skin that parted as blood ran down the boy's face

Whip whish, the backhand. Snap-whish, the forehand. Over and over, again and again. Young Nam tried to ward off the slashing switch with tiny, uplifted hands. His forearms bled where the branch hit. The whipping started to increase in speed as Young Nam's mother grew frenzied in her drunken madness. She shrieked and muttered obscenities, her arm thrashed the switch wildly. And the boy bled and whimpered and cowered in his corner.

His whimpering pleas seemed only to infuriate her more. The pain was intense and throbbing, each slash injecting a stunningly sharp spike of pain. With each slash, skin split over already-gashed and bleeding flesh. Blood splattered the walls in a fine spray of droplets. The blood stained the yellowed and peeling rice paper that hung from the walls by the dusty residue of long-ago glue.

Suddenly, his mother reached out for him. She grabbed him by the front of his shirt, lifted him off the floor, and brought him dangling and dazed to her face. The pain and the smell of alcohol were overpowering. Young Nam gagged and gasped as his mother's hold tightened at the front of his neck, and she breathed her alcoholic stench in reeking puffs of exertion in his face.

"I . . . HATE . . . YOU!"

She shrieked the words.

They burst up from the pits of her soul, driven by her heart's tortured rage and the pain of despair and self-loathing. She screamed the words at her tiny and gagging and bleeding son, words meant for the entire world, but vented and focused on the only thing over which she had power. Just as suddenly as she'd picked him up, she threw him back down, and Young Nam landed in a heap on an elbow that soon started to swell.

As he looked up, he saw his mother slump to the floor, first onto her knees, then onto her hands as well. She started sobbing violently. She did this for what seemed a very long time to Young Nam. He watched, too frightened to say anything. Watched as he huddled in his corner of his one room hovel-home. As she wept on her hands and knees, his inebriated mother mumbled things that were impossible to comprehend between her tears and erratic, labored breathing. Except for the words ". . . why did he leave *me*?"

Without warning, she vomited. It gushed forth in a solid liquid stream of yellowish-brown, splattering up from the floor when it hit. Putrid and watery. It spewed out of her gagging and drooling mouth, each convulsion of her body pushing out another watery stream of acrid and fetid vomit. It puddled onto the lumpy, uneven floor between her hands as her head hung low, hair falling down over her face and soaking in alcohol-laden, mucus-filled puke. The smell was nauseating to Young Nam.

The initial retching spasm of his mother had splashed him. He sat huddled and whimpering, vomit and blood mixed on his face. He breathed in the wheezing, involuntary inhalations that continued even after there were no more tears left to cry. He was very, very frightened. Abruptly, Young Nam's mother fell completely prone. Fell right into the pool of her stomach's prior contents, then rolled slowly over onto her back. Vomit coated her face and dripped from her hair. She slurringly whispered her son's name.

"Young Nam . . ."

"Yes, Mommy."

"I'm sorry . . . Little One . . . I'm so sorry . . . Young Nam . . . help . . . me . . ."

The words were slow and drawn out as her head lolled from side to side. Young Nam moved close to his mother.

"What is it, Mommy?" he pleaded in his tiny voice, fearful concern overcoming his pain and revulsion.

". . . I'm . . . dying."

With those words, Hee Ae convulsed once more, and her eyes rolled back as she lost consciousness.

"MOMMY! NO! PLEASE DON'T DIE! I PROMISE TO BE GOOD! PLEASE, MOMMY, PLEEEASE . . ."

He flung his tiny body on his mother's passed out form as she lay in her puke. He was terrified. All he had in the world was this woman. He had nothing and no one else.

The boy kept making his pleas to his unconscious mother. For all her anger and abuse, she was also the only one in his four-year-old world that showed him love. The only one who cared for him. The only one who ever held him, who fed him, and whose love he craved.

Four-year-old Young Nam believed the words slurred by his mother. He believed she was dead. He believed that she had just died and that there was no one to protect him, no one to love him, that he was all alone. He was filled with a mindless terror and loneliness beyond comprehension.

He was wrong in his belief. She wasn't dead, just unconscious from too much alcohol. But her death was real to him. He believed her words as small children do. In his terror and loneliness, he began to cry and shake uncontrollably, a wailing, desperate cry of anguish and fear from a four-year-old who believed that his mother had just died.

And that he was alone forever.

Chapter 3

Noah

Noah Lindquist felt the vessel surge and shudder beneath him as the ship struggled through the morning seas, slowly gaining on the harbor city of Busan, Korea. He hadn't slept well. Beyond the lack of comfort in the steerage accommodations, there had been his consuming thoughts and haunted memories. He wasn't sure now, as he stood in the clawing winter air, whether he had relived memories or whether they had been dreams.

It was a cold December morning in 1981. The sky was mostly dark, the deep violet of predawn. Venus, the morning star, hung low above the horizon, a single, stellar diamond glowing among the pink blush of the sun's rumored arrival. Water splashed against the cutting bow of a rusted and weary ocean-going ferry. The ship had known the gleam of new paint and well-preserved decks too long ago. The water surged and splashed and flung bow spray up against the faded paint of her name. It was written in Japanese, the slash and swirl of Asiatic brush strokes amid the streaks of rust and corrosion. The brush strokes said "Haru Maru"—Strong Spring.

Noah leaned forward and gripped the metal of the lifelines. The Sea of Japan was roaring in his ears and the salt-laden wind scraped and slapped at his face and whipped his hair as he stood on board the rusting hulk that plied the ferry lines between Shimonoseki, Japan, and Busan, Korea. Noah shivered from the chill as he began to think of what was to come and what once was.

At eighteen, Noah looked more like thirteen or fourteen, barely pubescent. He was slight and short. His face had a soft femininity about it, which caused his few years to appear even younger, except for his bushy-black eyebrows. His hair was dark chocolate with amber highlights that glowed like molten copper when the wind flipped a lock so it glinted in the sun. He had the clear expression of his genes. He looked like what he was: a random mix of Korean and Irish. His eyes epitomized it—green eyes staring out through an Asian slant. But those eyes contained a look that seemed too wary for a face so young.

The vessel had finally reached the outer islands that guarded the mouth of Busan Harbor. Noah felt it shudder as speed was cut. The approach into the harbor would be slow and cautious. The currents and winter winds made entry a tricky and difficult passage, especially in light of the heavy port traffic and the gaggle of anchored freighters and roaming fishing boats that choked the harbor approaches. As the ship slowly sliced the icy waters toward the harbor, the sounds of gulls, ships, water, and a waking city surrounded Noah's lone figure gripping the lifelines in the chill dawn.

He smelled the salt as the sea shattered against the ship's bow, heard the calls of weaving gulls and the growing vibrancy of the approaching city. The sun was coming above the horizon, shedding a thousand rays of dawning pink, yellow, and red. The Sea of Japan glittered like fool's gold along the distant eastern horizon and high cirrus clouds reflected the rose garnet of the rising sun.

Noah's green and wary eyes were focused elsewhere, not seeing the ageless spectacle of sunrise. His gaze was directed toward the closer, imminent harbor. Toward the city of Busan. And what awaited him there.

Busan was a bustling port city. In 1981 it was rushing headlong into the arms of first world industrialization, helping to pull Korea out of obscurity into the emerging ranks of the newly industrialized countries—a soon-to-be nouveau riche nation challenging the old-money states of the West.

Noah had been born in South Korea on Easter Sunday in 1963. He had been born with a different name, Lee Young Nam, and his mother had been a starving, poor peasant, the kind that graced the covers of *Life* magazine and *Time* when boat people, Asian refugees, and America's distant adventures were brought to the doorstep of middle America, the way the family cat would bring back the grisly details of its night's labors. And the alien Asian face would stare the thousand-year-old look from the magazine cover. A similar face belonged to his mother, a woman whom he had known as the center of his universe when he had been a tiny and frightened child in a nearly forgotten world of long ago.

Noah had never known the man who gave him his Irish half. He had been born the bastard son of that Korean peasant woman, fathered by a white cracker of an Irish-American soldier from a place called Alabama.

He was thinking of that woman and the fact that she was waiting for him in the approaching port.

He wasn't sure whether it was the cold, penetrating wind, or the deeper, imbedded memories that caused his body to spasm in shivers. He'd been thinking of things long buried in his brain and being, events he had not dared to relive, but now these countless memories were gushing back. He could remember so many things, even from when he was two years old, but each memory was a snippet, a looped movie of a scene from his early childhood. These scenes simply began and ended with no preamble or coda and often had no context. But each was complete and coherent within its endless memory loop. And they were not just his memory's photographic or moving picture, but had sound, dialogue, smells, touch, hunger, fear, and pain—always. Noah let himself open the curtain of his memory to watch the disjointed memory loops and to relive events from when he was a four-year-old.

THE SOUNDS WOKE HIM. And the smell. He lay in the dark and listened to sounds he did not want to hear and breathed air he did not want to breathe. He had heard the sounds too many times and knew the smell intimately. He knew their meaning and what tomorrow would bring because of them. Sex was a very familiar thing—and he was four years old.

The little boy wondered as he watched. Who was this animal groping his mother in his dark little home? He watched the shadow that was his mother on her back, watched her legs spread wide above the grunting animal's waist, watched her body jerk with the man's animal thrusting. He turned away from the frenzied movements to stare at the rough of the opposite wall and breathed the fetid smell of sex and listened to the prostitution of his mother.

Amid the groans and rhythm and breathing of the sex-made sounds, the boy heard the forlorn baying of an unknowable dog. He listened to shut out the world inside the little room. He listened to be as far away as he could while physically trapped in the grunting heat. He listened to drive away his fear.

But his fear never left.

As sleep eventually crept around the edges of his thoughts, the little boy knew there would be money in the morning and later some food. He also knew what else the morning would bring at the hands of a mother driven to madness by the liquor she would use to dull her shame and tame the monsters of her soul. The little boy whimpered quietly in the dark and his tears wet his stained pillow. Young Nam was afraid of the pain and drunken fury that waited for him on the opposite side of the far-off sunrise.

The lone dog barked small and distant beneath the cold stars.

The ship's horn startled Noah back to the present. He focused his eyes and looked around, self-conscious that someone might have seen him vacant and staring, his mind a million years and a thousand wounded hearts ago. No one was around. Just the continuing roll of the ship beneath his feet, making him shift his weight back and forth, his body grip and sway against the lifelines.

The day was brightening, if still no warmer. Noah could hear the gulls calling. He realized that he was getting wet from the flung mist that reached up from the ship's bow cutting its way through the salty water of the harbor, reached up in a prismatic blanket of tiny sea pieces. Each sheet of gossamer mist felt like a soft, icy caress. And each caress had left gathering layers of sea dew, slowly soaking Noah.

The December sea wind was penetrating. Noah could feel the cold of the silver chain and pendant he always kept around his neck, feel its sharp and metallic presence against his skin, even under his coat, shirt, and T-shirt. It made him think of how incredibly unlikely the string of events and circumstances had been that had brought him here, on a Japanese ferry pitching and plying toward a meeting with his long ago birth mother. A meeting that he thought could never take place.

The three lines of Korean script on the pendant given to him by his mother, the pendant that was now pressing its cold against his skin, was the last address he and his mother had shared in Korea along with her name and his Korean name. All in neatly engraved Korean letters.

His memory's library was playing one video loop after another. Each looping reel reawakened a particular time when he had lived another life. Some of the memories were first hand, others were what he had been told about events and people he might not have known or remembered directly. All these memories had always been an undertow throughout his young life that had pooled and pulled him, often subconsciously. He cast his memory's net into the dark, pooling waters of a past in which he had learned to stop wading for the fear and pain and unanswerable questions that lurked beneath their surface.

THE VOICES ROSE into the cloudless sky of summer, above the thatched roofs to mingle eventually with the midday sun.

"CRIPPLE . . . CRIPPLE . . . CRIPPLECRIPPLECRIPPLE!"

The words chanted in the bagpipe voices of small children. Piercing, gaining rhythm, cadence, and intonation. Rise and fall. Echo and chant. The tempo and pace quickening until the words fell apart, breaking against the mind's ear into meaningless syllables. Out of the verbal chaos grew a new rhythm and cadence that quickly gained strength and definition.

"SOUVENIR-BASTARD . . . SOUVENIR-BASTARD!"

Children are born neither good nor bad, but simply are born. Good and bad are thrust upon them as they grow older, by a world that defines itself in such terms and words. In reality, the world just is. And so children do things that just are, with little understanding and no guilt. So a child's cruelty merely is. Pure, simple, and terribly stark. It has not been dulled by drilled-in social rules and formalities, not sheathed in pretend politeness. It is a naked blade, cold and hard, glinting as it cuts and jabs and gores its victim.

Young Nam broke from the group of children, broke from the chanting and the torment. He fought free from the cutting, cruel jabbing and taunting surrounding him. Atop his scrawny body sat a head that appeared too big; his body had a belly that bulged with starvation and worms. His tiny legs pumped furiously as his spindly arms flailed in rhythm with those legs. Tears and snot and sweat were streaming down his face, bright shirt and shorts dirtied and torn. And there was blood that oozed from his lip and down his chin, blood that flashed bright red on his arms and knees as the toothpick limbs pumped their running motions in the sun.

Freedom was a pounding heart and gasping lungs and feet that carried him away from the chants, the profanity, and the guiltless, innocent cruelty of fists, kicks, and rocks thrown by other children. With his tormentors falling behind him—they had had enough fun and were not inclined to pursue more than halfheartedly—Young Nam ran as fast as he could. He ran with his blood roaring and pumping in his ears, ran until he reached the solitary sanctuary of a remote rice field. If freedom was a thudding heart, then safety was distance and solitude.

He ran until he couldn't run any more. He flopped his form down on a paddy dike. He dropped from exhaustion. The tiny boy gasped to still his rushing blood as he lay on the grassy rise, his boney ribs surging and falling rapidly in time with his gasps.

Young Nam had been punished—severely beaten—when he'd been caught crying. In Korea, little boys were supposed to become men someday. And men don't cry. Not Korean men. He had had that beaten into him as it was beaten into nearly all Korean boys. Physical punishment was the norm in Korean society. It was simply seen as the way boys are shaped into men.

But he was alone now. And he was not a man, but barely a four-year-old boy. The tears came unwanted and unstoppable. Shuddering sobs wrenched from the depths of his heart. Sobs that shook his tiny body as he lay curled on his side, skinny arms hugging bleeding, boney knees to his chest. Curled and fetal, wheezing with his mouth agape and his face contorted, blood oozed from his lip and mixed with the tears running down the side of his face to pool and drip from the corner of his mouth.

Young Nam did not know why his life was the way it was. Why the world seemed so pointedly cruel. At his age, there were a great many things that he did not know or understand. He didn't know how he differed or how racial difference or physical deformity were perceived. He didn't know the meaning of his differences from those around him. He didn't know the social implications of his separateness, how it impacted his mother, through what filters others saw him, and how it created a gulf between him and his society.

He only knew there were stares that were icy cold or shocked and repulsed, that the air could turn hostile or fill with revulsion in a heartbeat, that people young and old openly shunned him and flaunted their indifference to his existence. Young Nam had learned that danger and rejection lurked in every stranger. His reactions from today's incident—fear, confusion, humiliation, and pain—welled up from the dark, deep reaches of his tiny being and flooded his starving form.

As he cried, lost among a maze of nearly identical paddy dikes, hawks circled in great arcs overhead, riding the sun-warmed currents like sailboats of the air. They circled and called to one another, the sounds rising to vanish into the infinite heaven above.

As he stood at the ship's rail, gazing through the present into his past with time-distant, vacant eyes, Noah could still hear the hawks, smell the grass, and taste his tears. He had always known that he was from two different worlds, cultures of West and East, two races separated by continental distances. Yet he had never felt a member of either. He had always felt set apart, stared at, questioned, different.

Noah had always had to explain himself; he didn't seem to fit into any simple category. Perhaps it was partly because people like him were tied to a part of its history that America did not seem to want to remember. Although Noah had been born a decade after the Korean War, he was the product of its ongoing aftermath. Some historians refer to the Korean War as the Forgotten War. Unlike the Second World War, which is remembered and celebrated as a great victory for freedom and the American vision of democracy, or Vietnam, which is remembered as America's worst defeat, scrutinized and analyzed as an example of American policies gone wrong, the Korean War was neither victory nor defeat. Americans did not want their sons to "die for a tie," as the 1950s slogan had made clear. And America did not want to remember that more than 36,000 men did in fact die for a tie. Americans remember the Berlin Airlift, the Berlin Wall, and the Cold War. But they can't seem to find a simple category or narrative in which to put their Forgotten War. So it, and people like Noah, who are inherently linked to this forgotten chapter of history, are put into a closet that's rarely opened—the contents overlooked and unexamined and therefore unexplained.

This made Noah's search for identity and belonging harder than it might have been as he grew up. People guessed him to be Chinese, Japanese, or Vietnamese. But rarely did they guess Korean. Despite 36,000 deaths and decades of having more than 50,000 servicemen per year stationed in this distant, foreign, tiny country, Americans— always more focused on Europe, the West, and black/white racial issues—could find no national reason to have Korea register in its social conscience.

So Noah was left always having to explain himself and always finding his story too complicated to fit in a neat little elevator pitch. He had grown up envying those who could explain their place in the world, in society, and to themselves with a simple phrase: "I'm Irish . . . I'm Italian . . . I'm Navajo . . . I'm Jewish . . ." Americans did not seem to think it odd that such descriptions automatically meant being American, just a clarification of the version they were. Noah knew there could be negative stereotypes associated with such pithy descriptions, but usually not confusion or disbelief. He found that the simplest way to explain who he was when asked—and he was always asked, "What *are* you?"—was to answer, "I don't know, I'm adopted." It was simple, mostly true, and seemed to meet the need to fit a clear category that satisfied the questioner.

"Oh . . . *adopted* . . ."

But it wasn't just American society. Korean society had never accepted him as Korean either, but the reasons were different. Biracial children, like him, had been humiliating symbols of American domination and contamination to a society proud yet insecure in its history, culture, and ethnic purity. Up through the 1960s and into the 1970s when Noah had been an infant and a small child, it was not uncommon for Korean women to abandon their American-fathered children at birth. The shameful refuse of human passion, loves, and lusts, were left to die in the cold of a Korean winter, among the weeds and snow, left to die crying their infant wails for food that would not come and warmth that would not be given. Occasionally, racial crimes of murder claimed some who survived into adulthood. Racially mixed meant racially impure.

They were the unwanted human bycatch of two races and cultures that clashed on too many fronts, too many ignorances, and too many prejudices. They were what the military might refer to as collateral damage: an unfortunate but unavoidable by-product of political forces leaving their messy, bystander human waste. And, in the aftermath of the Korean War, those global political forces had resulted in 50,000 American troops—lonely, scared, and isolated young men, far from home—placed as sacrificial lambs to deter a much feared, ever-possible repeat of North Korea's Communist aggression. Those young GIs were placed among a populace that was devastated by a brutal civil war and struggling in national poverty. It was a poverty that made too many women sell themselves to scared and lonely American men. Collateral damage all around.

And Noah had not been fully accepted by American society. He wasn't white to a color-conscious country and he wasn't black—black/white being the obsessed, fractured racial fault line—but he was short and slant-eyed, and the average American couldn't notice any splash of Irish features. Nor would it have made a difference. Racially mixed was racially tainted. He wasn't white, meaning he wasn't normal.

A Chink, a Jap, a Gook.

In America, he represented a growing foreignness and a growing complexity creeping into the fabric of everyday life and America's social tapestry. Especially in the rural Midwest, Noah had grown up with the stares and the questions with no simple answers—for himself or those who stared and asked.

What *are* you?

Where are you from?

No . . . I mean *originally*?

In his rural America, as in Korea, he was an outsider. Contaminated blood, shot through with foreignness. Neither claimed him a native son, and Noah, for his eighteen years of life, had felt an outcast of both. Noah's story was just too far outside the common boundaries, known reference points, and comfort zones of most Americans or Koreans for either to connect or care. The conversation would naturally end with his mostly true, but overly simple answer, and the response: "Oh . . . *adopted* . . ."

Noah had been adopted by third-generation American Swedes who had four children of their own before they plucked him out of a Korean orphanage. He'd gone from rural Korea to rural, American Midwest heartland when he was almost seven years old. He thought of his midwestern family, his blonde brother and sisters. He could see the faces of his parents, a picture that floated into his mind's eye like a sepia toned photo: long Scandinavian faces radiating the reserved Lutheran midwestern morality of their heritage and upbringing. He could see their earnestness staring at him from behind those long, high noses, through deep-set eyes. He remembered when he had first met his mother's bright blue eyes, that earnestness, as he came off an airplane on a cold winter night.

But that memory was much later, well after the ones running their looping scenes in his brain now. He thought about what would happen today in the slowly approaching port; it occurred to Noah that his story was not getting any simpler. He refocused his thoughts on those earlier events and the life he had shared with his Korean mother.

Chapter 4

Hee Ae

A s mealtime approached, he came home. And she knew immediately what had happened. She paused long enough to look up at her son from her squatted position. The tear trails down dirty cheeks, the blood still oozing from his lip and one knee, the torn shirt, the bruises and scratches, all told a familiar story, plain as words on a page. She looked back down and resumed scooping the pickled cabbage from its sunken earthen pot. She would be making *kimchee* for dinner, the spicy, hot cabbage dish that defined Korean cooking.

Though her face remained impassive, her chest snapped taut with impotent, mounting fury and guilt. Guilt that surfaced like some ugly sea creature broaching the waves of her conscious thoughts. Pain's venom stabbed fang-driven into her heart.

It's your fault, whispered the grotesque sea serpent of her guilt. *You are the reason; your sins are paid by your son, over and again. Your sins.*

As she rose to carry the cabbage to her cooking area, she stole another glance at her tiny child as he pumped the hand pump near her in the courtyard, the water coming out in fitful splashes. He deflected the pump's water onto his face, washing the day's humiliation, at least the visible traces, from his face. The pump looked huge next to the four-year-old, and he had to reach up for the handle and use his weight to bring it down. He didn't ask for any help. He never did. And he never spoke about what happened, but moved in silence until he had shoved it all away somewhere inside himself.

It must have been some of the other children, she thought with mixed anger and relief—relief because children rarely caused serious injury. But she knew that, as this had not been the first time, it would not be the last. And it would only get worse. She turned out of the courtyard with her cabbage and walked briskly to where she was preparing the rest of her meal in the cooking pit near her room. It was a rare luxury to have so much food to prepare, even a chicken. And it was thanks to the generosity of her landlord. His generosity highlighted her extreme poverty and brought on a sense of shame in Hee Ae for what it forced her to do sometimes to get what little money she could; she tried to keep her leaden shame crammed below her conscious thoughts. Her face was frozen and unreadable.

As Young Nam washed himself, Lee Hee Ae took the rice pot off the charcoal block she used for cooking and started scooping rice mixed with barley into small metal bowls. She finished making the kimchee. She set the rice and a boiled chicken along with the kimchee on a low, black lacquered table. It had mother-of-pearl inlaid in a floral design at each corner. She carried the table into the one room that was home for her and her son.

The room in which Hee Ae was setting the table was about twelve by ten feet. It had one small window, high up and near a corner. The window was covered with rice paper, but no glass. The paper let in a feeble light. The walls were covered with rice paper that served as a kind of wallpaper, as was the floor, though a different, more durable version. Both were equally uneven, wavy and bumpy. The wallpaper was yellowed and peeling along the seams and in the corners, where the glue had long ago turned to dust. The cooking area was a semi-outdoor, half-enclosed dirt-floored pit. It was connected by paper-covered sliding doors to the room.

There was no electricity and no plumbing for water or toilets,

only the communal hand pump connected to its well back in the
courtyard, surrounded by sunken clay pots that stored various
foodstuffs and a reeking, open-pit communal outhouse located
outside the farmhouse's enclosed walls. Hee Ae cooked using
cylindrical charcoal. She bought two or three pieces from the
charcoal peddler when she could afford it. The cooking pit's floor
was sunken, a few feet below the room's floor level, and was located
partially under the room's floor, with the smoke vented through a
chimney that ran under the room. This made a part of the room's
floor heated and warm to the touch and was the extent of heating in
the Lees' tiny home. But too often Hee Ae did not have the money
for charcoal, and there was no heat.

The room was part of a larger, thatch-roofed farmhouse that
contained a few stables and a small courtyard, fenced in with straw
and wood. There was a time when the farmhouse would have been
home to one extended family. Not so long ago, a time when most
farm families owned their land and worked it and lived together,
aunts and uncles, brothers and sisters, children and grandchildren,
all would have been farming the family's land and tilling the farmhouse's rooms. Each room would have a different, but blood-related
nuclear family. But now, the rooms were half empty, with the occu-
pied ones serving as homes to the likes of Lee Hee Ae, the remnants
of the past owners serving as landlords.

The crude structure of rock, mud, and straw walls, dusty orange-
brown, rough and pockmarked, rose to meet an ancient, gray-
brown thatched roof. In the rafters and awnings pigeons roosted,
their droppings making white and gray runs down the walls.

When it was time, she called him. They ate in silence, mother and
son. She thought how small he was as he shoveled mouthfuls of rice,
mixed with barley, using his oversized spoon. Despite his size and
starving-boy fragility, he had something hard and untouchable in him,
she thought. She wondered about what was inside his so-young soul.

It scares me sometimes. Maybe it's just me seeing things, maybe it's my fears and guilt, but I swear I can see a look in his eyes, a look a child his age shouldn't have, a sort of hard knowingness. It's such an unfeeling kind of knowingness, fueled by what seems like a cold, adult-world detachment. A look that understands too well.

And what does he understand about me? Can he love with that sort of thing inside him? Do you love, my little son, do you? Do you love me?

Young Nam picked up a piece of chicken, eating greedily. He licked off the skin that stuck to his fingers before having more spoonfuls of rice. He didn't eat like a normal child. His was an efficient, urgent devouring like the starving animal that he was. He wasted none of his food. He had learned that substantive food was a rare item in his life. After cleaning all the meat off the chicken limb, he methodically ate the cartilage off the joints and cracked open the bones and sucked out the marrow.

Hee Ae watched, walking the shadowy halls of her thoughts.

He looks like his father. The same freckles, the same green eyes, the same American looks. And where is his father now? The old pain was still there. *How can my heart still hurt after these many years? After knowing that I was nothing to that American. But he had told those lies that I so wanted to believe . . .*

She thought of her son's quick mind. Her boy caught on to too many things uncomfortably fast. She thought of the potential that would never be for her son. She thought about how her son's life would simply be wasted by his poverty and the prejudice of his Korean world, the crippled limits of his deformity . . . and her own limits and demons. And she thought of the waste that was her life.

It was lonely in the echoes of her thoughts.

Hee Ae decided not to ask about what had obviously happened today. Nor would she punish him for crying. Childhood would end soon enough. What little childhood her son had, she would allow him that childhood tonight. He had obviously suffered enough for today. And she knew there would be more suffering in her son's future. Her boy may not fully understand how he differed, but she knew. Hee Ae knew that her boy would only grow to be more outcast and rejected in his Korean society. He would have plenty of opportunity to have his manhood tested then.

She continued to watch him. She watched and slowly strolled through those lonely corridors behind her eyes, halls with closets of memories and anxieties and guilt that rang with the fading echoes of laughter, agonies, and silence.

It's surprising how loud silence can be.

Chapter 5

Hee Ae

J ust wait a sec' will you, Hee Ae? What is your problem? Let me get the water off the fire and I'll be there," Hee Ae's friend yelled over her shoulder as she lifted the still-boiling water off the charcoal fire and onto the low table.

"We promised that we'd be there at four o'clock and now it's almost four-thirty!" Hee Ae's voice sounded wee and tiny as it filtered in from outside. But it still sounded fully irritated and impatient.

"What about Young Nam? Do you want me to carry him?" The woman looked down at the tiny tot of a six-month-old, sitting amid an encircling wrap of heavy blankets, a bottle of diluted formula clutched in one chubby hand.

"Oh, don't worry about him. He's all wrapped up in his blan- kets so he can't fall over—and he's sitting up pretty well without them anyway. So, he'll be fine. He's got his bottle, and we'll be right back . . . so, let's get going! We're late!" Hee Ae was in a hurry. Another friend had come up from Seoul to the dreary little village of Munsan where Hee Ae lived, and she was dying to catch up on what was happening in the big city.

At thirty-six, Hee Ae had a lot of rough mileage under her belt. She was by no definition an angel. Innocence had long since been stripped away by the sharp talons of a bitter life; been stripped away by a childhood and adolescence under the rule and abuse of a subsistence existence and Japanese occupiers; been stripped away with her clothes, as they had been torn away by a drunk, abusive, former husband who

had beaten her on their wedding night; been stripped away by years
of poverty and the constant struggle to stay alive. It had been stripped
away by the promises of many men and one particular man—who
had so shattered her heart and her life that neither would ever quite
heal—her son's father. The wound was still too fresh and was mostly
the driver of her current urgency.

So, she liked to party, to smoke, to drink, to find an excuse to laugh,
if only in the temporary intoxication of alcohol and a few friends.
And she needed to laugh, because she was so afraid of the times
when she wasn't laughing, when she was alone with her fractured life,
bleeding heartache, and the burden of her infant. She was afraid of
the lonely, struggling days and the lonelier nights trapped with the
mindless demands of a baby who was always hungry. She was afraid
of the emptiness of existing just to live. And she was afraid of a love-
less world, where she had desperately hoped for love in the seductive
lies of betrayal—and now searched in the embraces of too many, only
to find the same emptiness and pain after the lust.

She could not help but feel a deep, innate love for her son. But the
pain of what his father had done to her rose up in equal parts with
her love for her baby every time she looked at her infant son's face.
And in her pain, she sometimes resented the weight and responsibility her infant placed on her. Sometimes the pain of betrayal and
the burden of motherhood strained her life to the breaking point.
Her burden was worsened by the clear fact of her son's mixed racial
makeup. He was her living, breathing, and very public crime against
Korean racial purity; and being noticeably unmarried, her society
judged and condemned her. Her son was deemed the clear and convincing evidence of her monstrous moral failing.

Sometimes she just had to get away from it all, from the haunting,
hurting memories that lingered in the shape and lines of her son's
face and the color of his eyes. And the shame of the judgment of the
present, of all those who saw her as a whore for foreigners.

"Okay, okay, I'm coming!" Hee Ae's friend called to her as she waited impatiently outside. "Let me just take the water off the fire. I'll put it back on for dinner when we get back." The woman looked down again at the baby, swaddled in blankets, shaking his formula bottle and staring around with his big, weirdly-green infant eyes. She patted his head as she got up from setting the boiling pot of water onto a nearby low table.

Poor little guy, your mommy will be home soon.

She gave a last look over her shoulder at the tiny, wrapped-up form as she went through the door, a form that waved tiny and pink hands in the air, the kind of aimless flailing that babies tend to do. Pink and plump and tiny perfect little hands. The woman trotted out to catch up with her friend, Hee Ae. They both hurried up the unpaved road. Behind them, the gurglings and noises of the infant broke the silence of a still and vacant room.

What now? Hee Ae felt exasperated. She strode over the gravel with determination. She'd been gone only a few minutes, well, time had sort of slipped past, so maybe it was closer to forty-five minutes. Then the gnarled-up shopkeeper from down the street had popped his head into the little bar where Hee Ae had been drinking with her two friends. He bobbed his mass-of-wrinkles head in greeting and gummed toothless words, words that said that there was some horrible noise coming from her friend's place.

What the hell? Hee Ae had thought.

"You'd better go see if it's Young Nam," Hee Ae's friends had said.

So, she'd left. And now she walked in quick, clipped steps of irritation. As she approached her friend's apartment, screams that seemed impossible to be coming from anything human, much less a tiny infant, hit her like a hot and dangerous gust of wind. Hee Ae had never heard such a noise from her son or any other child. It was something more animal than human, the kind of semi-human screams heard only in the worst of a hot mid-summer nightmare dream, a whisky-fed dream, a fever-driven dream. They were the kind of screams that clutch the soul and grate against the marrow of one's bones. Fear ran its icy finger up her spine and worry puckered her brows into a sudden mash of black and plucked liner-painted hairs as her step quickened to a trot.

Oh God.

Oh God Oh God Oh God Oh God . . . !

The unspoken prayer streamed through her head as her breath whistled between clenched teeth and cheap lipstick. Whistled out in gasps as she stumbled over potholes in her high heels. She reached the sliding door, yanked it aside, leaving the remains of three broken and splintered fingernails, unnoticed, imbedded in the wood around the door's handle. The animal screams now filled her head, high-pitched and gasping, yet somehow guttural.

She burst into the room where she'd left the swaddled little form with the aimlessly waving pink and perfect little hands. With her infant son's screams washing over her, she stood frozen. The scene leaped into her vision and slammed into the core of her brain. She stood there for a second that seemed an eternity as time seemed to stop, allowing the sight before her to bore home to the core of her awareness, permanently stamping the scene into the very fibers of her brain. She stood there a second that was an eon, a second when her heart and time stopped.

Her son lay half in and half out of the still boiling-hot water that had been taken off the fire and placed on the low table. His left forearm and hand were immersed in the brutally hot water, propping him up. His other hand was flailing and thrashing violently, splashing in erratic, jerky spasms of pain. The water was trickling slowly out of the tilted pot, pouring onto the baby's shirt and chest. Blistered welts had formed, red and swollen, where the water had splashed his face. His left hand and both forearms were lobster-red, blistered and welted. Where he had touched the heated metal of the pot itself, his skin was scorched and gaping. The baby's mouth was stretched grotesquely wide into a frozen scream that never stopped, but it wasn't just his mouth—his whole face was frozen in lines of an instinctual, primal, animal fear and pain. That animal soul of anguish poured out from that scream-frozen, contorted face with its angry red welts and blisters. It spilled out in wave after shrieking wave from a tiny and red open mouth as the scorching water boiled his body's baby flesh.

As Hee Ae broke from her stunned trance—eyes impossibly wide and hands clutched up at her gasping mouth—she jumped toward her infant son. She started screaming "Oh God" over and over, mimicking the terror-filled screams of her son. She grabbed the infant away from the water in a move that was guided by instinct alone. Through her shock and horror, a cold, distant, and inhuman corner of her mind noted with fascination that pieces of her baby's hand and arm floated in the water, white and frothed, looking just like the boiled meat it was.

As she put the infant down, she realized that the bright and cheery little red shirt he wore was soaked in unbearably hot water. When Hee Ae went to remove the shirt, ragged pieces of her son's chest tore away, clinging to the fabric the way chicken skin sticks to the fingers of picnickers eating at a Sunday barbeque. She flung the shirt and the clinging, boiled skin aside and looked around wildly.

She finally spotted it, the chamber pot that sat discreetly in the corner of poor Korean homes of the time, filled with the piss of distressed bladders. She snatched it up, sending the lid and urine splattering against floor and wall. She emptied the remaining piss over her infant son, splashing him with the acrid fluid. Hee Ae hoped that the urine would help prevent infection.

The hospital had been a horror. White-jacketed foreigners jabbering in foreign gutturals as they cut away pieces of her baby's boiled skin, flesh, and fingers. She'd been lucky to have gotten her son there as fast as she had. An American Army jeep had stopped as she had held her dying son in her arms, stumbling along the dirt road that led to the American military base, where she knew there were doctors. The ride had been a bumpy blur; her arrival had been a flail of arms that lifted her tiny Young Nam away. And she stood there watching those giant and hairy beings in their white coats, jabbering their gibberish, and cutting away at the flesh of her infant son. All the scenes had been permeated in the red wash, rising blood of her fear. And her monstrous guilt.

Eventually, an interpreter had told her that her son might actually live. But it had been close. Hee Ae had been very close to having a boiled and dead son. But there would be a long road of recovery and agony for the baby and, later, the boy. He'd have to survive infections, surgeries, and skin grafts. But for now, he was still alive.

Chapter 6

Ellen

NOVEMBER 1968, ST. PETER

Ellen Lindquist answered the phone on the third ring. She prided herself on being efficient and prompt in everything she did, including answering her home phone. It was three o'clock in the afternoon on Tuesday, November 5, 1968. It was a slightly breezy day with winds gusting to fourteen miles an hour and temperatures in the mid-forties. The weather mattered in Minnesota—especially when heading toward winter—and Ellen lived in St. Peter, a small farming community in south central Minnesota. It also was election day, and Richard Nixon would beat Hubert Humphrey—Minnesota's own—for the presidency of the United States of America. Ellen, of course, had already gone to her designated polling location and had cast her vote.

"Hello, Lindquist residence. Ellen speaking."

Ellen answered the phone in a pleasant, cheery voice, saying the phone greeting that she had taught her four children. She always made sure to set the example, even if the children were not around. She spoke with the classic Minnesota yah-sure-ya-betcha accent. But like all Minnesotans, and Midwesterners in general, she thought she didn't have an accent and that all newscasters spoke just like her.

Ellen was a trim, attractive woman of thirty-eight. She had the classic blonde-haired, blue-eyed combination of her Swedish heritage and an air of energy and efficiency that hinted at her nursing school training. She smiled easily and often and had a musical laugh that she always ended with a descending exclamation of "Oooohhhh, deeeaaaarr."

"Mrs. Lindquist?" the voice asked, sounding small and distant in her ear.

"Yes, this is she."

"Good afternoon, Mrs. Lindquist. This is Julie Benson, with Lutheran Social Service."

"Oh, Miss Benson! It's good to hear from you. What a nice surprise! We are all so excited about our pending 'stork delivery' and working to get everything ready. Is everything okay?"

Ellen's face broke into a smile as she spoke into the phone.

"Mrs. Lindquist, I'm afraid I have some disappointing news. Your boy's mother has changed her mind and has reclaimed him. He is no longer available for adoption."

Ellen's face immediately lost its just-formed smile and she stared blankly, unable to think of what to say, just holding the phone against her ear. She felt like she'd just been kicked in the stomach. She could feel herself struggling for breath, even though she was simply standing in her kitchen on a brisk, sunny November afternoon.

No . . . this cannot be. This cannot be happening!

"Mrs. Lindquist? I'm so sorry . . . hello? Are you still there?"

"Yes." Blankly.

"It's what we call a disrupted adoption. It's rare, but it does sometimes happen. And we do, of course, respect the mother's wishes. And it's the law."

"Of course."

Ellen's gut kept hurting more, like there was a blood clot building from the phantom kick that was turning into a blood knot that was growing and tightening. She could feel her heart beating faster and harder. She was having a hard time focusing on Julie's words.

What was Julie saying?

". . . so if you're interested in exploring this alternative, I can get the process started."

"I'm sorry. What alternative?"

"I know that this is all quite sudden, and it must be hard for you. The other boy? You may recall that there was another boy that may be available. We think that he still is. But he has some medical issues, and that's why we all agreed on the first boy, even though he was a bit older."

"I see. And Lutheran Social Service is certain that it's final with our boy?" Ellen still thought of the boy, who was no longer going to be remotely "her boy," in her head and heart as her boy.

How could God let some woman take my boy away from me?

"You're certain that she won't change her mind? Has anyone tried talking to her?"

There was a silence on the phone that stood between Julie Benson and Ellen Lindquist a few seconds too long.

"Mrs. Lindquist, LSS would never attempt to talk a birth mother out of any decision she makes. We must respect the wishes of the birth mother and can never be perceived as pressuring a mother in any direction. I'm sure you realize that."

Another uncomfortable silence, two breaths beyond a polite duration.

"Yes. Of course." Ellen could feel the tears starting to form in the corners of her eyes and building their watery volume, threatening to burst the confines of her eyelids. She could feel the sobs pushing to get out in tandem with the threatening tears.

Ellen needed to get off the phone.

"This is all just so sudden and disappointing, Miss Benson. . . . Thank you for letting us know and for mentioning the alternative. Umm, you know I'll need to discuss all this with my husband. Please give us a few days, and we can call you back and let you know."

"You bet. Of course."

"Good-bye, Miss Benson."

"Good-bye, Mrs. Lindquist."

Ellen heard the click of Julie hanging up and the sound shifting to the dial tone of a dead line. She stood there with the dead phone against her ear and began to cry. She cried almost without sound, but her body shook with silent sobs.

Oh, God! It hurts so much, Lord. Losing this boy hurts so bad! It hurts because it reminds me of my real loss, of my real boy . . . God! How can you take away two boys from me?

The flashback nightmare started again. The feelings of it, the gut-wrenching anguish of it, and the black abyss of her loss. The black hole that had taken her son still sucked at her soul and her faith.

My God, my God, please help me through this!

Ellen Lindquist was a very God-fearing woman. She was raised surrounded by the strict traditions and beliefs of a spare and fervent Lutheran faith and morality. She believed in her God and in the sacrifice of her God's son, as example and atonement for her and all sins. She had held her beliefs all her life, from her earliest memories.

But there was a time in her life when it all was in doubt, when the chill night of her anguish and anger, rage and broken heart had made her question God, good, sacrifice, and her prior unquestioning faith. And it had happened on a June day in 1957. She remembered the bleeding, the fear, the pain. And the unending loss that still filled her with a void, despite four beautiful children.

You don't ever heal or "get over" the death of a child. Never.

Chapter 7

Ellen and Elmore

JUNE 1957, MINNEAPOLIS

Elmore Lindquist was driving faster than he would normally drive. Elmore was a very predictable man. He always obeyed traffic rules, speed limits, good manners, and his wife. And he always filed his taxes early. He was an accountant, after all. But today, this clear Friday afternoon on June 21, 1957, Elmore was driving way past the speed limit.

"I'm bleeding Elmore! I'm bleeding! Oh God! It's getting worse. It's NEVER felt like this before! There is something wrong! Elmore . . . HURRY for God's sake!"

Elmore gripped the wheel in his big hands without thinking as he pressed the gas more and shot a glance to his right and saw the fear on his wife's face. The Bel Air's engine revved under Elmore's encouragement. He was headed to Swedish Hospital in Minneapolis, and he couldn't be bothered to stop for the red light that he careened through—didn't slow a bit, only pushing the gas more. Swedish Hospital had been founded in 1889 and had a nursing school from where Ellen Lindquist—now frozen in the passenger seat of a speeding 1955 Bel Air with a bleeding pit in her swollen abdomen—had graduated.

Elmore bumped and skidded into the emergency entrance to the hospital. He slammed the car into park, not bothering to engage the emergency brake, and pushed out of the driver's seat. Without closing his car door, he ran around the front of the car and yanked the front passenger door open. He bent down and lifted Ellen up with one arm under her knees and the other under her armpit. Ellen wrapped her arms tightly around the back of his neck and pressed her face into his chest and under his chin. Adrenaline fueled Elmore's long strides toward the emergency room doors. Elmore was a big man, standing six feet two and tipping the scales at over two hundred pounds. He had no trouble carrying his petite but pregnant wife.

It hadn't dawned on Elmore that he should have let Ellen wait in the car while he went and got help and a gurney. There was no way he was going to leave his terrified, bleeding wife alone. Not for a second. He pushed his way through the doors turning and using the back of his free shoulder.

"MY WIFE NEEDS A DOCTOR NOW!"

Elmore was known for having an amazingly loud, deep, and authoritative voice. Driven by his own fears and pounding heart, that voice now sounded like the command of the Almighty himself.

Elmore's guts were trying to crawl out of the back of his throat. At least that's what it felt like. His wife was in emergency surgery where doctors were rushing to get their eight-month-old baby out of Ellen's belly. Elmore sat in a cheap Naugahyde chair in the OR waiting room at Swedish Hospital. His big frame was bent over with his elbows on his thighs just above the knee. His hands were folded—clenched—as if in prayer, except for his thumbs, which were sticking out and pressed against each other, their knuckles white with the pressure. Elmore's chin was pressing down on top of his folded fingers. His blue-grey eyes were blank and staring, but not seeing anything. He had a habit of chewing his tongue when he was thinking or stressed. His tongue was bleeding even as he kept chewing it.

Placenta previa.

Elmore had never heard of it until ten minutes earlier.

"We need to do a c-section immediately. Your wife is bleeding

profusely, and she's in danger. And your baby's heart rate is danger-
ously slow. It is likely in distress from your wife's placenta previa."

That's what one of the attending physicians had told Elmore as his
wife had been taken to surgery. What Elmore learned was that placenta previa was a condition where the embryo attached low in the
uterus, which meant that the placenta grew from that point of low
attachment and ended up covering the cervical opening, often in
the last trimester of pregnancy. There is no known cause and often
there are no symptoms, until a woman one day has vaginal bleeding.
And the blood will be bright red. In a few cases, the bleeding may
be significant and endanger the mother and the unborn child. It can
also be accompanied by contractions and premature delivery.

All of this had happened to Elmore's wife. And he would be
learning other unheard-of words before this day was done.

Thank God that the Carlsons were home, thought Elmore, as he
stared with his unseeing eyes.

The neighbors next door to Ellen and Elmore's home in Hopkins,
a new suburb of Minneapolis, were the sort of neighbors one would
expect to find in suburban Minnesota in 1957. The Carlsons were in
their early thirties with three children. Sandy volunteered for everything, was active in her church, and was a thrifty housewife—as
stay-at-home moms were referred to—while Ed worked for 3M in
sales. Sandy Carlson was looking after the Lindquist's two children,
three-year-old Christina and one-year-old Karsten. Christina had
been crying when Elmore had dropped her off with Sandy.

The three-year-old had never seen her mother cry or be so
uncontrollably upset. She couldn't understand why her mother kept
slamming down the phone after asking for Daddy at work. It scared
her to see her Mommy crying and talking to herself. And when her
Daddy had finally come home, he too seemed very upset and didn't
play with her like he usually did when he came home from work.
The girl's parents were like gods in her three-year-old world. Seeing

these titans clearly frightened and acting so strangely scared Christina very much. Years later, when Christina herself had had children, and they in turn had children, she would still remember this day clearly. Especially her fear and unnerved bewilderment.

Placenta previa. What in Sam Hill's name is a word like previa, *anyway?*

This question came to Elmore's mind. He never swore or used profanity, not even in his own head. The closest he ever came was saying, "What in Sam Hill's name" when others would have used "hell" or "damn" or "fuck." He was thinking of many things at the moment. He was thinking how much he loved his wife, how lost he would be without her, how she gave him so much purpose and direction. Ellen planned everything, organized everything, and drove everything—in a good way, at least from Elmore's perspective.

Time limped by as Elmore sat in his Naugahyde chair, with his praying hands and pressing thumbs, while his mind filled with agonizing thoughts and his guts kept threatening to crawl out of the back of his throat. He unthinkingly chewed on his tongue.

Chapter 8

Hee Ae

D o you have to smoke, Mommy? I don't like it. It smells bad."
Young Nam's high-pitched protest caught Hee Ae
by surprise and snapped her back to the present with a
silent, but seemingly thunderous screech of mental gears reverber-
ating in the corners of her brain. She hadn't even realized that she
was smoking, but she saw a burning half cigarette in her hand, its
glowing tip creating an upward curl of smoke that had thinned and
spread and made a growing haze in the air.

"Did you enjoy your food, Young Nam-ya?"

She changed the subject, ignoring the boy's complaint. Her son's
plate was completely empty, except for the crushed and gnawed
bones of what were once pieces of chicken. The little boy had
sucked the marrow and chewed the cartilage from every bone, leaving only a pile of bone splinters.

Hee Ae had barely touched her food. The flood of memories had
washed clean her appetite, and her stomach had an acid, sour feel.
The cooked chicken reminded her too much of her child's boiling.

"Mmmmm! I just *love* chicken, Mommy!" Young Nam exclaimed.
"How come we don't have chicken more often?"

It was a question Hee Ae could not help but take as an accusation,
if not an outright indictment, trial, and conviction. Even at his age,
the boy knew that he and his mother were very poor. He saw that
others had many things—clothes, food, toys—that he did not. From
as far back as he could remember, his world had always been this

way and whenever he had asked his mother for such things, she had always given him the same answer: "Because we don't have enough money, Young Nam-ya. We are too poor."

Hee Ae felt the question and accusation stab and twist inside her acrid stomach. She felt guilty for so many things. She felt guilty for crippling and deforming her son. She felt guilty for being a less than ideal mother who enjoyed too much her times away from her maternal responsibilities—with friends, men, or inside a bottle. She felt guilty for the cruelty toward her son that she could not stop or prevent—from the world or from her own hand. But maybe most of all she felt guilty for their poverty and the lack of everything in their lives.

"You know we don't have enough money to buy chicken. This was a gift from our landlord. He is a very generous man, so make sure you give him genuine thanks tomorrow. Anyway, if we were rich, you'd want to eat chicken every day and soon you'd get sick of your favorite food!"

Hee Ae hoped that she sounded as casual and teasing as she was trying to be. Trying to sound lighthearted while lifting the tonnage of her heart's guilt.

"Plus, I thought you liked cabbage soup. And the rice. We usually have enough rice for you."

The boy looked at his mother with what she took to be an accusing glance before quickly looking back down at his empty plate with its splintered, sucked-out remains of what was once a chicken's leg, thigh, and wing. She could see that he was still very hungry. She hadn't been able to feed him anything the entire previous two days. Whenever he complained about being hungry, she had told him to drink water. It would at least physically fill his belly, temporarily beating back the cries of his stomach. But of course, there was no nutrition in water and the cries of hunger would come back, screaming louder and filling the boy's head with little other thought than of food.

"Here. You can have my chicken, Young Nam-ya. I'm not hungry." She actually was quite hungry; she had not eaten in the last couple of days either. But despite her body's hunger, her appetite was gone, replaced by a need to placate her son's questions and her conscience. With her last statement, Young Nam's face lit up as only a child's can, sending a shot of warmth through her body.

"Yummy! Yummy! Yummy! Thanks, Mommy!"

His tiny body quickly leaned forward and grabbed Hee Ae's plate, sliding it in front of him. He was the picture and personification of glee; if he had been thinking any accusing thoughts, they were already a forgotten memory.

Korea is a sternly hierarchal society and dictates elaborate rules and behaviors for social interactions. There are rules about children's behavior toward adults, rules governing behaviors between genders, and strict rules of behavior between superiors and subordinates, where elders—especially men—are expected to be given deference. Children are expected to obey, to listen, to wait their turn. Young Nam knew better than to ask for his mother's food, so his surprise and delight were real and very genuine.

As her son started devouring what had been her portion of chicken, Hee Ae leaned back and took a long drag on her cigarette. She got her cigarettes from the American soldiers that she did odd jobs for, such as sweeping their quarters—and sometimes other, more personal things. She smoked constantly, and her cigarettes were always running short. It was another weakness of hers that consumed resources. Getting paid in cigarettes didn't leave her with money to feed her son. But she needed her smoking to deal with her life. Just like she needed her drink.

She savored her cigarette.

Her cheeks sucked inward as her lips clenched her cigarette in a tightly puckered grip. She took the smoke deep into her lungs, holding it before slowly blowing it out in a lazy stream. Her lips formed a sideways "who" shape out of the right side of her mouth. As usual, she ignored Young Nam's earlier protest. Today she had bought her smoking right with a gift of boiled chicken. Through the cigarette haze, she watched her son chomping away. She could see how tiny and skinny he was, how bloated his belly was, knew how full of worms that belly was. She could see by the skinny tininess of him that hunger was a constant element in her son's life—as it was in hers.

Chapter 9

Noah

The ferry was coming up on Yongdo Island that makes up the west side of Busan Harbor. It would need to steam past the sea walls that jutted out from Yongdo Island and from the opposite Busan peninsula. Noah became aware that other passengers were now coming out to watch the harbor scene in the bright but blustery morning. Most were Korean. He could tell by their conversations. He could speak and understand Japanese, which he'd learned over the last six months living in Japan as a Rotary International exchange student. He didn't speak or understand any Korean. Ironically, he had forgotten his native tongue, but could speak the language of Korea's historically hated enemy, Japan. But he remembered nearly everything else about his life in Korea. Clearly, Korea had changed as dramatically as had Noah.

The man who had created the post-World War II South Korea, officially the Republic of Korea or ROK, was an extreme autocrat with the un-Korean sounding name of Syngman Rhee (which rhymed with wingmen pee, Noah thought, the first time he'd read about the man). Rhee's regime had been overthrown in 1960 by nationwide student riots. The fragile democratic government that took his regime's place was weak and ineffective. South Korea's military leadership feared that a weak ROK government might be seen as an opportunity for the North to attack and accomplish the communist unification of Korea that it had failed to do in 1950. So in 1961, a talented, ruthless, and highly ambitious general named Park Chung Hee—whose daughter would one day be elected the

first woman president of the ROK—led a military coup and established a new, military regime. There would not be free elections
again in the Republic of Korea until 1988. Noah's earliest years and
all his childhood memories of Korea were of a military state.

The military presence was everywhere. Soldiers, jeeps, trucks,
and tanks had been a pervasive, normal everyday part of Noah's
distant, young life. At five o'clock every day the Korean national
anthem would play from public loudspeakers everywhere in the
entire country. All traffic would stop, both vehicles and pedestri-
ans. Everyone would turn toward the nearest South Korean flag
and salute or stand at attention, including Noah as a tiny boy who
thought this was how the world was everywhere.

Since the division of the peninsula at the end of the Korean War,
North Korea had used subversion, terror, and sabotage tactics against
South Korea as part of its continued efforts to topple the South
Korean government and achieve reunification. This effort originally
used military infiltration, border incidents designed to raise tensions,
and psychological warfare operations aimed at the South Korean and
United Nations armed forces as well as the civilian population. Noah
had grown up listening every day to propagandistic speeches being
broadcast across the border from North Korea through enormous
loudspeakers that could be heard clearly in his village, which lay just
south of the division between the two Koreas. Infiltration by North
Korean military agents was common. Over time, however, there were
clear shifts in emphasis, method, and apparent goals.

The 1960s saw a dramatic shift to terrorist methods and violent
attempts to destabilize South Korea, including commando raids and
incursions along the border that occasionally escalated into firefights
and artillery duels. The incursions peaked in 1968 when more than
566 separate infiltrations were reported, including a bizarre, seemingly Hollywood-scripted commando attack on the South Korean
presidential palace by thirty-one commandos of North Korea's 124th
Army Unit, its elite Special Forces.

Noah had grown up hearing of and seeing terrorist killings, hearing the thud-thud-thump of gunfire and the ground-shattering boom of artillery and tanks rumbling and clanking through the countryside where he lived. Until he was nearly seven years old, Noah only knew the threat of war, random terrorist attacks, and unexpected murderous violence as the normal state of the world around him. It would shape his views, fears, and phobias and put an experiential distance between him and nearly anyone else he would ever meet or know. Not knowing intimately the pervasiveness of military force and threat, the violence of a terrorist war, a war of infiltration, sabotage and murder in young Noah's world is to never truly know anything about Noah Lindquist or the boy he once was.

The knife sank deep into the man's chest with a slip-thud, all the way to its hilt. It had been driven by the hand and arm of a young lieutenant in the Democratic People's Republic of Korea's—North Korea's—elite Special Forces commando unit. The man gave a gasp of pain and surprise. The lieutenant gave a sharp, brutal twist to the knife, using all his adrenalin-driven strength, and the man started to strangle out a scream of pain. But it was cut off as the commando's arm and hand held the man with the strength of trained muscles, fear, and hate. He held the man from behind, his left arm coming from under the man's left armpit and gripping the man's head from behind in a classic half nelson. He gripped him with the remorseless will of those who have been trained to kill for ideological reasons.

The man's struggles grew weaker and his breathing became ragged and gurgling. Then suddenly the struggling stopped; the breathing quit in a long sigh, but the body still twitched and quivered. The lieutenant carefully lowered the dead man to the ground, careful to minimize any noise, and removed his knife with a forceful jerk that took a surprising amount of effort. The knife came out with a wet slurp.

The commando noticed for the first time that the man he'd just killed had been carrying traditional Korean ceremonial foods. These foods were offered to ancestral spirits when a family member visited the grave of a parent or grandparent, observing traditional customs and offering remembrances and respect to the departed, usually shortly after midnight on the anniversary of their death.

That's why he'd been out after dark, well after curfew, thought the lieutenant.

Too bad. Now you're part of the honored dead.

The lieutenant was part of an assassination squad, which was itself part of a larger thirty-one man commando unit that had been ordered personally by North Korean leader Kim Il Sung to assassinate the South Korean president. The commandos had trained for two years for this mission. They had practiced every conceivable attack scenario on an exact mock-up replica of the South Korean presidential mansion.

On January 21, 1968, a cold, moonless night, they had infiltrated across the Demilitarized Zone—the DMZ—between North and South Korea. This was the stretch of no-man's-land that was established along the 38th parallel.

The lieutenant's unit had been quietly circling wide of a small village called Munsan, which was just south of the DMZ. Each of his unit's men carried sixty-six pounds of equipment. He had been ordered to reconnoiter ahead of his unit along a footpath the commandos had come across.

The lieutenant was proud of being an elite warrior on a personal mission of glory for his Great Leader. He would be one of only ten who would survive to return to the North. He would kill again during this mission, in which ultimately at least eighteen people, in addition to twenty of the commandos, would be killed. Only one commando would be captured alive.

Chapter 10

Ellen and Elmore

JUNE 1957, MINNEAPOLIS

Mr. Lindquist? You need to come with me right now." On the word *now*, Elmore's eyes suddenly focused on where the word had come from. He saw that "now" and all the words in front of it had come from the mouth of a very tall nurse; some would call her big-boned. There was a blue Bakelite name tag on her white uniform above her left breast that said "Swedberg" in yellow engraved letters.

Elmore swallowed and tasted blood. He'd been chewing his tongue harder and longer than he'd realized. He stood up instinctively from his black Naugahyde and steel-legged chair and saw that Nurse Swedberg's eye level was only an inch below his. She was very Nordic, with a square-jawed, almost masculine face. The white uniform accentuated her bigness, especially the white nylons that made her calves look enormous. She had a complete sense of authority and purpose about her that made people rise to their feet, just as Elmore had done. She had a surgical mask in her left hand and was holding it out to Elmore.

"Please take this mask and put it on, Mr. Lindquist, and follow me."

Elmore took the mask from Nurse Swedberg with his right hand, grasping the strings from Swedberg's fingers. She wore no nail polish, but her nails were expertly trimmed and pink with cuticles that were neatly pushed up in perfect parabolic arcs. Her nursing training made her compulsive about such things as grooming nails and cuticles. She had surprisingly delicate, long-fingered hands that contrasted with her overall bigness. Swedberg turned and started walking, her huge calves propelling her longs legs out of the OR waiting room and toward a set of double doors that had a long, narrow vertical window in each next to the metal push plates that met at the centerline where the two doors touched. The word *PUSH* in all capitals was stamped into the metal plates.

Elmore hurried to catch up to Nurse Swedberg as they passed through the swinging double doors. He noticed that the vertical windows in the doors had wire that crisscrossed in a diamond pattern in the glass.

How institutional, popped into Elmore's mind, to his surprise.

"What's the matter? Is there a problem, nurse? Where are we going?" Elmore interrogated as he drew abreast of Swedberg and her propelling calves.

"Your wife was given general anesthesia because we had to do the surgery as quickly as possible."

The nurse didn't look in Elmore's direction when she spoke, but kept her square, Nordic, masculine face pointed forward, eyes glued down the hallway to guide her striding pace through and among the people, objects, and equipment that filled the hallway along its length.

"We've removed the baby by c-section and have stopped your wife's bleeding. Your wife should be fine, but she is still unconscious from the anesthesia . . . but, your baby . . . I'm, . . . I'm afraid there's a problem."

Stride, stride, stride. Turn left. Stride, stride . . . Elmore had to catch up.

"A problem? What problem? What in Sam Hill's name is the matter! Is the baby going to be alright?"

Stride, stride.

"I'm afraid your baby has a serious problem. It's meconium aspiration syndrome. MAS. The doctor has done all he can and is afraid your baby may not make it. That's why we need to hurry, Mr. Lindquist."

Swedberg's face never changed from looking straight ahead, and she extruded an air of authority and purpose as her mighty calves pushed her body forward, stride after long-legged stride. Saying words such as "meconium aspiration syndrome" only reinforced her air.

Meconium? What the HELL kind of word is that!

Elmore actually said the word *hell* in his head. He shocked even himself. He'd never actually formed such a word in his brain, even during his Army boot camp nightmare when he'd been sleep deprived and screamed at by deranged, sadistic, Southern, redneck drill sergeants, who particularly didn't like soft college-boy Yankees such as Elmore.

He knew the word *aspiration* and knew the meaning of the word *syndrome*.

But *meconium* sounded like something you'd find in the periodic table in a chemistry book, next to strontium or rhodium. Some rare sort of metal. And what was it doing being aspirated or syndromed in a *baby*? And how did it have anything to do with a word like *previa*?

Elmore didn't have a clue what in Sam Hill's name the word meant, other than that it was something medically bad. And that it was doing something horrible to his just-born baby.

Meconium aspiration syndrome or simply, MAS, is usually not serious and is not too uncommon. MAS can happen before, during, or after labor and delivery when a newborn inhales or "aspirates" a mixture of meconium and amniotic fluid, the fluid in which the baby floats inside the amniotic sac. Meconium is the baby's first feces—poop to be scientifically precise—which is sticky, thick, and, of all colors, dark green. It is usually pooped out by the fetus in the womb during early pregnancy and again in the first few days after birth.

If inhaled or aspirated by a baby, meconium can partially or completely block the baby's airways. Although air can flow past the sticky, fetal poop trapped in the baby's airways as the baby breathes in, the thick green poop becomes trapped in the airways when the baby breathes out. The aspirated meconium can get further and further inhaled into a baby's lungs and can irritate or clog the baby's airways, making breathing moderately difficult to potentially impossible.

Ellen Lindquist's surgeon would have been well versed in all textbook symptoms and probably could have recited them from memory. When Ellen's baby was removed through a caesarian section, her baby had all the symptoms of MAS except one: postmaturity. Ellen's baby was just under eight months old. Her doctor inserted special instruments into the baby's trachea to remove the thick, green feces that was clogging the trachea and listened to the baby's chest with a stethoscope for sounds in the lungs. It was clear that the baby had been at least partially deprived of oxygen while in the womb, probably caused by the bleeding and excessive loss of blood from the placenta. The baby's breathing was heavily labored, and it was clear that its lungs were not inflating properly.

The doctor had repeated the suctioning and the intubation, while the baby had been placed under a heat lamp and onto dry towels. Despite the repeated suctioning, no more meconium was coming out. The heart rate continued to be low and weak and the breathing shallow. The baby was blue and moving only feebly.

"Get the father in here, NOW!" Ellen's doctor had said. There wasn't much time, and Nurse Swedberg had gone to find Elmore Lindquist and bring him to the OR.

Here, put on this surgical gown," ordered Nurse Swedberg as she and Elmore arrived outside the OR that contained Ellen.

She had put a surgical mask on her face so her words came out muffled, but no less filled with her constant aura of purpose and authority. Elmore grabbed the garment and slipped it over his white, short-sleeved shirt with a thin, dark blue tie—he was an accountant for Pillsbury and it showed in his attire. Swedberg also finished tying her surgical gown's strings behind her back. Lindquist and Swedberg were standing in front of the doors that led to the operating room.

"And, Mr. Lindquist, please put on your mask as well. We don't want your wife getting any infections. She is very exposed right now. Once we enter the OR, you must listen to what the doctor tells you and comply immediately. Are you okay with blood and graphic medical situations? Yes?"

Nurse Swedberg locked eyes with Elmore and nodded her head; Elmore obediently nodded as well. How could you resist the efficiency, energy, and authority Swedberg radiated?

"Sure, Nurse Swedberg. I can do this for my wife and baby."

"Okay. Here we go."

Swedberg pushed open the OR doors with her back, walking backwards into the operating room. Elmore followed.

Oh Lord . . .

Elmore saw Ellen on the operating table, and Elmore's knees went weak and his heart grabbed his ribs from the inside and wouldn't let him breathe. She was unconscious with tubes in her arms that dripped fluid from bags of blood, plasma, and other fluids hanging from metal, vertical holders. There was an intubation tube that came out of her slack mouth. She was covered in beige, surgical linens except for her protruding belly, which was cut open and held gaping by steel spreaders that were covered in blood. Her abdomen looked like butchered pork belly, showing layers of red muscle and whitish fat, all smeared in Ellen's blood, which also stained the linens all around her cut, stretched belly. Inside the layers of cut meat that made up Ellen's gaping abdomen, was a deeper, bloodier, redder mass of gore that was her womb.

Elmore's vision was narrowing and blackening at the margins; the scene immediately horrified, sickened, and frightened him, and his heart gripped ever tighter to his chest cavity. His breathing grew more shallow and rapid. And his thoughts became a repetitive prayer.

Oh Lord . . . Oh God . . . Oh Lord . . . Oh God . . .

Elmore had lied. He wasn't very good with blood and gore— not for Ellen, not for his baby, not for anyone. His father-in-law was an avid fisherman and hunter, and although Elmore joined him frequently in these activities, he always let Ellen's dad dress out the deer they shot. He would find ways to keep busy, ostensibly helping the older man, but they were really just tasks and ways to distract himself from the blood, guts, and gore. The sight and smell of all the blood and bowels always nauseated Elmore, despite having grown up on a farm. But Elmore's dad raised corn, wheat, and vegetables; there were no animals raised for slaughter on the farm where he'd spent his childhood.

What horrified Elmore the most was that Ellen looked so inanimate, like some dead object made of cut meat, waiting to be sliced up further. Ordinarily she was so full of energy, drive, and life, with her pert blondeness, intelligent blue eyes, and quick musical laughter, and her "Oh, dears!" Ellen always made all the plans, took care of all the details, and was the drive behind Elmore's big, gentle, easygoingness. Ever since he had met her, he realized how lost and pointless he felt without her and her organization and purposefulness.

And it horrified him to see that clearly there was no "Ellen" on that table, no purpose, no plan, no drive. What accentuated the look of deadness was the color of her exposed belly skin. It was tainted yellow and jaundiced from the iodine that was used to disinfect her abdominal area where now the steel implements, smeared with her blood, were keeping the cut muscle and gore open. Surrounding Ellen was a group of people who looked like they were gathered for some weird KKK ceremony, all dressed in loose-fitting beige garments, wearing masks, gloves, and surgical caps, looking identical expect for their varying heights and staring eyes.

Elmore stood transfixed. He could barely hear the sound of his breathing, made loud and whistling through his mask, over the pounding of his heartbeat rushing his pulsed blood through his ears. His head felt the way it did when he stood up too fast.

"Mr. Lindquist, I'm Dr. Bjorklund."

The words came from one of the gowned and masked figures who moved toward Elmore. His beige surgical garments were crusted in blood that had turned brown and iron-rust.

"I'm Mrs. Lindquist's surgeon. I assume that Nurse Swedberg explained the situation to you?"

Elmore nodded.

"Good. Now, Mr. Lindquist, my colleague, Dr. Karlson, will start cleaning and suturing your wife. We had to do the emergency c-section because your wife was bleeding badly. The placenta had torn due to the previa. We were able to get in quick enough and were able to stop the bleeding. But she did lose quite a lot of blood."

Elmore nodded. He focused on Dr. Bjorklund's voice and fixed on his eye so that he wouldn't have to see Ellen and the blood and work that Karlson was doing to her.

"Will she be okay?"

Please! Dear Lord, let him say yes!

As if on cue: "Yes, Mr. Lindquist, I think so. We didn't have time to give her a spinal, so she'll need to recover from the general anesthesia. As long as that goes well, she should make a full recovery."

All the while Bjorklund had been talking, he'd been moving from behind the operating table and come around toward Elmore, and now he was moving to the farther side past Elmore. Elmore just noticed the little table with dirty towels and a lamp over it. A very small blue form was on top of the towels. It was his baby—a boy. Elmore noticed that no sounds were coming from the wrinkly blue infant and he was not moving but lying limp on his back. His tiny chest was barely rising and falling. The tiny boy had a blue knit cap on his head and a small tube coming out of his mouth. A nurse in surgical gown, gloves, mask, and cap was beside the baby, her eyes looking from the baby to Bjorklund and to Elmore. The eyes looked very concerned and sad.

"But, Mr. Lindquist, I'm afraid that your baby is a different matter. We have tried all we can. The baby clearly had been in distress for some time while in the womb, generating and swallowing a significant amount of meconium."

Dr. Bjorklund paused and looked down at the tiny blue baby with his tiny baby blue cap. He looked back up and directly into Elmore's eyes.

"I'm deeply sorry to tell you that your son is not going to survive. He only has a little more time. He is not getting enough oxygen, and there is nothing we can do at this point. Mr. Lindquist, we are a Lutheran hospital and we brought you in here so that you could be present to witness your son's baptism, before it's too late."

Elmore's vision went dark around the edges and the scene grew small and seemingly distant, as if seen through a tunnel, and he suddenly could not breathe. And his chest felt like a black hole was inside, sucking his heart and lungs and ribs into its crushing center. He felt nothing else. Not the floor beneath his shoes, not the ventilation moving his hair, not the tear suddenly escaping his right eye and traveling down his cheek toward his chin. And his mind was completely blank, except for one thought—a prayer really.

Oh, my dear God no. No. No. No.

Chapter 11

Noah

The Citation V private jet was sitting on the tarmac near the passenger exit area of the general aviation terminal—GAT—of Charlie Brown Airport in Cobb County, Georgia, just to the east outside of Atlanta, off I 20 and I-285 North. Noah could see the sleek jet through the security gate at which he was stopped. The jet had two large twin turbofan engines on either side of its dart-shaped fuselage, just behind the wings and immediately before the tail. The highly aerodynamic shape was accentuated by the red, blue, and tan striping down each side. The striping indicated this Cessna Citation V Encore+ was operated by NetJets, Inc., which leased the plane to Noah's employer.

Noah leaned through the driver's side window to hold up his access card to the sensor. The gate started to slide to the left on rollers, and Noah pushed the button on the armrest of his Mercedes S420 to roll his window up automatically. It was eighty-two degrees with ninety percent humidity in early July 2000, but once his window was up, the temperature and humidity inside his S-Class Mercedes returned to coolness and comfort. The double-layered glass also completely shut out the roaring whine of near and far jet engines at the airport. He was glad that he'd gone for the slightly older model of the S-Class. He didn't like the looks or the cheap feel of the current model, the first made by the merged Daimler-Chrysler Corporation. His S had heft and stature, like a tank, but the elegant ride and trim package you'd expect from the flagship car of

Mercedes Benz—the original German company before it watered itself down with Chrysler. With the double-layered glass that had a polymer internal layer, sound waves crashed against the car's windows and windshield and lost all energy, leaving the interior silent as a tomb. He pulled through the now open gate and drove over to the passenger parking area at the GAT. Noah was talking into his Bluetooth earpiece as he came to a stop and shut off the engine.

"Debbie, please make sure that the Air France flight is all set for me Sunday evening, and that I get the first class upgrade. I'm going to need to sleep on the way to Brussels, and Air France's first class seats go completely flat. I'm going to need that."

Noah Lindquist was talking to his executive assistant, Debbie McKinsey. Noah liked Debbie because she was so incredibly efficient and anticipated his needs and requests even before he thought of them himself.

Just like Radar O'Reilly.

He hadn't thought about the TV series M*A*S*H in forever, but yup, Debbie was definitely a Radar O'Reilly.

"Already done, Noah. You're confirmed for international first class on AF 3679 departing at 17:36 on Sunday, July 2 and arriving into Brussels at 8:54 Monday morning, July 3. I have your car and driver all set to pick you up upon arrival, and you're booked in a nonsmoking suite at the Conrad Brussels Hotel, where the board meeting will be held on Tuesday. I booked you starting Sunday night, so that you'll be able to check in when you arrive Monday morning. Anything else, Boss?"

"Yes. Make sure you follow up with the strategy team regarding the PowerPoint slides. I need them emailed to me by Sunday so I can review them on the flight to Brussels. I will need to go over the board presentation with our CEO on Monday afternoon. Project Pacific Blue is his current top priority."

"Sure thing. You got it Noah."

Noah Lindquist opened the car door as Debbie's voice was talking in his left ear and got out into the Georgia July heat and humidity. The morning heat was heavy and oppressive. It would get up to ninety-one with ninety-six percent humidity by midafternoon. But Noah would be in a much cooler place by then. The Citation was awaiting his arrival to take him there.

"Okay. Thanks. Good work as always."

"Thanks. Call if you need anything."

"Oh, wait . . . did you get everything set up on the plane?"

"Of course! 'Bye!"

"'Bye, Debbie."

Noah hung up his Motorola dual band, tri-mode phone. His was the latest in mobile phone technology as of summer 2000. He worked for the largest telecommunications company, after all. His phone worked anywhere in the world, except Japan and Korea, which had their own unique transmission technology. And his company paid for all charges, including international roaming, which was amazingly expensive.

As he took his Tumi roller bag and his Bally briefcase from the trunk of his silver 1997 Mercedes Benz S420, Noah Lindquist looked exactly like what he was, a top executive for a very large global company. He moved in a world where people knew they were the elite, and like dogs who mark their domain and were always attuned to the scents around them, they were keenly aware of the right labels, the correct brands, and flaunted a carelessness toward the most outrageous price tags.

His title was Senior Vice President, Strategy and Corporate Development. He reported directly to the CEO, who would become Chairman and CEO of AT&T within a couple of years. Noah was responsible for all strategy and strategic business planning worldwide, as well as all mergers and acquisitions and corporate investments for a global joint venture of AT&T and

British Telecom with revenues in excess of seven billion dollars and offices in fifty-two countries.

At thirty-seven years of age, he was the youngest of the seven-person top executive team—by a long way. He knew he was extremely lucky to have the position that he did and the career successes he'd enjoyed to date. Noah had leveraged an MBA and a stellar earlier Navy career—he had been the only officer in the US Navy ever to earn the coveted Surface Warfare Officer board qualification on an aircraft carrier as an ensign, the most junior officer rank—into a successful international corporate banking career, which he then used as a springboard into corporate mergers and acquisitions work and executive status. He was very indebted to the lessons that Ellen and Elmore Lindquist had taught him, the right education, an open American social system, and particularly to a few key people who had taken a chance on him.

Thanks for believing in me, thought Noah as he remembered his BellSouth boss, who had seen something in him when he was a corporate banking VP and had given him a chance of a lifetime, hiring him into BellSouth and the globe-trotting, elite world of international mergers and acquisitions. Very few made it to this level within a top global corporation and got to do the work he did, and Noah knew more than anyone how improbable his journey had been.

A whole lot of luck . . . and a bit of hard work—and the hand of God, thought Noah. He routinely put in twenty-hour days, seven days a week and had taken only three weeks of vacation—total—since graduating from college fourteen years earlier. His current CEO, toward whom Noah also felt great gratitude, had decided to take a chance on him and had recruited him away from BellSouth and elevated him to his present position—and told him he had a Trojan work ethic. Noah knew that whatever it was, it came from trying to live up to the organization, drive, and purposefulness—and above all the duty to do one's best, always—that his mother, Ellen Lindquist, had drilled into him.

Step up and take on the hard jobs that no one wants and do them well, Noah . . . and do the things you hate about them as well or better than the things you love about them.

Noah could still hear his mother's voice in his mind's ear saying those words, because she had said them so often.

Noah had learned early in life how to fit in, to mimic, and to conform to the expectations of his surroundings and the people around him. Being innately different, Noah had learned the value of minimizing all other controllable differences. The circles he now moved in would have noted and approved of his attire, his branding, and he knew he fit in perfectly. It was expected and an innate part of his current job. He was impeccably dressed in a dark blue Savile Row tailored, summer-weight wool suit that was exquisitely fitted to his trim form, with pant creases pressed to a wrinkle free, remarkably perfect edge. His pant cuff indented—"broke"—just the right amount over the front of his gleamingly polished black Salvatore Ferragamo leather shoes. His black leather belt effortlessly matched his shoes. His immaculately starched and pressed Lord and Taylor white broadcloth shirt was French-cuffed, with just the exact tasteful amount showing below his suit sleeve. Each cuff was pierced by a solid sterling silver Tiffany cufflink that looked like a corded knot. The left cuff was embroidered with his initials NLPL. Noah Lee Peter Lindquist. His Omega Speedmaster watch peeked out from under his cuff, just below his initials. Noah's light blue Ermenegildo Zegna silk tie was expertly knotted in a half Windsor and perfectly offset his shirt and suit.

He strolled through the automatic doors out of the locker-room humid heat into the almost too-cold air of the GAT passenger departure area, pulling his Tumi behind him.

Noah could see through the far, opposite exit that led to the tarmac that there was a little, navy blue carpet leading up to the entry ladder steps of the private plane that was parked on the tarmac about fifty yards from the terminal building. Noah strode through the GAT lobby and through the exit onto the tarmac, toward the waiting jet. The copilot was standing there in his uniform—dark blue trousers and white short-sleeved shirt with a blue tie and black epaulettes with three gold stripes. He greeted Noah.

"May I take your bag for you, Mr. Lindquist?"

"Sure. Thanks, Mike."

Noah handed the roller bag to the copilot who followed him into the plane with the bag.

"Good morning, Mr. Lindquist. I'm Captain Nelson," greeted the senior pilot as Noah entered the cabin of the Citation V. "We're cleared to take off as soon as you're seated and ready. We should be wheels up in fifteen minutes and about two hours twelve minutes of flight time between here and Mankato Regional Airport."

"Thanks, Captain. Good morning." Noah flashed Nelson a warm smile that showed perfectly straight white teeth, thanks to braces in junior high.

"Your Glenlivet 18 is next to your seat, and we'll have your Crab Louie salad for lunch, just as Debbie requested."

Radar O'Reilly . . . she really did get everything set.

Noah settled into the large, cream-colored leather seat, surrounded by cherrywood trim and a table of inlaid cherry and maple. The fawn-colored suede leather-covered walls of the plane glowed from recessed, indirect lighting. Noah grasped the tumbler of eighteen-year-old single-malt scotch that was there next to his seat.

Yes, I know it's nine o'clock in the morning, but I need this.

His thoughts turned to the reason for this flight, and a particular thought popped into his brain.

Crap! I can't believe I forgot!

"Hi Debbie, it's Noah . . . yes, thanks, the scotch was ready . . . and the salad . . . yes. Hey, real quick before I take off. I need you to have flowers ready for me to bring to my mom. Call Mary's Flowers in St. Peter. She likes roses and lilies . . . what?"

Noah stopped to listen to Debbie McKinsey talking into his left ear through his Bluetooth earpiece, his green eyes looking vaguely at the polished cherry bulkhead at the front of the passenger compartment. He nodded and raised the scotch to his lips and took a sip.

"Of course. You already took care of it . . . driver already told to pick up . . . roses and lilies in an arrangement. Okay. Great. Thanks."

"Mary said she was particularly proud of the arrangement, since she knows your mom. Safe travels, Noah, and I hope your visit goes as well as it can with your mom." Debbie's voice communicated her genuine concern.

"Thanks, Deb. It's not going to be easy seeing her, given the situation. This fucking board meeting . . . I won't be able to be with her at the most crucial time. I can only go now. Jesus fucking Christ. How can she forgive me . . . ?"

"You're a good man and a good son, Boss. Hang in there. Safe flight."

The plane had been taxiing for some time. He buckled his seat belt as the plane turned onto the runway and the engines suddenly started to scream, and he was pushed back into the big leather chair. Noah shut off his cell phone and ended his call with his executive assistant as the plane started to rise into the air.

Jesus, how do you tell your mom that you can't be at her side when she most needs you, because of your job . . . I feel like such an asshole. How did your priorities get so fucked up, Noah . . . Jesus H. Christ . . .

He took another, longer gulp of the expensive scotch and the ground fell away from beneath the sleek jet as the wheels were raised into its belly and disappeared into the aerodynamics of the plane's lines.

Chapter 12

Ellen and Elmore

JUNE 1957, MINNEAPOLIS

Elmore held his wife, her tears soaking and staining his thin, blue tie. Her body was violently shaking with each sob. Her hands were grasping, clinging to Elmore's shirt as her knuckles stretched white and pointy in their vise grip. Elmore stood there next to Ellen's hospital bed. The railing on his side was down and she was half sitting, leaning into Elmore and crying racking sobs into his shirt and tie. As he stood and held her, his own tears were silently brimming and rolling down his face. They gathered on his chin and dripped, one by one, onto Ellen's bedsheet.

"I had him baptized, Sweetheart."

His wife's sobs turned into a louder, longer, screeching, rising, scream of a howl.

"Nurse Swedberg did the baptism . . . she was amazing. He opened his eyes when she splashed the water on his head."

Elmore was talking through the screeching and moaning, the desperation of pain and agony being vocalized by his wife in her completely broken, soul-torn sorrow. He paused to sniff—snort in the snot of his nose—to keep anything from running out. He couldn't reach his handkerchief that he always kept in his trouser pocket. He needed his hands to hold his shattered wife.

"They wanted a name to baptize him under . . .

"Sweetheart, I couldn't ask you, and we hadn't really discussed a name . . .

"I knew you had one in mind and would have taken care of all that . . . if . . . if . . . so, so I picked one that I thought you'd want . . .

"He was baptized as William Olof . . .

"I held him until he died . . .

". . . it wasn't long."

He could only say a few awkward words at a time. Elmore's tears were coming more freely now. He could do nothing to stop them but stay silent and stoic, other than the words he was struggling to say. Elmore had never hurt like this before. It felt like there was a hole inside of him, as if a core, unrecoverable part of him had died, as surely as his son was dead, and it was sucking his thoughts and his marrow—even threatening to suck his soul—away into agony and oblivion. Holding Ellen seemed to be the only thing keeping him from falling into that well, that piece of death that had made a hole inside him. And his faith.

Elmore was not a philosophical man by any stretch of the imagination. He was an accountant for a reason. His imagination didn't stretch far, and he liked numbers and rules and concreteness. And at a time when the black hole of his pain and despair was threatening to suck away his very will to exist, the strict, clear, simple rules of his religion and its duties and promises of salvation and deliverance from his excruciating pain and loss were an anchor to which he could hold—barely. This deeply personal, tragic, and horrific day, Elmore's faith—and Ellen's struggles with her faith because of this soul-ripping day—would have life-altering consequences more than a decade later for the Lindquists as well as for strangers on the other side of the world.

As his tears rolled silently down his face, and he held his wife in her gripping, wailing agony, he only knew that he'd done his duty as a father under the dictates of his church. Elmore had followed the rules, and he hoped that would help him through this nightmare of incomprehension and pain. Everyone's identity is shaped by the society and environment to which he or she is exposed. For Elmore and Ellen, the critical element in shaping their identities was the Lutheran church.

The Lutheran church in America was far more fractured in 1957 than it is today and far more conservative. Lutheranism and the Lutheran church has its roots in the Reformation movement led by Martin Luther in the early 1500s against the practices of the Catholic church at the time, especially its ornate symbolism, veneration of saints, and selling of absolution for money and "works." Lutherans are Protestants, literally "protest"–ants, those who protested against the practices and certain beliefs of the Catholic church.

Protestors reject practices and activities that epitomize their opponents, and that rejection helps to distinguish protestors and to form their identity. So Lutheranism embraced puritanical practices, rejecting the complex, rich ceremonialism, artifacts, and hierarchical structure of Catholicism. Lutherans embraced a personal relationship with God, rejecting a belief in the need for a special priestly class to act as intermediaries. They embraced simplicity and austerity; rejected elaborate worship, most ornate symbols, most saints; and fervently rejected conspicuous consumption. Many Protestant sects, including certain denominations of Lutherans, abstained from alcohol, smoking, and sometimes even dancing and certain types of music. Piety was a virtue to be aggressively, if humbly, pursued.

Lutherans, however, share with Catholics, in addition to the general tenets of Christianity, the belief in infant baptism. Lutherans baptize babies because they believe that babies are included in the Great Commission, the general command in the Gospel of Matthew that states that all nations should be baptized. And Lutherans believe that the proper interpretation of "all nations" includes infants. But there was a more vital aspect of Lutheran belief that drove Elmore's actions this searing day.

Elmore was a Swedish Lutheran by every definition. He was of 100 percent Swedish stock, his grandparents having emigrated from Sweden in the 1850s. He would one day trace his family history back to the 1560s and to an area of central Sweden called Dalarna— all Swedish, all Lutheran. He had been instructed throughout his childhood, as had his wife, in what is known as the Augsburg Confession. It is the founding summation of the beliefs and principles of the Lutheran church and how it differed from Catholicism. It was written and proclaimed in Augsburg, a Bavarian town in the center of southern Germany, in 1530 against the edicts and wishes of the Holy Roman Emperor and the Pope.

The Augsburg Confession was drilled into young Lutherans during *catechism*, a word derived from Greek that means to teach children by word of mouth, especially in religious matters. Elmore and Ellen both went through Lutheran catechism so that they could be formally recognized—confirmed—in their faith when they were in their early teenage years.

Especially through the first half of the twentieth century, one could not fully understand or appreciate the thoughts of a person such as Elmore or Ellen, or the actions of a surgical staff of a Swedish Lutheran hospital in 1957, without understanding something of what was taught, retaught, and transmitted through the generations for more than four hundred years and had shaped the actions around a young couple's heart-shattering tragedy.

Lutheranism articulates the belief that baptism is critically necessary because human beings are inherently sinful—born with original sin—and therefore can never be worthy of salvation, or as Luther put it, "justified before God." No act, deed, or will of a human being could earn or cause God to give this justification and salvation.

This is the key to understanding why Elmore did what he did, why Ellen's doctors and nurses did what they did. This is the key to give true understanding—authentic meaning—to what many outside their Swedish Lutheran world would perceive as a pointless ritual act. Lutherans' pivotal belief is this: Only by spiritual rebirth through the waters of baptism can a person be recognized as a child of God and be offered the grace of God. Children, therefore, are baptized as a church's most holy gift to them, a promise of God's salvation.

Luther preached the "little church" model of the family, likening a family to a church and the father as the family's head and minister. Luther wrote in his *Large Catechism*: "It is the duty of every head of household at least once a week to examine the children and servants one after the other and ascertain what they know or have learned of it, and, if they do not know it, to keep them faithfully at it."

With such a duty to instruct their children in their religion, Lutheran fathers in particular had a clear and sacred responsibility not to deprive their children of baptism and thus the potential to be received by God into eternity. Elmore was a very good father and a Swedish Lutheran by every meaning of those words, including doing his duty as a Lutheran father, even as a part of his soul died with his tiny, blue, infant son.

"Dr. Bjorklund said he was too underdeveloped to consciously feel any pain so . . . so . . . he didn't suffer . . ."

Elmore struggled out the words, whispered in his normally booming bass, through his silent tears.

Ellen's only response was her raging sobs and cries of uncomprehending grief.

Officially, they hadn't given their son a name. William Olof Lindquist was a name for God's ears alone. The tiny blue baby boy with the streaks of dark green meconium on his body was born—and died—as "Baby Boy Lindquist" according to his birth certificate and his death certificate, both issued on Friday, June 21, 1957, in Hennepin County, Minnesota, USA. The records would note that his

71

mother was Ellen Ilsa Lindquist, married to Elmore Olof Lindquist. Baby Boy Lindquist's body was donated to science.

There was no funeral, and there was no memorial service. Ellen would be too angry at her God and too broken in her world, her pain, and her faith to endure those rituals. And Elmore would lumber and silently endure, as he did in all things, the sucking black hole of death in his core forever linked to a fragile, limp form that had died in his arms. And he would hold onto Ellen in the night—and to the rules that dictated the duties of his life—to anchor him against the pull of that darkness.

Chapter 13

Young Nam

JANUARY 1968, MUNSAN

The boy had woken up alone. He could see his breath coming out in white puffs in the room's still cold air. He could hear roosters crowing in the distance, coming across the snow-covered rural landscape of frozen rice paddies that stretched away outside the walls of the cramped, barely lit room. There were no more charcoal briquettes to burn to create any warmth under the room's floor, and Young Nam shivered under his blanket as he lay on his futon mattress that was too thin and did not insulate well enough against the room's ice-cold floor. His mother had not come home last night, which was not unusual.

She had gone to Seoul to peddle some refurbished junk and black market cigarettes that she had gotten from American GIs. His mother would ride the crowded bus the thirty-five miles to Seoul and would have to pass through the many security checkpoints that were in place to detect North Korean infiltrators—and black market smugglers like Hee Ae. She would hide the cigarette packs in her long winter undergarments, held in place near "feminine" locations by rubber bands to elude casual pat downs. The boy remembered the times that he had been taken along with her and how anxious and afraid he had been when the South Korean soldiers had come aboard the bus. She had made him also carry packs of cigarettes under his clothes, betting that soldiers would not search such a tiny boy. Young Nam and his mother would stand in the aisle of the bus because they could not afford to pay for seats. The boy's legs usually could not take the two hours or more it took for the bus to make its way from Munsan, his village near the DMZ, to Seoul, the capital city. The frequent stops the bus made to off-load and pick up passengers and for security check points made the short-distance journey into an endlessly long ordeal for anyone and an eternity for a small boy. But, because he was so small, he could usually sit on the floor of the aisle without taking up too much room. Whenever the soldiers came on, they would demand to see papers from selected passengers; apparently those selected looked suspicious, guilty, or nervous. Or were just capriciously selected out of a soldier's spite.

The soldiers all seemed so huge to Young Nam. They were dressed in dark olive-drab uniforms. The boy had no idea what any of their insignia meant. But he did notice that their high, laced leather combat boots were polished to a black mirror finish and the metal lace hooks sparkled in the sunlight. He also was impressed by their huge black metal-barreled assault rifles, which had semi-polished wood stocks. These rifles were M14s, produced and supplied by the United States to the ROK army. These had originally been designed and produced to replace the older, Second World War era M1 rifle. The US military had already decided several years earlier that the M14 was inadequate and had replaced it with the M16-A1, which in its A2 variant is still the standard US military assault rifle used today.

The little boy saw that each soldier carried one of these enormous wood and black steel weapons, holding them at the ready, and that each rifle had a clip locked into its magazine slot just in front of the trigger guard. The uniformed men would surround the bus as it came to stop at a checkpoint. When the driver opened the bus door the three soldiers would enter. Two would take positions: the last to board would be in the front door well, the first soldier to board would stand at the front of the aisle, each with rifles at the shoulder, covering the passengers. The second soldier in line would sling his rifle and go down the aisle, demanding papers at random, searching packages, and conducting intermittent pat downs. Young Nam would sit on the floor almost shaking with fear of being caught with the black market cigarettes his mother had stuffed into his baggy, oversized pantaloon-like pants that were the traditional Korean attire. He was so small that she could only put a few packs around his groin and thighs, and the boy was sure that the soldiers could see them bulging out.

Young Nam would be too afraid to make any move and unconsciously held his breath while the soldier came down the bus aisle in his huge, gleaming black boots. He could count every lacing rivet and feel the heel-toe thud-thump of each step. He didn't know what would happen to him if he were caught. He'd seen people removed roughly at gunpoint from the bus in the past. He never found out what happened to them once they were left behind and the bus had roared off. All he knew was that he didn't want to be one of them and be in that sort of trouble. His heart and pulse fluttered at hyper speed as he sat and waited to be discovered. But he never was. Not yet.

His mother had told him she would also be visiting some of her family that lived in Seoul. Hee Ae did not visit them often due to her circumstances—divorced from her Korean husband and raising a crippled half-American illegitimate son. A couple of her siblings still interacted with her, but it was always awkward and always very strained. Her circumstances were analogous to that of an ill-educated, single, divorced Southern Baptist white woman raising a half-black, out-of-wedlock son in rural Alabama in 1923 and going to visit her white-cracker kin in Selma. Awkward and strained were clearly understated descriptions of the circumstances and situation. Hee Ae rarely brought Young Nam along on such visits.

It was hard enough to see him endure the coldness of strangers, but to expose him to the equally cold reactions of family was just too much for Hee Ae to witness and subject her small boy to.

The conflict of wanting to give her son the warmth of family, but knowing that such family warmth was not in her control and not hers to give, was just one more torment for her to endure. It never dawned on her that there was anything not completely right about leaving her son alone. She just did what she had to do, given what she had—and didn't have. As a mother, of course she worried and constantly felt the sinister whisperings of her guilt in her tortured heart, but Hee Ae had no choice. There was no social safety net in Korea in 1968, no state-mandated pensions or social security—not in a country where electricity still did not reach many parts outside of cities, where clean water and sanitation were a work in progress; not in a country where one in five infants born did not live to see their fifth birthday.

Family was the social safety net, its mesh made of mutual obligations, ties of blood, lineage, and familial fidelity. Hee Ae's net was tattered with gaping holes—torn by foreign blood, promiscuity, and a broken, bastardized lineage, and unfulfilled and failed fidelity. What few bonds remained were unable or unwilling to support the weight of her and her son's needs.

Hee Ae would be making another visit. It would be a place she'd only been to once before, to talk with people she'd never met since, about a topic that choked her throat and left her feeling like she would vomit. But, like so many things about her life, she had to do what she had to do, with little choice and only bad to horrible options.

Chapter 14

Ellen

All through dinner, Elmore could tell that Ellen was very upset. *I should have called when I got the note at the office saying that she had gotten a call from LSS . . . but I didn't even have time to get to the voting booth to vote for Humphrey.*

Ellen had made a broccoli hot dish, which people outside the Midwest called a casserole, and placed it on the table. Already on the table were a bowl of boiled, canned green beans and another bowl with a salad of leaf lettuce, tomato slices, and cut cucumbers with croutons and Bacos brand artificial bacon bits. There was also a serving plate with slices of white bread and a side dish of margarine. Ellen always made sure that every meal had all four food groups: protein, vegetables, grains, and dairy. Everyone had a glass of two percent milk in front of their plates.

The Lindquists always ate dinner together at the small Formica-covered, fake wood-grained table in their tiny kitchen. The table created a sort of partition between the kitchen and the laundry area, making them into two separate, tinier rooms, even though they were really just one room with a fridge, sink, and oven at one end, and a washing machine and laundry sink at the other.

Elmore always sat at the head of the table, with his back to the one wall, and led his family in saying grace before starting to pass around the food. As the head of the family and Luther's "little church," not only did he lead family prayers, he also started the passing of the food, serving himself first. And the food was always passed to his right, making the bowls and plates go counterclockwise. Ellen sat on the side of the table to Elmore's right and two slots down, with her back to the kitchen part of the room. It was the position most easily able to leave the table and get anything in the kitchen. Ellen always arranged things with an eye to efficiency and purpose.

Between Elmore and Ellen, to Ellen's left, sat five-year-old Carla Lindquist, the youngest of their four children. Carla was a beautiful towheaded, blue-eyed girl, her hair so fair that it looked translucently golden. People remarked when they saw childhood pictures of Ellen that she and Carla could be identical twins at the same age. If the word had existed in 1968, those people would have used the word *clone*. But it would be years in the future before "clone" would come into everyday language. Across from Ellen was Karissa, nine years old, with blondish, light-brown hair and hazel eyes that looked out through cat-eye glasses. Unlike her siblings, she was athletic and highly social, with a gang of other tomboy girls that she always palled around with. Next to her on Karissa's side of the table was Christina, now fourteen and in tenth grade—she had been skipped a grade ahead. Her blonde hair had turned light brown and her blue eyes radiated with intelligence and teenage impatience. Sitting at the foot of the table was twelve-year-old Karsten, the only boy in the Lindquist household. He was a tall, thin boy with finely formed facial features, blondish hair, Buddy Holly glasses, and pale blue eyes that tended to stare off into space—literally. He was consumed by science fiction, reading about and daydreaming of interstellar space and far-off galaxies full of aliens who inexplicably were attracted to buxom human females from Earth.

The children could also sense that something was wrong. It was in the way their mother was silent, except to say grace and short, terse commands to sit up at the table and pass the food as it was handed to them. They could also see it in the way Ellen had violated her paper napkin, gripping it in her right hand and turning it into a crumpled, tightly wadded paper ball. Her hand would repeatedly open and turn the napkin ball a little in her hand, before crushing it again, a little tighter. Christina could see that her mother's bright blue eyes were rimmed in red and bloodshot and that her lipsticked lips were smashed into a thin red line. Christina, Karsten, Karissa, and even little Carla, knew not to cross their mother, especially when she was crushing the paper life out of a perfectly innocent napkin. The normal babble and arguing of children's voices around the dinner table was replaced by the random clinks and tinks of forks against the CorningWare plates and salad bowls.

The Lindquists ate off CorningWare at every meal, except on special occasions. Their plates, salad bowls, and the hot dish serving bowl—all white with the signature CorningWare blue flower pattern, available for purchase through the 1968 Montgomery Ward catalog—were created in 1953 by Corning from materials originally developed for a US ballistic missile program.

The family finished dinner as the four children exchanged looks and glances among each other and at their mother's clenching and unclenching hand. Even the family's cat knew enough to slink out of the kitchen and disappear down the stairs to find a dark hiding place. The rest of the evening would be similarly tense and quiet.

The kids were all now in bed and Elmore and Ellen were in their pajamas, light blue, formal sleeping outfits with dark blue piping around notched collars and turned up cuffs. Ellen would never have allowed anyone to sleep only in underwear. And certainly not in the underwear that had been worn and sweated in during the day. Ellen was already in bed, staring at the ten o'clock news on channel 3 on the bedroom TV. A weather map was being displayed showing curved red and blue lines, the blue ones with little evenly spaced triangles on them and the red ones with evenly spaced little half circles, documenting moving warm and cold fronts. The volume was turned too low to hear what the announcer was saying.

"I got your message from the department secretary that Julie Benson from LSS called today. Sorry Sweetheart, but I was tied up in faculty meetings and student advisory sessions all day and couldn't call back."

Elmore pulled back the covers on his side of the bed and got in.

Ellen's gaze turned slowly away from the TV and the flickering weather map, and she faced Elmore and locked her eyes onto his.

"She took our boy away . . ." her voiced trailed into a glottal hiccup.

Elmore knew that her tears were not far off, and he reached over and pulled his small wife close into his large arms and the cold little death hole inside him sucked at his spine and sternum.

"Oh, Sweetheart . . ." was all he could manage to say.

"How can God do this to us . . . again, Elmore?" Ellen started shaking in his arms.

Elmore held his wife's blonde head to his chest, feeling her warmth contrasting with the cold that now was suddenly at the pit of his being. And Ellen pressed herself into Elmore's big presence and felt her doubts start making their heretic, subversive arguments in her head.

A loving God . . . really? What's loving about taking away my son? After I answered his call he does this!

Oh Lord! How can I do my life's mission if you destroy me again!

Ellen cried out to the empty silence in her heart and gripped Elmore's pajama shirt in the tight fists of her hands.

Chapter 15

Young Nam

He had not eaten anything the day before and now his stomach was demanding that he do something to alleviate the hollow craving ache of hunger. As he lay shivering under his blanket, he kept thinking of food and the ache in his stomach intensified. Along with a growing agony in his bladder. He had been needing to urinate for a very long time, but was unwilling in his little-boy terror to leave the safety of his blankets while it was dark. Now the urgency of the pent up urine was unbearable. Young Nam had to brave the cold. He had only a couple of sweaters that he always wore during winter, including the one he was wearing now. He slithered from under his blanket, careful not to pull it back and let out the warmth that his small body had created between blanket and mattress.

He slept in his clothes, which he wore for days at a stretch, sometimes weeks. He only had a couple of sets of pants, shirts, and sweaters. And three pairs of socks. But only one pair of shoes and one coat. They weren't actually shoes, just the rubber protective mudguards that one pulls on over real shoes, what people in the Midwest of a certain older generation call "rubbers."

Although meticulous about washing his hands and face with well water from the hand pump in the common area, he did not have the luxury of bathing, except for once every month or two at a public bath, where there was hot water and a small pool-like bathing area that was always crowded and filled with strangers who were all women and girls. His mother brought him into the female bathing area of the public bath so that he could stay with her—he was still small enough. People thought he was two years old, maybe three. He was actually four.

His mother would have him soap up her back and scrub it with a washcloth. Young Nam always noticed how much dirt and dead skin came off his mother's naked back when he did these infrequent scrubbings. He always fatigued his arm muscles scrubbing this way and that way. His mother would sit with her back to him, and he would stand behind her and his eyes would be level with her shoulders. She would return the favor, with him standing with his back to her while she was sitting behind him. Other than his back, he had learned to wash himself by the time he was three.

Young Nam both looked forward to and dreaded these bathing events. He reveled in the warmth and abundance of so much water—he could literally swim in the public bath. But he was highly self-conscious of all the stares and pointed fingers. Not because he was a male among females. Not at all. Because of his grotesque scars and deformed hand, arm, and chest. He could see the revulsion on people's faces, the skittering away from being too close to him. The way other children would point and dare each other to go touch the grotesque kid. He hated his naked repulsiveness. He clung close to his mother to hide behind her, crossed his arms over his boiled-scarred tiny chest, and hid his left arm under his right one.

But in a public bath, there was no place to hide. And all his deformity and repulsion were gawked at, whispered about, and nakedly displayed.

But this morning, he missed the warmth of those baths as he scampered over to the chamber pot in the small room's corner, his ears stinging from the cold. The fluid that was in the vessel was frozen. It was solid in its brownish-yellow, frozen "urineness." The chamber pot came up to his upper thigh, and he had to stand on his toes to pee cleanly over its lip. His pee came out in a steamy torrent that sent up a small cloud of white vapor and started melting the frozen urine in the pot where his steaming hot stream hit and splashed. The feeling of release his bladder gave as it pushed out its liquid agony was so all consuming that the boy felt nothing else for the entire time he stood on his toes and peed. He didn't feel the cold. He didn't feel his hunger. He didn't feel his nighttime terror.

Just the glory of his bladder's release.

The boy did not know when his mother would come back. Sometimes she would be gone for several days. He knew that bad things roamed the night, and he had been very frightened being alone in the dark. Young Nam's imagination always ran wild and he saw terrible things in every shadow, certain that every sound was made by something horrible moving in the night. Korean folktales were filled with ghosts and evil spirits, and in a land of ancestor worship, people truly believed the dead roamed the night, in spirit if not in body. And a little boy completely internalized as verified truth all those stories and walking dead beliefs. Only fatigue and exhaustion, which made him suddenly fall into the unconsciousness of sleep, finally gave him sanctuary from his raging terror of the dark and what it hid. Now, in the frigidly cold morning's grey light, his fears were beat back for another day.

What would happen this cold Monday in January would mark the shivering little boy forever and, because of this day, he would become even more terrified of the night and its darkness well into his adult years.

The boy was walking in his flimsy rubber non-shoes through the snow, staying on the mostly packed path. It was colder outside than it had been in his small room, because the wind was gusting. It moved the frozen, ice-glazed branches of the bare trees and shrubs next to the path. Young Nam knew that the path was little used. It led to a small burial plot that held markers of some of Munsan's honored departed loved ones. But the boy knew that he wouldn't reach the plot for at least a mile or more.

His destination was an area of fallen trees that was well before the burial mounds and stone markers. That's where his dinner could be found. Or so he hoped. His stomach now felt hollow and achy. A dull, constant, consuming urge kept demanding thoughts of food be thrust into his brain—thoughts he couldn't stop or control. He had to find something to eat, and he was making his way in the cold, blowing, winter-gusted winding path.

His village of Munsan was really just a small collection of farm houses and a main dirt road that had one strand of power line looping along its length, held up by uneven and slanted power poles. In the village, the roadsides had dilapidated sheds that passed for shops and stores, mixed with vegetable and local cooked-food stands and peasants selling other odds and ends. In winter the stalls were mostly empty except for the occasional soup and rice vendor or a farmer pushing *kimchee*. It was just too cold on this gusty Monday to be sitting alongside a pot-holed road, hoping someone would come by.

The village was situated on the south bank of the Imjin River at the edge of the DMZ. It was close to Panmunjom, where the armistice was signed and the United Nations Joint Security Area was located—the only official point of interaction and close proximity between North Korean and United Nations forces. Munsan would stay a small, rural backwater, which boasted a train station that was closest to North Korea in all of the ROK. In the early part of the twenty-first century, an economic boom and temporarily thawed relations between the north and the south would cause a small real estate bubble, but nothing that really put the place on the proverbial map.

Munsan's only real claim to a place in broader history was its role as the location for the original first point of attack by North

Korean forces on June 25, 1950, starting the Korean War. The battle is considered one of the most decisive and more successful examples of a surprise attack and would be celebrated as a great victory over the capitalist South Koreans—America's stooge and lapdog—in the Democratic People's Republic of Korea for decades into the future. The ROK army would tell the story of those battles around Munsan that June of 1950 differently. They are remembered as days of heroics, astonishing loss, sheer bravery, and the horrible cost of blunting an overwhelmingly powerful force and conducting a successful retreat.

Young Nam could feel the wind through his winter coat, which was new and too big—his mother wanted to ensure that he wouldn't outgrow it for next year—and into the colorful sweater that he wore. Unfortunately, it was not made of wool, but of polyester, and did not retain heat or keep out the wind as well as wool. But it sported bright reds, blues, and yellows. Koreans favored bright colors, especially reds and bold blues. But Koreans also were attracted to spring like pastels of light, baby blues and hot pinks. Even the men. The new coat was a gift from some rich Americans who, for reasons that the boy could not understand, gave away money to poor strangers like him so that his mother could buy him a coat. Young Nam couldn't imagine having so much money that he would give it away to strangers.

The boy kept his hands in his coat pockets to keep them warm. Especially his left hand. He knew he needed to protect it from the winter wind and cold. Scar tissue is not like regular skin. It has no sweat glands to give moisture or protective oils. Skin scars, for example, are less resistant to ultraviolet radiation, are dry and non-self-oiling, harder and are less pliable, and do not grow at the same rate as normal skin. This often creates contracture through tightening of the skin, creating pulling, limited movement, and slight to gross misshapenness and deformity.

For four-year-old Young Nam, it meant that his left hand and arm had become curled and shrunken. Four of his left fingers' scars had grown together, making it impossible for him to open his hand or uncurl his fingers, except for his first finger. His stump of a thumb similarly could barely open. His left hand was essentially a small pincer with a pointing finger that could open and close only part way. It would ache in the cold and become dry and cracked in the desiccating low humidity of winter air. The cracking usually became severe enough that the cracks would start bleeding, sometimes getting infected as skin gaped open allowing germs and other pathogens to gain access to inner tissues. His mother did not have the means or the knowledge to treat his cold-cracked, bleeding, aching left hand. He had no lotions, no sterile ointments, and no warm water easily available to ease the constant ache.

So the boy protected his hand as much as possible. Keeping it in the warmth of his pocket. He did almost everything one-handed.

The goal of his trek through the steep, rugged, Korean snow-covered terrain was to dig up insects, mostly—and hopefully—pill bugs and maybe some bees. In summer, insects were more plentiful. Ants were everywhere, as were grasshoppers. In warmer times, when spiders were plentiful, Young Nam would fashion a loop out of scrap wire that he could get from a trash heap and tie it to a thick stick or branch with string. He'd sweep the wire loop through multiple spider webs, creating a massive, combined web across the wire loop's opening. The boy could then use the spider web-enclosed loop as a net to capture big, fat grasshoppers, dragonflies, and crickets. Once victims had been caught in the web of spider webs, Young Nam would pull them off and put them into a bag for safe keeping until he got back home. The beauty of the spider web net was that he could capture multiple insects and did not have to remove them immediately. When he did take one from the sticky net, there usually was a hole that was made where the web tore away with the insect. But that was easily mended by sweeping the loop through a few more spider webs. For this reason, the boy loved spiders. And where most children and many adults had an unreasoning fear and revulsion to spiders, Young Nam never did, and never would in his adulthood. He never ate spiders, however, because he valued their web making so much more.

Even as a four-year-old he had figured out the truth and wisdom in learning the value of fishing rather than just eating a fish. The webs could feed him today, tomorrow, and the next day. Eating the spider that made the web would feed him only today. The boy loved spiders for being his little helpers.

In winter, it was all different. No spider webs were available to make a sticky net, and there were no flying insects available anyway. Few insects survive cold winters, and those that do usually hibernate or are deep in the soil. But some survive by creating glycerol, a type of antifreeze that courses through their bodies, allowing some insects to hibernate through the freezing temperatures of winter.

Pill bugs cannot survive temperatures below twenty-one degrees Fahrenheit, but they can survive by finding warm enough environments, such as compost heaps. Bees survive winter temperatures by huddling together and amassing body heat inside their hives, eating the stored honey for energy to vibrate their wings, which creates body heat.

Young Nam was on a hunt for pill bugs, as it was harder to find wintering bees. Pill bugs actually are crustaceans, as are crabs, lobsters, and shrimp. They are sometimes called roly polies because they curl up into little balls when surprised. The boy had eaten them boiled as well as roasted. He planned on roasting the ones he hoped to find today. It took less fuel to simply heat up a pan than it did to boil water, and he knew that there were no charcoal briquettes left, so he would need to use firewood that he had to collect. At his age, he couldn't read or write, but the school of starvation, cold, and poverty had taught him more than most boy scouts would ever learn about survival.

He had learned that he could find pill bugs in natural composts, such as piles of heaped-up vegetation, dead grass, leaves, and rotting wood that can form in forests around fallen trees and trunks. The vegetation decays through the action of microbes that consume the dead vegetation, wood, and cellulose as food. Their metabolic action of digestion, of converting the dead matter into chemical energy, gives off heat as a by-product, just like human cells do. If a decaying mound of vegetable and wood matter is large enough, its microbial action will raise the temperature enough so that insects, like pill bugs, can survive winter temperatures.

And roasted pill bugs, though he did not know it because he had never tasted water crustaceans, can taste a bit like shrimp.

Young Nam was now shivering, and his feet were too cold to feel anything. But he was almost at the turn in the little path where the pile of rotting trunks, leaves, grass, and other fallen vegetation was composting and playing host to his next meal. As he picked his way along the snowy path, he was looking ahead. Something caught his eye, up ahead and off to the left of the path. As he got closer, the boy realized that what he saw was a piece of *songpyeon*, a traditional Korean rice cake filled with beans, nuts, or other similar foods. It lay there just off the path. His mouth started watering. Somebody must have dropped it, but it looked good. He hurried to pick it up, his shivering momentarily forgotten. As he stooped down, reaching for the songpyeon, he noticed that there was another one, half hidden in the tall, dead grass poking up through the snow. He rushed over to pick that one up as well. Then he saw that there was a whole scattering of food.

How could this be? It's all over the place! And a whole bunch of it . . . oh, boy, it's RICH people's food!

The boy started gathering the food—fruits, rice cakes, pastries, meats, nuts, fish—and stuffed them into his pockets and piled them in the crook of his left arm. They were frozen, but he tried to eat the pastries and was able to get several frozen bites. He was busy picking up the food, bending over, and moving to the next piece that he found. He didn't notice that he was moving off the trail, deeper into a stand of leafless brush and brown, dead grass and deepening snow. Suddenly the boy stopped and dropped all the food he had gathered.

His landlord—the nice man who had given his mother the chicken last summer—was staring at him from the snow.

Young Nam started shaking, not from the cold but from an onrush, a tsunami wave of instant terror. The boy's heart started pounding his raging terror as a thundering drumbeat within his chest, and he no longer felt the cold or the wind.

There was blood all over the white garments worn by his landlord. The shaking, tiny boy knew that they were special clothes worn when going to honor one's ancestors or departed parents. The boy's eyes took in the scene of bloody horror and locked onto his landlord's eyes.

The man's eyes didn't blink.

They stared sightless and shocked through the boy to some infinity beyond. The gusting wind flapped the dead man's sleeves and blew strands of his hair over his face, across the staring, shocked, infinity-locked eyes. The movement of the clothes and hair made the stiffness and nonmovement of the body that much more noticeable. There was frozen blood, still red because the cold had preserved it from oxidation, which was caked around the man's mouth and down his chin in a frozen, frothiness. His body was set in an awkward, unnatural pose with a leg tucked under his prone body and the other leg splayed out at an angle. His left arm was bent and partially raised, and the fingers of that hand were blue and claw-like, reaching to the cold sky. The right arm was up over the man's head against the ground. There was frozen blood on the fingers and palms of both cold blue-white hands. And there was a grotesque amount of blood covering his chest, abdomen, and sleeves. It was splattered onto the white trousers, and his right foot was bare—frozen blue and whitish—the shoe nowhere to be seen.

The little boy had stumbled upon the prior night's efficient work of the North Korean commando. It was a scene that the boy would never get out of his head, and it would fuel his fear to nearly an uncontrollable phobia of what the night and the dark might hide. He would struggle with this phobia for years to come.

Young Nam was shaking violently now. In his own way, he too was frozen, but with a crazed, primal terror that that seemed to have no limit. The boy's immediate coherent thoughts were that he himself was about to be killed, that whatever had done this was still here, waiting in the dead waving grass. He expected to have something leap out at any instant and tear him limb from bloody, torn limb.

A word started screaming in the tiny boy's brain, spreading panic from out of the primitive, reptilian part of his brain the way a locust plague might spread across biblical fields. A black, buzzing, spreading, devouring, all consuming, world-ending panic.

RUN!!

Chapter 16

Noah

Noah felt the jet's acceleration easing and the flight path begin to level off. Private jets have much more power-to-weight than commercial airliners, and the Citation V's leap into the sky was thrilling. Not only were the speed and acceleration much more intense, the climb angle was much steeper than the gentle one-gravity acceleration and looping climb of a commercial plane. Noah loved the feel of speed and power that pushed him deep into his plush, cream-colored, calf leather chair. He looked out his window and watched the lush green, tree-filled Georgia landscape grow small and distant. As the plane leveled out to its cruising altitude, the engine and outside noises faded into the background, muffled by the abundant insulation and suede leather of the cabin's curving walls and glowing, softly lit ceiling. The powerful Pratt & Whitney engines were well behind the cabin and so were almost silent when cruising.

Noah had been on many private jet flights, too many to remember them all. As an executive at BellSouth Corporation, before his current AT&T-British Telecom global position, when he had been in charge of many of the international mergers and acquisitions initiatives for the huge southern phone company, he'd often traveled on one of the twenty-one corporate-owned jets—the BellSouth Air Force as he and other executives liked to jokingly call the fleet of planes. He'd often flown across the Atlantic aboard the large Falcon 900, built by the French Dassault Aviation company, the only tri-engine corporate jet.

For Noah, the plush cabin, the private airports with few or invisible security hassles, and swift access to destinations on the other side of the world were normal and unremarkable.

He loosened his perfect half-Windsor knot on his silk tie. His jacket was already hanging in the closet, taken by the copilot when Noah had embarked the plane.

"We're at forty-five thousand feet and headed to Mankato Regional Airport. Flight time remaining, a little under two hours."

The copilot had just entered the cabin and made this announcement. Private jets fly much higher than commercial airliners so that they do not crowd commercial flight paths. It also means the air is thinner and so gives less resistance, allowing private planes to travel much faster, both speed through the air and, especially, speed over ground. Additionally, coming in and out of smaller, regional airports meant few or no airport holding patterns that eat up time.

The copilot disappeared briefly behind the front bulkhead and reappeared with a tray of food. It was the Crab Louie salad that Debbie McKinsey had ordered for Noah. The ornate tray was set down in front of Noah, the crabmeat already removed from the legs and heaped in a mound on top of a bed of fresh-cut romaine lettuce.

As is evident from the salad's name, the main ingredient for Crab Louie is crabmeat. Variations of the salad are many, and Noah's had all the usual ingredients, plus some—hardboiled egg, tomatoes, asparagus, olives, and chopped green onions. What all Crab Louie salads had in common was "Louie" dressing, made from mayonnaise and red chili sauce. Noah always had the dressing served on the side, never mixed with the salad's ingredients.

Noah loved the salad. Especially the way Debbie ordered it, with a massive amount of crabmeat. Along with the salad was served an assortment of specialty breads and his favorite mineral water, a bottle of ice cold Badoit, pronounced "bod-wah," a little-known brand of mineral water obtained from natural spring sources at Saint-Galmier, France, and carbonated by countless years of underground filtering, sieving through granite rocks and subterranean gas deposits. The water is named after Auguste Badoit, who began bottling the water in 1838.

"Thanks, Mike," Noah said to the copilot, as he accepted a dark blue, soft Egyptian cotton napkin. The crew always made sure that the napkin matched the passenger's suit color so that no white or dark lint would be visible on a passenger's suit trousers or business skirt.

As he started to eat his salad, Noah's thoughts ran to his mother, Ellen Lindquist. He had always been in awe of her discipline, organization, and industry, her willingness to take on thankless tasks and meet any responsibility head on. These were traits that she had worked to instill in Noah through her example and explanations. He knew he could never match her, however he might try. She just was beyond human in her sense of duty, organization, and purpose.

I wouldn't be here except for her faith and example . . .

Although he loved her for just being his mother, he loved and admired nearly everything about who she was as a person. But he had never expressed his admiration and love to her. Noah and his mother—or any of his family—rarely talked about their feelings. It just wasn't the Swedish way. So in one sense Noah had never gotten to really know Ellen Lindquist, her emotions, fears, or hopes. Ellen was his mother, not his friend. His family didn't swap personal secrets among themselves. He knew it had to do not only with her particular traits and values, but also her upbringing and Swedish immigrant heritage. He thought of how she had worked to pass on those traits and that heritage, culture, and family lore to him, and how he had internalized much of it, because of and through Ellen's example.

Ellen Lindquist had just found *the* hard job that she wanted to take on. Her pulse started quickening as she read further into the magazine article dated January 1968, her thoughts were starting to form an explosive idea.

Dear Lord . . . !

Ellen Lindquist never shirked responsibility. That was what had drawn her to nursing in her youth. It was a hard job that offered clear responsibilities and held one fully accountable to meet those responsibilities. Ellen enjoyed taking on hard jobs and doing them well. She had excelled at Swedish Hospital Nursing School for exactly this trait. And because of her intelligence. She had been known as the student that took on any job—the more thankless, the more filled with drudgery, the more menial, the more you could count on Ellen to step up and tackle it head on.

Ellen supposed that she got this trait from her parents, who both had this straightforward approach to life and its tasks. Her maiden name was Swenson, born of Ilsa and Magnus Swenson. Neither the Swenson line or her mother's family, the Linns, have a history of dreamers, artists, or out-of-the-box thinkers. The families' histories were unremarkable, except in the consistent level of just doing what had to be done: working farms, moving from poverty in Sweden, settling the prairies, growing families and crops, and being faithful to the Lutheran church.

Ellen's mother was the oldest of eight children, all girls. Without any sons to help work the small farm northeast of Minneapolis, Ellen's mother's parents put all the girls to work doing the many chores that had to be done to make a farm operation survive in an era when there was no electricity or combustion engines. There was only animal and human muscle—mostly just human female muscle. Ellen's mother would often remark in her later years to anyone who would listen, but mostly to her grandchildren, that her father never complained about not having any sons; he only celebrated and cherished each and every one of his daughters. Her sisters would confirm this in conversations at family gatherings where they constituted a senior council of blue-haired matriarchs. Their husbands, all strong, able men, joked among themselves, out of their wives' earshot, that they all knew who drove the agenda bus in each of their lives—the Linn sisters and the particular one they happened to have married.

Ellen's mother had learned and passed on to her daughter that the sooner you tackled the hard job, the sooner it got done. And no job, no chore, nothing ever worth doing, went away. And it never got done on its own. And no one ever came along and did it for you. Ilsa Linn and her sisters had also learned that if a job wasn't done right, then they usually had to it again, and you had to take the time to undo what you hadn't done right in the first place, making the chore that much harder. The Linn sisters had a creed that they lived by and taught their children: do it now, do it right—the first time, every time.

As the oldest child in her family, Ellen's mother internalized and rebroadcast this mantra more fervently than any of her sisters. She had to set the example, and she had to do much of the mothering as her younger sisters kept being born. Ilsa's parents, Per and Marie Linn, and her in-laws had come from an area of southeastern Sweden known as Småland and were brought over by their families as children in the 1850s. These early Swedish immigrants settled in the Chisago Lakes region of what was then the Minnesota Territory. Their story, according to Swenson and Linn family legend, was part of the basis for the four novels by Swedish author Vilhelm Moberg who wrote *The Emigrants, Unto a Good Land, The Settlers,* and *The Last Letter Home.* The series of novels told the story of destitute Swedish immigrants settling into the Chisago Lakes area, about fifty miles northeast of Minneapolis, in the Minnesota Territory of the 1850s. These books, the first of which was published in 1949 and which most Americans likely have never heard of, were famous among Swedish Lutheran Americans. As the Pilgrims were to Plymouth Rock and to Americans in general, this fictionalized tale—based on real interviews and oral histories—was almost required reading for Americans of Swedish descent.

The series describes the hardships and utter poverty faced by rural families in Småland, Sweden, an area known for having little arable land and rocky, lake-filled hills. The story relates the heart-wrenching decisions the people of a Lutheran church community had to make between starvation and leaving for the New World, knowing that if they left they would never see their homeland or extended families again. And it relates the hardships, separation, and longing for family that settling a new land brought, even as these families eventually triumph and prosper in their new home.

Ellen was very proud of her mother and father, her grandparents, and their family lore and heritage and always thought of herself as "Swedish Lutheran," just as did her husband, Elmore, and everyone else they knew who was of the same ethnicity. One said "Swedish Lutheran" in the same way one said "Pennsylvania Dutch,"—although the "Dutch" was a corruption of the German word *Deutsch*, which means, not surprisingly, "German."

Being Swedish Lutheran was just who Ellen was and who she thought her people were. To be Swedish meant being Lutheran, and people from Småland were very Lutheran. Even today, Småland is significantly more religious (meaning Lutheran) than Sweden in general. Among Swedes, people from Småland have a reputation that is reflected in the traditions of the Linns, the Swensons, and all their neighbors. Some people suggest that the harsh conditions throughout the history of Småland have forced the inhabitants of the region to be inventive, and, oddly enough, cooperative. Even among themselves, Swedes acknowledge that Swedish people in general are hardheaded and stubborn. "Cooperative" is not often used to describe a Swede.

An old Swedish encyclopedia, *Nordisk Familjebok*, describes the inhabitants of Småland in this way: The Smålandian is by nature awake and smart, diligent and hard-working, yet compliant, cunning and crafty, which gives him the advantage of being able to move through life with little means.

A running joke local to Sweden is that Smålandians are "very economical," meaning sometimes modestly frugal to more commonly utterly cheap. Ingvar Kamprad, the founder of global cheap furniture giant IKEA (started in the Småland town of Älmhult) and a native of Småland, is quoted as saying that the Smålandian people are seen as the Scotsmen of Sweden. This may offend some Scotsmen, but probably would be readily agreed to by anyone familiar with the culture and habits of Scotland and Småland.

Ellen laid down the copy of *The Lutheran*, a magazine sent monthly to many Lutheran homes in the United States. She had been reading it with extreme interest. Her excitement was growing uncontrollably as she read more and more of the article.

She had just found a hard job that she felt called to take on. It would be her new mission.

Her heart was beating noticeably in her chest with anticipation and a fever she didn't understand. And for the first time in a very long time, she felt a certainty—a rock solid absoluteness—in her life, suddenly replenishing a faith that had ebbed away, just as her tiny blue boy's life had ebbed away while he had gasped for breath. It was as if God had reached down and tapped Ellen on her shoulder and whispered in her ear.

I have a job for you, Ellen, and maybe a way to help your unhealed, gaping loss—the dark pit of doubt and anger that I see in you.

Ellen couldn't wait to talk to Elmore.

The Lutheran magazine today describes itself thus:

> No other magazine offers members of the Evangelical Lutheran Church in America the range of inspirational and informative stories found in *The Lutheran*.
>
> Delivered directly to subscribers' homes each month, *The Lutheran* is recognized for its award-winning content and

design. It is an excellent adult education resource. In-depth study guides are developed for two or three articles in each issue. The stories and guides range in topic from current issues in church and society to spiritual formation to inspirational stories about individuals and congregations, and cover both global and local stories.

It goes further, making the point that:

As a partner in God's mission, *The Lutheran* shares with the ELCA's diverse membership the stories of God's people living their faith.

The Lutheran offers:

Stories to enrich your faith

A forum for tough issues

News you'll find nowhere else

Although this is a current description, the spirit of it could have been easily applied in 1968, when Ellen Lindquist had read an article—news that she had found nowhere else—that would re-inspire her faith and change her destiny and her life forever.

Chapter 17

Noah

Noah looked up from the book he was reading in the small coffee shop. *Kissaten.* The Japanese word for coffee shop popped into his head. Noah was starting to be able to think in Japanese—or at least a few words and phrases of it—after the several months he'd been living in Japan. He was spending a year in Kumamoto as a high school exchange student.

"Kon-nichi-wa, No-a. O-genki desu-ka?" The American-accented Japanese came from the coffee shop's entrance.

Hi, Noah. How are you?

"Hi, Brad! I'm fine. I didn't know that you'd gotten back from Korea! How are you?"

Noah had replied to Brad Jackman, an American expat he'd met a few weeks after he had arrived in Kumamoto, where Brad had been living for more than two years. Brad spoke Japanese fluently, if still with an American accent. He had dropped out of the University of Washington and decided to go to Japan to study aikido, having been exposed to the martial art during his college sophomore year. Brad's father was a contracts lawyer with a large Seattle law firm and didn't understand his son's decision to drop out of college to pursue some exotic Asian karate thing instead of following his example and attending law school.

Brad couldn't think of anything more boring and empty than becoming what his father was. Brad had a need for meaning, for additional dimensions to his existence. Not religious in any way, he instinctively sought a spirituality that he thought was missing in his classes and classmates at UW. Brad's grandfather had left him a small sum of money upon his passing when Brad was in seventh grade. He decided to use that money to underwrite his quest for spiritual enlightenment, a potential glimpse of which he had discovered through a UW martial arts club. Brad was hooked on the rigor, the philosophy, and the spirituality he saw in aikido.

Aikido is a Japanese martial arts discipline that was developed by Morihei Ueshiba in the 1920s. By the time Ueshiba died of liver cancer in 1969, he had founded and launched a global martial arts movement that endures to this day. In his later years, he looked strikingly like the martial arts master character in the movie *Kill Bill 2*, right down to the long white hair, the flowing white Fu-Manchu mustache and beard, and the inscrutable stare of a true master.

Ueshiba developed aikido as a blend of his martial arts studies, philosophy, and religious beliefs. Aikido's founding master's goal was to create a martial art form that followers could use to defend themselves while also—as crazy as it sounds to nonpractitioners—protecting their attacker from injury. Aikido blends the defender's movements with the motion of the attacker, redirecting the force of the attack rather than opposing it. When executed correctly, aikido requires very little physical strength.

Different approaches to aikido have developed, depending partly on when certain followers studied with Master Ueshiba. However, they all share techniques learned from Master Ueshiba and most have concern for the well-being of the attacker. This strange combination of opposing yet protecting one's attacker intrigued Brad. So he had come to be a novice, an initiate, in one of the most famous aikido *dojos* in Japan, the Manseikan Honbu Dojo, founded in 1954 in the city of Kumamoto, Japan.

"Yes. I got back Friday. I figured I'd find you here," Brad said to Noah with his signature grin splitting his freckled face and offsetting his red hair as he stepped further into the little coffee shop. The Japanese just loved Brad's classic redhead features. They thought he was some sort of human-ish alien, until he started speaking to them in Japanese.

In 1981 Japan had just emerged as a reborn player on the world stage and there were relatively few foreigners in Tokyo, but in a backwater place like Kumamoto in the eastern center part of Kyushu, Japan's southernmost home island, there were only twenty-six in the entire province or prefecture. And even fewer in the city itself.

The "here" that Brad was referring to was one of Noah's favorite hangouts. It was a small, hole-in-a-wall coffee shop a couple of blocks south of the Shimotōri Arcade, near the main shopping drag of Ginza Dori. The coffee shop was called Blue Note and always had jazz playing through speakers that were tucked into the shop's corners. Noah would take the bus to Blue Note from his homestay where he was placed as an exchange student. The homestay family was nice enough. The father was a schoolteacher at a girl's junior high school and the mother was a stay-at-home mom. The family had three children, ages nine, five, and three. Other than the father, none of the family spoke any English. At eighteen, Noah wasn't used to being with little kids, especially ones jabbering in Japanese, and he would come here to get away from the noise and constant requests to play from the two younger kids, especially on a Saturday, like today.

Brad came over to Noah's table in his slightly odd walk, like his feet were somehow too small and he had to step quickly and with a roll not to put too much pressure on them. Noah always figured it had something to do with his aikido training. But maybe not. Brad pulled a chair opposite Noah at the small table. It was one of the first things that Noah had noticed when he arrived in Japan: the tables, chairs, and sofas, even though they looked Western, were all slightly lower and smaller. When sitting in these Japanese versions of Western seating, Noah was always reminded of sitting in a grade school classroom chair after he had grown up.

Jackman took off his black wool seaman's watch coat and hung it on the chair back before sitting down. It was November, and today was a cold day for Kumamoto, with a flat, grey overcast sky. A coffee shop server came over, wearing a simulation of a French horizontal-striped shirt and black pants, with a long, white French waiter-looking apron. He set a small glass of water in front of Brad. Water was never served with ice in Japan or in any part of the world, for that matter, outside of the United States. It's something most Americans who travel abroad find very annoying.

"Hey it's good to have you back. You increased the population of non-Japanese in the city of Kumamoto by ten percent," Noah said as Brad thanked the waiter in Japanese for the water glasses that had just been set down. Kumamoto City had a population of around one million, but Noah was right, only about a dozen foreigners.

The waiter nodded his head and gestured to the glasses with his hand as he bowed and departed for the kitchen in the back. Brad called after the waiter and asked in his perfect American-accented Japanese for a large coffee.

"What? The foreign population doubled in the two and a half weeks I was gone?"

"Well, people heard that you weren't around and figured it was safe to move in."

"Well, guess they're all gonna be packing and leaving then!"

Noah closed the book he had been reading, *The Chrysanthemum and the Sword: Patterns of Japanese Culture*, written by anthropologist Ruth Benedict in 1946. It was one of the first twentieth-century analyses done of Japanese society, its norms, culture, and people. It helped explain some of the unfathomable, extreme Japanese behavior that Americans had witnessed during

World War II. Noah knew it was dated, but it had been available to purchase and he needed help in understanding Japanese culture and the people around him.

"So how was Korea? Cold, I bet," Noah asked, remembering the cold of his early childhood.

"Yup. And you know what else? Koreans have the most perfect, straight teeth. Really! No shit. Compared to Japan, it was like the first thing I noticed!"

Americans stand out in other countries, because putting braces on children is not a common practice anywhere else in the world. Certainly the British don't do it, nor the French, nor the Japanese. Unfortunately, Japanese have smaller bodies and heads than Brits or French, but about the same-sized teeth. Less real estate, more crowding. American expatriates in Japan always talk about how jammed and crooked teeth are among the Japanese.

"Really? That's what you noticed first? I knew you were weird, Brad."

Noah still had a retainer cemented onto his lower teeth and wore a removable one at night.

"Whatever, man. But it's true. And they *don't* do braces; it's just natural."

One of the things that had bothered Noah most growing up as the only half-Korean person and one of only a few visibly racially different people in St. Peter, was how he got lumped into any and every Asian category.

Chinese! Japanese! dirty knees—look at these!

Racism was too lazy to correct its own ignorance. Bothered by his own lack of knowledge regarding Asia, since his arrival in Japan Noah had been reading and learning—with great surprise—about the vast differences, not just between Asia and the West, but within Asia itself: among Chinese, Japanese, and Koreans. Most Americans, or maybe most Westerners, like Europeans, Brits, and French, think that there is little difference among Japanese, Chinese, and Koreans. Westerners rarely can tell these ethnicities apart physically.

Hell, they all look the same to me!

But the cultures and languages are very different, much more different than, for example, French, German, and Italian. The Chinese language is completely unrelated to either Japanese or Korean. Finnish and Hungarian are more closely related to Korean and Japanese than Japanese and Korean are to Chinese. Chinese is what linguists would call a multi-tonal, monosyllabic language, whereas Japanese and Korean are atonal, polysyllabic languages. What this means is that in Chinese Mandarin, a word like *ma* can have several meanings depending on the tone and context (for example a rising tone, like when an English speaker asks a question) and that different inflection can change the entire meaning of a phrase.

Korean and Japanese, though distantly related as languages, are no more so than English and Danish. And unlike English and Danish—and Spanish, German, Finnish, or Italian—Korean and Japanese have fully unrelated writing systems. Korean is completely different from either Chinese or Japanese, but written Japanese does use a significant number of Chinese characters, called *kanji*, along with two different syllabaries of forty-six symbols, called *kana*. A syllabary is a phonetic writing system consisting of symbols representing syllables. Because the characters of the kana do not represent single consonants (except in the case of the sound "n"), the kana are referred to as syllabaries and not alphabets.

Unfortunately for written Japanese and for centuries of students in Japan, the spoken language existed well before there was writing to go with it. The first written language that Japanese speakers encountered was Chinese. Early written Japanese tried adapting Chinese writing by one of two methods: using the Chinese characters phonetically to sound out Japanese words, like some sort of very complicated alphabet, or using the Chinese character that had a meaning, like "mountain" in Chinese to represent the word *mountain* as spoken in Japanese. Over the centuries parts of both methods survived, and Japanese today uses two syllabaries, which are derived in two different ways from simplified versions of Chinese characters to phonetically "spell out" syllables. But Japanese also use kanji, full Chinese characters, to represent the root meaning of many words. The Japanese Ministry of Education has limited the total number of kanji required to be learned to 1,945, but most newspapers limit kanji use even further, to about 1,000 characters.

Korean is written using a true alphabet consisting of twenty-four letters representing vowels and consonants. But unlike the letters of the Latin alphabet, which are written sequentially, Korean, or *Hangul*, letters are grouped into blocks, such that letters for the word *han*, grouped together to make the word, look similar to a Chinese character or a Japanese kanji. Therefore, although the word *han* may look like a single character, it is actually composed of three letters denoting the sounds: "h," "a," and "n." Koreans are very proud of their alphabet. Legend attributes the creation of the alphabet to King Sejong the Great, the fourth king of the Joseon Dynasty, in 1443. In 1940 a document from 1446 was discovered that clearly laid out the reasons and creative process for the promulgated Hangul. In explaining the need for the new alphabet, King Sejong explained that the Korean language was fundamentally different from Chinese; using Chinese characters to write Korean was so difficult that only privileged aristocrats could read and write. The majority of Koreans were effectively illiterate before the invention of Hangul.

October 9, the anniversary of the date of the alphabet's promulgation to the people, is a national South Korean holiday. The event is celebrated even in North Korea.

Written Chinese contains approximately eighty thousand characters and was standardized some two hundred years before the birth of Christ. Modern Chinese, however, uses only about thirty-five thousand characters. Written Chinese is not an alphabet or a syllabary but is pictographic or logosyllabic, meaning a character usually represents one syllable of spoken Chinese and may be a word on its own or a part of a word. Even though there is one written Chinese language, spoken Chinese is a group of closely related languages spoken by more than 1.2 billion people composed of at least fourteen different groups. None of these groups speak a language that is related to Japanese or Korean.

The differences in the languages reflect the vast differences in the cultures and histories of these countries and ethnicities. Essentially, Westerners are simply wrong in their assumption that all Asians are similar. All of Europe, including Russia, is much more similar and related—culturally, linguistically and racially—than are China, Japan, and Korea.

N oah looked into Brad's grey eyes. *Wow. I think he's really serious about being impressed with Korean teeth. Go figure.*

The waiter returned to the table. He set down a steaming cup of very dark aromatic coffee. The cup would not have been characterized as a "large" cup in the United States. But in Japan, Americans were always amazed by how small the "regular" cup was. This one was large, by Japanese standards.

"Domo." Brad thanked him and reached for the white cup on its saucer, steaming with the vapor of the coffee's molecules drifting into the shop's November air, and took a small slurp.

"They got good joe here."

"Wouldn't know. I don't drink that stuff. Coffee smells like it should taste amazing, but tastes like crap, like boiled tar or something."

"It's an acquired taste, my friend. Wait 'til you're pulling all-nighters at that fancy college you got accepted to in Virginia. I guarantee you that you will acquire a taste for it very quickly, especially since you're going to be studying nuclear engineering."

Noah picked up his cup of Japanese green tea. This he could handle.

"Hey, I need to return your necklace and pendant . . . and I brought something back from Korea for you."

Brad reached into his coat pocket and pulled out a small silver chain with a flat silver oval pendant. The pendant was engraved on one side with a floral design and was smooth, except for some small, engraved words, on the other side. The words were written in Korean, in three lines. He held the chain and pendant out toward Noah.

"Thanks, Brad. I'm glad you didn't lose it."

Noah pulled it over his head—it was a tight fit—and tucked the chain and pendant under his shirt.

"It's one of the only things I still have that my mother gave me."

Noah looked at Brad Jackman and didn't want to ask.

Brad would have said something if he had . . .

Noah's thoughts were controlled. He needed to guard against thinking about some things. There was no point—and a deep fear—in touching what lurked under some of his avoided thoughts.

Don't go there, Noah.

"Well, I wasn't going to lose it, asshole. Anyway, I returned it to you. But I said that I brought back something from Korea for you."

"Brad, you didn't have to get me an *omiage*"—the Japanese word for a gift one brings back from a trip to give to friends and family members. It was considered highly impolite in Japan not to bring back omiage from a trip.

"I think you've been living here too long when you start getting people like me omiage."

"I didn't. You don't rate it, and I'm not that Japanese. Here."

Jackman was holding out a letter-sized envelope toward Noah.

"It's a letter from your mother. I found her."

Noah Lindquist's breathing froze and he stared at the envelope in Brad Jackman's hand, outstretched in front of him.

Chapter 18

Hee Ae

L ee Hee Ae stood outside the gates to 305 Sangmoon-Dong (Sangmoon Street) in the Sungbuk district of metropolitan Seoul. The entrance had two red brick entry pillars, a bit taller than a full-grown man. The gate and the pillars were ludicrously out of place in this snowy outskirt of Seoul. They looked like the entry to some Virginia plantation, made of red brick and wrought iron. And in fact there was an odd, almost Southern-looking main building visible up the curving drive beyond the gates. It looked like a red brick hybrid of a Southern courthouse and a Southern Baptist church, without the steeple and the white cross.

But it definitely did not look like it was a building that belonged in the brown dirt and grimy snowiness of a treeless remote outskirt of the capital of a third world, Asian country. One would almost expect to see the legs and feet of the Wicked Witch of the West sticking out from the foundation stones, as if the building had been suddenly dropped on top of her after being picked up from some place in Fluvanna County, Virginia.

Hee Ae had taken the bus from the main terminal near the center of Seoul, transferring from the one she had taken to reach the main bus terminal. A green placard on the right-side pillar had "KOREA SOCIAL SERVICE, INC." written on it in raised, goldish letters in English. In much larger print the same thing was written in Korean Hangul. It had been seven months since she had been here. She stood for a very long time and made all the arguments over and again in her head. She felt like she would throw up at any moment, and the taste of bile was real and bitter in the back of her throat. Her demons and guilt-serpents were frothing in her conscience and her ruptured thoughts.

She had first heard of this place from another woman who worked at the "club" she had worked at—a club that entertained only men, only American military men. She had learned that this woman's girl-friend had used this place to solve her problems and responsibilities. She learned that there were eager, rich American parents who were waiting to lavish America's unfathomable wealth and endless plenty upon Korean children. Especially if the children weren't really Korean, but were American. She learned from this woman that her friend was now happily living her life and that she had her life *back*. No more shame. No more stares and pointing fingers, no more explaining what already was starkly clear yet could never be explained. Nobody wanted to hear the excuses of a grade-school educated, dirt-poor whore, holding her foreign bastard son's hand.

Hee Ae heard how this woman's friend had started a whole new life by leaving her old one behind within these gates, the ones before which Hee Ae was standing. This other woman had even subsequently gotten married to a Korean husband from a reputable family that actually farmed land.

You could have a husband again! A good one this time . . . no one would need to know or find out about your half-breed American child . . .

You could move and start your life all over! No more being worth a few American dollars! No more being just meat. No more being used, reviled, shunned, isolated . . . lonely . . . and drunk to stop the pain of all the loneliness, of being shunned, of being used.

So why was this so hard? She heard the voices in her head again: *Your son would be so much better off being spoiled, pampered, educated, and fattened by god-like, immortally wealthy Americans.*

He would live and grow up among these golden Olympians on their far-off perfect mountain top among the clouds of plenty, safety, and limitless bounty. He could live and grow up among his people— Americans! He could grow up away from Koreans and their ancient, demanding, tribal, exclusionary clannishness, their petty and lethal bigotry . . . and away from YOU! Your drunkenness, your poverty, your anger, your harm . . . remember: YOU CRIPPLED HIM!

My god! The Americans maybe could fix his hand. Erase his scars! She'd heard stories of the magic of American medicine. Had they not saved little Young Nam when he should have died—boiled to death—from what she had done to him? What more might the miracles of America and American medicine be able to do?

You must do this!

But I can't.

Because I love him too much. So much it truly hurts.

I can't let him go . . . I just CAN'T . . . !

But your love is not enough . . .

Her thoughts and her heart, her demons and her cravings, her hopes and her terrors erupted inside her. The voices argued inside her head. Point and counterpoint. One set of hopes arguing against another set of hopes. All this torment and battle invisibly raging inside the soul of a small woman standing with a thousand-mile expressionless stare through slanted, Asian eyes, their pupils dark as midnight with torment and confusion; standing in front of a gate that could have been at home in the Shenandoah Valley rather than outside of Seoul, South Korea.

Chapter 19

Noah

Noah could see the famous Busan lighthouse that stood as a lonely, gleaming white sentinel on the grey rock that was splashed in thundering, icy cold, chaotic surges of spray on the southern point of Yongdo Island at the entrance of Busan harbor. His ferry was slowly thrumming and shuddering past the landmark, putting the lighthouse to her port side. He tracked it with his green eyes as it slowly fell astern on the ship's port quarter.

The lighthouse had been standing as a beacon to ships coming into Busan since 1906. It had been built under Japanese initiative and control a year after Korea became a protectorate of Japan under the Portsmouth Treaty, which ended the Russo-Japanese War in September 1905. The war had several inconclusive land battles, but only one very conclusive naval battle, the Battle of Tsushima Strait, in which the Japanese fleet sank two-thirds of the entire Russian navy. It was the last time that a defeated naval force of one nation officially surrendered at sea to the victor after a pitched battle.

President Theodore Roosevelt invited the warring parties to a treaty conference in neutral America. Through his back-channel negotiations, he was able to get the parties to sign a peace treaty on September 5, 1905. A key concession to which he got the Russians to agree was giving control of Korea to Japan. For this, Theodore Roosevelt was awarded the Nobel Peace Prize in 1906, the same year that the Busan lighthouse was erected on its lonely, sea-thrashed perch, looking across the Sea of Japan from Korea toward Japan.

While he gazed at the lighthouse sliding by, Noah Lindquist was consumed by his thoughts and memories. And his anxious anticipation—*dread? fear? elation?*—of meeting his flesh and blood mother for the first time since he was a six-year-old. The letter that Brad Jackman had given him a month ago, during their meeting at the Blue Note kissaten in Kumamoto, was tucked inside his breast pocket. It had been from his Korean mother, handwritten in Hangul, the alphabet that King Sejon the Great had promulgated in 1443 so that little-educated peasants, like his mother, might become literate.

Days after Brad's breath-stopping, shocking news, Noah had been able to find someone through his host family's father who could translate the letter for Noah. Translated, of course, from the twenty-four lettered alphabet of Korean into the 1,945 kanji and two, forty-six kana syllabaries of Japanese. He had had to further translate it from Japanese into English, with its twenty-six lettered Latin alphabet. Noah's birth mother said in the painstakingly translated letter that she wanted to see her son again. Would Noah be willing to meet her in Busan?

Noah had met Brad through another American expat, Rusty Carlisle. It was a purely chance encounter and introduction, and Noah and Brad had only crossed paths a few times after that first meeting. It was during one of those path crossings at Rusty and his wife's home, located in the eastern outskirts of Kumamoto in Ozu-Machi and halfway to the beautiful national park surrounding the conically-shaped Aso-Yama, the long-dormant volcano in the center of Kyushu, that Noah learned Brad was planning to travel to Korea.

"Over two years in Japan, and I've never made it to Korea," Brad said, between mouthfuls of homemade *sukiyaki*.

Sukiyaki is a Japanese stew-type dish, cooked and served in the *nabemono*, a Japanese hot pot. Sukiyaki consists of thinly sliced beef, which is slowly cooked or simmered at the table along with vegetables and other ingredients, like tofu and the Japanese mush-room, *inoki*. All of the ingredients are simmered and browned in sukiyaki sauce, which is a mixture of soy sauce, sugar, and *mirin*, Japanese sweet rice-wine vinegar. Before being eaten, the ingredients are usually dipped in a small bowl of raw, beaten eggs that each person has at his or her setting.

Because of its beefy savoriness, and the fact that everything is fully cooked, it's the one authentic Japanese dish that is compatible with and highly liked by Western palates. Traditionally, like many stews and hot dishes everywhere, it was considered a winter comfort food. But Rusty's Japanese wife knew how much he liked the dish and knew that the two other Americans would also like it. Plus, it was easy to make, essentially letting the meal cook itself on the table, with Rusty stirring the sauce and the ingredients. The modern nabemono was now electrically powered and heated, so you could cook and keep the meal warm by controlling the thermostatic temperature control as you ate.

The four of them sat around a low, traditional Japanese table in the middle of a tatami-floored dining room that had sliding wooden doors covered in white rice paper. The doors were open, even though it was a cool, early October evening, and the diners were able to look out over the beautifully manicured bonsai garden that comprised the view from the dining room. Each of the four sat on a square cushion, cross-legged. Noah could only sit in this fashion for short periods, before a leg or foot would start to go numb. He'd then shift his position and uncross and recross his legs to get blood flowing back to the numb limb, which would quickly feel uncomfortably weird and full of pin pricks as the blood brought feeling back.

Noah decided to sit on his knees. He could do this position for extended periods of time because he had done it through years of being on his high school wrestling team. His left foot was tingling and pin-pricking him like a hatter's pin cushion, so Brad's words at first didn't connect to anything conscious in Noah's brain.

"Blah blah, blah, blah. Blah . . . Korea."

What?

Noah's brain finally put the noises together into words and the meanings attached to them.

"Korea? Why are you going there?" Noah asked.

"Because, man, I'm going to head back to the States next spring. Go back to UW and finish college. And I can't tell people that I spent almost three years in Japan and never traveled anywhere else! Anyway, Korea is so close and it's cheap to get there. Also, I have a friend who is studying the Korean form of aikido, called hapkido, at a dojo in Seoul. So I have a place to stay and something interesting to do."

"I hear that hapkido is just a Korean renamed version of aikido. Is it really very different?" Rusty asked as he stirred the sukiyaki and shifted his gaze toward his wife and smiled.

"Kinu-chan, sukiyaki wa tottemo oishi-n datta-yo!"

Kinu, babe, your sukiyaki tastes really good!

Rusty spoke perfect Kumamoto-ben style Japanese.

"Thanks, Rusty. I'm glad you like it."

Kinuko Carlisle replied in perfect English, with the right amount of Japanese accent, so that she sounded like an Asian Bond girl commenting on some matter for 007 played by Sean Connery.

In fact, Rusty Carlisle looked an awful lot like Sean Connery, the actor who most popularized the character of James Bond. And Kinuko could definitely pass for being a Bond girl. She was shockingly beautiful, the kind of perfect beauty that makes men—and women— turn their heads. The kind of beauty that literally takes one's breath away for a moment, before the brain kicks the autonomic nervous system to start doing that breathing thing again. She had grown up in wealth and privilege. She was a graduate of Tokyo University, Japan's number-one ranked university, and her family's lore was that the family belonged to former Japanese nobility.

Rusty Carlisle was a forty-year-old former US Navy F-4 Phantom fighter pilot and a Naval Academy graduate. He had done two tours flying off aircraft carriers in the Gulf of Tonkin, one in 1965 and the other in 1967. His ships had been the USS *Coral Sea* and the USS *Oriskany*.

Rusty exuded the "right stuff" of a fighter pilot. Athletic, dark-haired, Sean Connery looks, a cleft chin, and a swagger that could be spotted two football fields away. That swagger now had a slight limp to it. He had had to punch out of his fighter plane on the return from a bombing mission in 1967. Ten miles short of the pitching flight deck of his carrier, the *Oriskany*, his Phantom's two engines both flamed out. He was out of fuel, probably caused by shrapnel that had severed some critical fuel lines. It's what pilots call a double flameout. Anyone who's watched Tom Cruise in the movie *Top Gun* has seen a dramatization of a double flameout. It's the scene where the character Maverick has to eject, along with his buddy and RIO, radar intercept officer, Goose. And Goose gets killed in the ejection.

Rusty had an actual double flameout happen to him and had to eject for real. Rusty's RIO luckily didn't get killed. He was fine. But Rusty clipped a knee on the edge of his Phantom's cockpit when the explosive charge under his pilot's seat blew him out into the skies of the South Pacific at the rate of 306 miles per hour. The impact shattered his left knee and after reconstructive surgery, a lot of hardware, an artificial joint, and years of physical therapy, he could walk almost normally. Just the slightest limp in his fighter jock swagger. But it ended his fighter pilot days and any thoughts he had of a navy career. After being discharged on disability, he landed a job with McDonnell Douglas, assisting in F-4 pilot training at Atsugi, Japan, where the United States has a naval air base near the ancient city of Kamakura.

At Kamakura sits one of the iconic images of Japan: the huge, green bronze statue of Amitahba Buddha—the *Daibutsu*—that sits cross-legged with his hands ceremoniously held on his lap, with the palms up, finger tips touching, and his thumbs and forefingers of each hand forming two circles, his huge head slightly bowed. It's been sitting there since 1252 on the exact same spot where it was erected.

It was in front of the *Daibutsu* that Rusty Carlisle met Oda Kinuko. She was as shockingly beautiful in the spring of 1976 as she was now in 1981. Rusty was looking to ask someone to take a photo of him standing in front of the iconic statue using his Nippon Kogaku K. K. camera (the company succumbed to public pressure and officially changed its name to what everyone called its cameras—Nikon—in 1988).

He approached this take-your-breath-away, beautiful girl, who was standing among a group of other young women, all in variations of the popular bell-bottomed, women's polyester pantsuit of the day. But she stood out. Literally. In addition to her stop-the-presses looks, she was a head taller than her friends. And Rusty swaggered over with his slight limp and tried to ask in his very limited Japanese.

"Sumimasen, shashin totte kudasai?"

Excuse me, take picture please?

All the young women turned and looked at Rusty, who stuck out as the only *gaijin*—foreigner—in the whole temple complex, wearing his bell-bottomed jeans and tight, floral-patterned, wide-collared polyester shirt with his Nikon FT2 handing around his neck like a brick, weighing more than one and one-half pounds. His Ringo Starr-style mustache spread above his smile. He was looking only at Kinuko.

She stared for an awkward moment—thinking—then said in her perfect, Bond girl, Japanese-accented English, "Of course, I'd be delighted to."

She liked his looks and the aura he exuded. And she always would.

B rad responded to Rusty's question, waiting for the older man to finish stirring the sukiyaki so that he could put more on his plate.

"Not really, Rusty. I hear that it's totally different from aikido now, but that it may have started based on aikido. Supposedly, a Korean guy growing up in Japan in the late 1800s learned aikido and brought it back to Korea. It sounds pretty cool. That's why I'm going to check it out."

"When do you leave?" Noah inquired.

"In two days. I'm taking a ferry from Shimonoseki. There're some really cheap fares. The boat arrives in Busan, and I'll take the train up to Seoul after touring around Busan for a day or two."

Brad made money as a private tutor teaching English to housewives and children of wealthy Japanese families around Kumamoto. He made surprisingly good money, but, given that he didn't work full-time, he needed to be frugal. Plus, the discipline of living in the aikido dojo had made frugality an ingrained habit for Brad Jackman.

Teaching was a high-status profession in Japan, as well as in most East Asian countries, especially if one taught at the college level, but junior high and high school teachers were held in very high esteem as well. Even elementary teachers basked in the reflected social status of being a *sensei*, "teacher," or sometimes translated as "master," like how the martial arts student character, played by actor David Carradine in the 1970s TV series *Kung Fu*, always called his teacher "master"—though in a very obviously fake, pseudo-Chinese accent.

As a half-Asian kid growing up in America in the 1970s, it always struck Noah as more than odd—insulting?—that Hollywood preferred to use Caucasian guys to play Asian men in any leading role. Asian males do not align with Western standards of male beauty, attractiveness, and masculinity. Asian females, however, do match Western parameters of femininity, female beauty, and attractiveness. Hollywood rarely uses white women to play Asian women. Noel had felt this difference in perceptions and standards throughout his teenage years.

"Hey, Brad. Do you think you might make it to the DMZ between North and South Korea? I hear it's a pretty interesting place to visit."

When Carlisle asked this, Noah looked at Rusty, trying to read his face.

When Carlisle had learned that Noah had been awarded a US Navy scholarship to college, the older man had taken a special interest in Noah and had often invited him to dinners at his home. Noah had shared with Carlisle that he had been born in Korea and that he was half Korean. Everyone always asked him, "Are you part Japanese?" (substitute Chinese, Vietnamese, or whatever Asian country the person happened to be most familiar with). Carlisle had been no different. So Noah had explained that he'd been adopted at a young age. This opened up a new dimension to the relationship that had formed between Carlisle and Noah.

"Yeah, I thought I might," Brad reached for more sukiyaki from the *nabemono* pot. "It seems like a pretty interesting situation to see firsthand."

"Noah, I think you should ask Brad."

Noah looked from Carlisle to Jackman.

"Ask me what?"

Brad dipped a piece of tofu into his dish of raw scrambled egg before slurping it into his mouth from his *hashi*, his chopsticks.

Noah felt very awkward and his gut tightened. The Carlisles and Brad were all looking at him, waiting for him to answer Brad's question.

Noah had struggled all his life with not belonging, being the foreigner, the odd one, the one who looked different, in Korea as well as in America. He didn't know Brad Jackman very well. Brad and Noah had never had a conversation about Noah's race, whatever it was, or anything else very personal. Brad had shared that he was from Seattle and Noah had explained that he was from St. Peter, Minnesota. Mostly, Noah had listened to Brad as he talked about aikido and living in a dojo. Noah had been in "watch and learn" mode since arriving in Japan. He did not know any Japanese before arriving in the country and had been drowning in his ignorance of the language and the culture.

He relished times, like this evening, when he could speak and hear English. Since only his homestay father spoke any English and his schoolmates spoke none, Noah struggled each day, all day, trying to make himself understood in the little Japanese he had picked up and went through his days understanding almost nothing of what was said around him. Essentially, he was a very miserable, lonely teenager. And he greatly regretted choosing Japan as his exchange country. He had had a choice. Now he regretted not choosing England or Holland or Australia. But he had wanted to see what it would be like not to be the only Asian in the room, the way he felt every day in St. Peter. What would it be like not to be stared at?

And he had thought . . . *just maybe, there might be a chance . . .*

He didn't think much beyond such initial unformed thoughts about the possibility of going to Korea.

He was so close . . .

Maybe I could ask Brad to look for her . . . but all I have are the address and names on my chain's pendant. Even if Brad were willing, how could he find her with just two names and an old address in a foreign country where he doesn't speak the language and knew only one person, who also was a foreigner?

Chapter 20

Ellen

The article that Ellen had read in *The Lutheran* magazine completely captivated her and created a true epiphany. For people who are not religious or are casually so, Ellen's epiphany would be hard to believe or truly grasp. How does one actually hear God's voice or truly feel God's touch? Surely it's simply all in one's mind and one's imagination. But it's not imagined, but real, to those who believe. And Ellen was raised to believe and had just found her belief reborn, stronger than ever.

The article articulated the duty of each Christian and Lutheran in a way she had not grasped or thought about until just now—and she was born and bred to understand duty, way down deep in her bones. The article had spoken to that bone-deep grasp of duty.

Ever since the death of her infant son, she had struggled with her core beliefs—of all that had been drilled in through her catechism training—in secret and in silence. She hadn't even shared with Elmore how shattered her beliefs were in the basic tenets of the world she had accepted all her life. Her faith felt empty and forced.

How can there be a loving God? How can he be just? If God wanted to punish me, why kill my innocent son? Where is the meaning? Where the HELL is the GOOD in any of this?

These thoughts and feelings had never receded since that horrible June day, more than ten years ago; they were always swirling nearby, waiting for a bad day, a tired moment, an injustice in her world, and then the thoughts would strike—quick and fierce and snarling, screaming the accusations.

Where is your justice NOW, God? Where is this fabled love NOW? And where was it THEN? Why did you kill my son??

But now, she was feeling a rush in her pulse. It was like suddenly seeing again after driving through a blizzard. The words in the magazine immediately caused a connection in her brain, set in motion a series of thoughts that unexpectedly seemed to shine an illuminating light through the darkness of her loss, doubt, anger, and pain. Her faith and her grasp of who she was as a Lutheran woman seemed miraculously, gloriously reborn.

Ellen embraced responsibility and mission. The harder it was, the more she threw herself into the task. Ask any of her classmates at Swedish Hospital Nursing School in Minneapolis or the blood drive volunteers at the community hospital in St. Peter. Ellen Lindquist was *the* go-to girl. And, now, it was crystal clear in Ellen's mind: God had reached out to her as *his* go-to girl, to do an exceptionally hard task. What she knew, deep in her bones with a certainty that had been missing for too long, missing since her tiny blue boy had died a gasping death, was this: God was calling her!

"For God so loved the world, that he gave his only begotten Son . . ." Ellen could quote the entire Bible passage by heart. And so she did, in her head. And the thoughts came.

All the suffering of these lost and abandoned children . . .

I could never have understood . . . never have truly appreciated my life . . .

What if . . . what if . . . God—MY God—let me feel HIS pain, what HE felt at the loss of HIS own son . . .

. . . that I may TRULY understand the magnitude of his love for the world!

What if God allowed my son's death and caused such a terrible void to be ripped into my heart that I might have the need, the SAME undying ache that he has, and fill it with . . .

. . . one of these destitute, lost, lonely children?

Oh Lord, this will be hard, but Ellen's blood could feel the truth of
her belief. This was now her mission and the answer to all her accusations and pain at her God. Ellen Lindquist had been hearing about
international adoption for some time. But in the 1960s, international
adoption was essentially synonymous with adoption from Korea.

Korea, or more correctly, South Korea, has been *the* example for
international adoptions. Reliable data on adoptions of any sort
are very spotty, with international adoption the best documented
because of the US government's tracking of immigration. Some esti-
mates put total international adoptions into the United States since
WWII at more than 250,000 children, with approximately 150,000
of those children coming from Korea. During the 1950s and 1960s,
adoptions from Korea essentially created international adoption as
a standardized practice and ultimately enshrined it in law. Eighty
countries have ratified the 1995 Hague Convention on Protection of
Children and Co-operation in Respect of Intercountry Adoption. The
United States ratified the convention only in April of 2008, but Korea,
surprisingly, has not ratified it yet.

According to Charles G. Chakerian, one of the leading researchers on international Korean adoption and notable for researching
and writing contemporaneously about events he was investigating
in the 1960s, child abandonment started to soar in Korea starting
in the mid-1950s. Korea was a society where the norms and strict
Confucian, male-dominant family codes had lagged behind social
realities. Between 1955 and 1970, a total of 80,520 children were
abandoned, with urban poverty as the reason stated for half of the
cases, followed by disability, family break-up, neglect by parents,
illegitimacy, and prostitution.

Every one of these reasons pressed their daily weight in little
Young Nam's life in 1968, when Ellen refound her faith and
embraced her new mission.

Researchers Chin Kim and Timothy Carroll contend that 4,494 mixed-race children were adopted internationally from Korea between 1958 and 1974. According to the Korean Ministry of Health and Welfare, the children who left the country during this first stage of international adoption from Korea were predominantly girls. The main country of destination was the United States where Korean children would dominate international adoption for thirty-eight years in a row.

In 1964 a nonprofit company, Korea Social Service, Inc., began to process international adoptions; it was the first agency to be entirely run by Koreans. Several others followed, along with existing international adoption agencies, like Holt International. At the beginning of the 1970s as many as seven agencies operated in the field: Seventh Day Adventists, Child Placement Service, Catholic Relief Service, Holt Children's Services, Korea Social Service, Welcome House, and Eastern Child Welfare Society.

There has been much literature and discussion on the topic of Korean intercountry adoption. Korea is unique, not only in the magnitude of absolute numbers of children adopted into foreign countries and the sustained duration of this phenomenon, but also because of the staggering percentages involved. At the peak of international adoption of Korean children, approximately one and one-half percent of ALL live births in Korea ended up being adopted by overseas foreigners, adoptive parents who were preponderantly white and American. And eighty to ninety percent of ALL births to single mothers in Korea were placed into orphanages and potentially available for adoption. This is in contrast to less than one percent of American children born to single mothers.

There have been critical voices, both within and outside of Korea, regarding Korea's history and practice of international adoption. In the 1970s, North Korea strongly criticized its southern counterpart through its national, propagandist newspaper *The Pyongyang Times* for "selling thousands, tens of thousands of children . . . to foreign marauders." This criticism received international attention when some of these articles were reprinted by left-leaning Western newspapers, especially in Sweden. Feelings inside South Korea are also conflicted and sometimes critical. According to a *New York Times* article published in October 2008, the ministry official who oversees adoptions at the Ministry of Health was quoted as saying, "South Korea is the world's 12th largest economy and is now almost an advanced country, so we would like to rid ourselves of the international stigma or disgrace of being a baby-exporting country." But if this sense of national shame, embarrassment, and disgrace over its practice of being the leading provider of children for international adoption for four decades is true, then how is it that Korea ended up in such a position? Many have theorized that there is something different or unique about Koreans and Korean culture and history that has been a factor in making Korea a "baby-exporting country."

Korean culture and history, even its current family law, uniquely emphasizes reverence for ancestors and the primary role of the male bloodline to define families. This strong tradition is based upon the Confucian emphasis on the primacy of family bloodline. According to some researchers, the male bloodline is the underlying definer of kinship and community in Korea. Adoption of a son was historically permitted for childless families, but only to preserve and pass on a family's name, and every effort was made to adopt a male child within the extended family, preserving the bloodline as closely as possible. Even today, the adoption of any child, but especially an unrelated child, is very rare, and some Koreans consider it shameful. In historical and modern Korea, the family name and lineage play a significant role in determining which of society's doors will be opened or closed, impacting everything from education, work, and career opportunities to the potential pool of marriage partners.

Especially through most of the twentieth century, strict social obedience to this blood-based family structure meant that a child in Korea who is without a biological family—especially one who does not have a Korean father—faced great discrimination, social stigma, and ostracism. Until quite recently, Korean citizenship was directly tied to Korean bloodline, particularly male bloodline. This meant that Korean orphans and mixed-race children of non-Korean fathers were not considered Korean citizens.

Nor were American-fathered foreign-born children considered US citizens. Under a quirk of US law, children of an American woman and a foreign man, even outside of wedlock, are automatically accorded natural-born US citizen status, no matter where they are physically born (subject to some residence requirements for the mother). But children born out of wedlock by an American man and a foreign woman outside US territory are not citizens. The American father would first need to formally petition the US government, under the Immigration and Nationality Act, to give his child citizenship. But the father's word is not enough. The petition must be accompanied by documentation that a blood relationship between the child and the father has been established by clear and convincing evidence. Therefore, most mixed-race Korean children at the time, like Young Nam, were technically stateless.

They belonged legally to no country.

And they had no citizenship anywhere on the planet.

Ellen knew a few families, distant friends of hers and Elmore's, who recently each had adopted a child from Korea. These people had adopted full-blooded Korean children. There was part of her—the politically correct part, though that term would not become popular until decades later—that admired these couples, their commitment to their faith, and to the "hip" new way of thinking that biology just doesn't matter.

Everyone who was educated and aware in 1968 "knew" that such things as "race" and "male" and "female" were just social constructions. If black people were different from white people, it was because of their respective social environments, not any biology. Ellen read profusely and read all the "in" books of her time. She was a bright, intelligent woman. Particularly, she knew that racism was not only increasingly unpopular in general, but particularly so among the educated elite, a social stratum in which, as the wife of a liberal arts college professor and herself a trained nurse, she certainly considered herself a member. And racism was also something that had become increasingly a sin in the Lutheran church, a sign of not embracing the grace of God. Her church increasingly preached the message that we are *all* created in God's image.

At the end of the 1960s, Korea's international adoption program suddenly seemed to gain worldwide popularity. In the West, adoption from Korea had become legitimized by a growing ideology (which was becoming increasingly accepted by the broad middle) that viewed and articulated such adoptions as a progressive, anti-racist act of rescuing a destitute child from the miseries and diseases of the third world.

Organizations like Lutheran Social Service extolled that "love is enough." If we are all created in the image of God, then bearing witness in the form of international adoption was a clear and visible way to live the message of the Lutheran church.

But the allure of Korean adoption had not been there for her. She wanted her son—William—back, not some foreign woman's Oriental son.

Just as Hollywood seemed to find Asians less than attractive, preferring white actors to Asian ones, Ellen was particularly put off by Asian men—the term used in the 1960s and '70s was "Oriental"—and was not very interested in things about Asia. She didn't like Oriental objets d'art and hadn't succumbed to the growing fad of decorating with Oriental accent pieces in one's home. She did own a few prints, a couple of lamps, and some Japanese teacups that she used as juice glasses. But these all were gifts, souvenirs that her one sibling, her older brother, Andrew, had given to her. She adored and idolized him. She always had and would.

Chapter 21

Noah

Noah was done with his Crab Louie salad. And his single malt scotch. Mike, the copilot, came and took the mostly eaten salad away. He piled up the sterling silver cutlery and Noah's used dark blue, Egyptian cotton napkin and lifted all of it off the glossy, cherrywood table.

"Would you like some coffee, Mr. Lindquist?"

"Do you have the Blue Mountain?"

"Of course, Mr. Lindquist. French press as usual?"

"Yes. Thanks, Mike."

Jamaican Blue Mountain is a classification of coffee. The coffee has a reputation that has made it one of the most expensive and sought-after coffees in the world.

The Blue Mountains are located between Kingston and Port Antonio on the island of Jamaica, the two points demarking the southern and northern limits of the mountain range. Rising to seventy-five hundred feet, they are some of the highest mountains in the Caribbean. The climate of the region is cool and misty with high rainfall. The soil is rich and dark—like the coffee it produces—with perfect drainage. This combination of climate and soil is ideal for growing some of the best and rarest coffee beans in the world.

Noah always preferred his coffee made in a French press. The French press used no paper filters that might absorb the coffee's delicate oils or impart a "paper taste" to the coffee.

Ironically, what is now commonly called a French press in the United States was first patented in Italy by a Milanese designer by the name of Attilio Calimani in 1929. The popularity of the device grew when the most successful brand of it was manufactured in a French factory that once made clarinets. This may be why it's referred to as a French press today. At least in America. The French call it *cafetière à piston*.

Mike brought out the French press with its fresh, incredibly aromatic Jamaican Blue Mountain just-ground coffee beans on the same ornate serving tray, along with a new dark blue napkin, a porcelain saucer and coffee cup, a sterling silver tea spoon, and an assortment of sugars and Equal. But no cream. Mike knew that Noah did not take cream in his coffee.

The copilot set down the tray on the table in front of Lindquist and reached over and slowly pushed the steel plunger of the French press down. He then picked up the press and poured the rich, almost-black liquid into the porcelain cup.

"Enjoy, Mr. Lindquist."

"Thanks."

Noah took a sip of the coffee, slurping the hot, dark liquid, which had been poured at 195 degrees. The Jamaican Blue Mountain was perfect. Richly coffee flavored, with a deep nuttiness, but no bitterness at all. He remembered long ago in a coffee shop in far away Kumamoto, telling Brad Jackman how he hated the taste of coffee. He had thought then that he would never acquire a taste for the black, bitter liquid. But four years of sea duty as a navy officer, standing endless hours of bridge watches at midnight or 2:00 a.m. escorting American-flagged Kuwaiti oil tankers through the North Arabian Sea and the Strait of Hormuz had nearly made him addicted to the caffeinated beverage. Noah always tended to become reflective on long plane flights, especially when traveling alone, like today. Reflecting on how he acquired his taste for coffee also reminded Noah of one of his most clear memories he had of his time in the US Navy. The day, recalled effortlessly in all its detail, had revealed to Noah the values and love—the amazing gift of her faith—with which Ellen Lindquist had surrounded Noah from the moment that she first met him as a frightened tiny boy.

IT WAS CHRISTMAS EVE, 1987. Noah was a young naval officer, and he had been at sea nearly 100 days straight escorting tankers through the Persian Gulf in the largest convoy operation since WWII. On this particular Christmas, his ship, the aircraft carrier USS *Midway*, was just outside the Strait of Hormuz, off the coast of Iran, as Iran and Iraq were approaching their sixth year of war with each other.

It was December 24 and Bob Hope flew aboard the aircraft carrier. Of course it wasn't just Bob. Oh no. He brought a bevy of beauties, with impossibly perfect bodies, with legs that never stopped, with perfect smiles and big hair. He came with singers and actors and beauty contest winners.

Noah was thinking back on previous Christmases while waiting for Bob Hope's show to begin. Christmas was his mother's favorite holiday, and she always pulled out all the stops and all her Hummel Christmas figurines. He could remember so many of the Ellen Lindquist orchestrated Christmases, but not all distinctly and separately. Many seemed to run together to where he couldn't remember which Christmas had brought him the Hot Wheels set and which brought him the blue blazer.

But thanks to his parents, there were Christmases throughout his past, when so much of America and the world around him was still so very new and he had found heroes who caught footballs and swung bats, heroes who he believed were just and fair and played for the love of the sport. Those Christmases were white and cold on the outside, but warm and glowing on the inside. As he waited for

Bob Hope's Christmas show to start, Noah felt so distant from the wonder of the season seen through the eyes he had when he was only waist high and his feet stuck straight out when sitting in his church pew.

He thought of his home and all the seasonal aromas. Breads and cookies that spread scented glory throughout the rooms and struck one in the soul with the first step inside from the winter wind. And other aromas as well. Aerosols that billowed from the bathrooms of the house, as they filled with too many Lindquist family women for the square footage of powder rooms, mixed with the mist of fogged-up mirrors and invisible, but staggering, perfume clouds.

Finally, the show got started with Bob Hope leading the way. Noah was shocked and surprised at how talented and engaging Hope was, live and in person. The show turned out to be better than Noah had expected. The iconic comedian actually was a very funny man with a wicked sense of looking at the world and twisting his words to make everyone laugh at their own worst weaknesses and gaffes. The show ended with Lee Greenwood leading Noah and the hundreds of other men standing crowded on the ship's hanger deck, singing as one, his most famous song: "God Bless the USA." The men hugged each other, pumped their fists in rhythm to the music, and belted out the lyrics at the top of their lungs into the Christmas Eve air of the Gulf of Oman.

But when the laughs and the singing were done, the reality of this Christmas and how far away it was from any of the Christmases he remembered crushed his soul.

After the show, Noah went to his bunkroom where he opened the presents that his family had sent him. He'd been sent a little "assembly-required" plastic Christmas tree. He had put the thing up in his tiny and crowded bunkroom. It was something that resembled the little Christmas tree in *A Charlie Brown Christmas*. Pathetic in a cute sort of way. He had also been sent a good couple of handfuls of his old and faithful Christmas tree decorations, like the tiny clothespin soldiers he had made back in first grade. Noah hung all those faithful, Elmer's Glue-dried-and-dripping decorations, decorations that had tiny red pipe cleaners for arms and colored cotton balls for hats. He hung all those decorations on the assembly-required, plastic Charlie Browny tree, and thought that his fellow junior officers might laugh. He didn't care.

Noah sat alone opening brightly wrapped packages that contained the presents sent by Ellen to represent the love and warmth of family. He sat and opened those bright boxes in the glare of the blinking lights of the plasticy, pathetic tree. And in the flashing hues, he was suddenly swept with a loneliness whose intensity he'd known before. It was so absolute, so profound and pure, a desperate longing that gripped his soul. And as he sat and stared amid the torn wrappings, so happy in their colors and cheery brightness, Noah cried.

He cried for his lost childhood when he had sat warm and safe between Ellen and Elmore at church on Christmas Eve. He cried for a world that needed men like him, in uniform, in harm's way, flung across the world.

In the tear-blurred lights and at that moment, Noah missed his family as he had never before. He missed the staggering perfume clouds. He missed the fogged-up mirrors. He missed the cooking smells. He missed each and every one of them in his crystal pure, absolute loneliness.

Noah believed in what he was doing. He believed in the duty he had as a US Navy officer. He firmly believed that societies grow and flourish only so long as there are those who are willing to sacrifice on their behalf. His mother had taught him this.

But theories and duty and abstract beliefs can seem inconsequential when a man is exposed to the icy winds of his utter loneliness. And in the winking lights of his plastic Charlie Brown tree, he wondered if he wasn't on the wrong path. Noah couldn't help thinking that, when it came down to the brass tacks of life, there really wasn't a whole lot else that exemplified the best of life than Christmas spent with family.

But then he also thought how someone as famous—who was such an American icon—as Bob Hope had traveled so far to give a show to him and his shipmates. How Bob Hope and Lee Greenwood and so many had given up their families at Christmas to come such a long way to reach out to men like him. Just to let them know that they weren't really alone—that they were all part of a society of shared hopes, shared dreams, and shared striving. It was then that Noah felt that he understood more clearly than ever the beliefs he'd been taught by his mother about Christ's birth and sacrifice: that God had taken on the frailty and limited form of humanness, that he might share in human joys and pains and lonelinesses and deaths. Noah suddenly grasped in his soul what his mother had always said: It is the wonder and hope and belief in the love of a God who would willingly share in the crushing mortality and limitations of his fleeting creations that is at the heart of Christmas.

Ellen and Elmore Lindquist's teaching found its mark that far away, floating Christmas. Noah came to understand as never before what Christmas was for his mother. For Ellen Lindquist, Christmas was not in the glitter and props and material objects offered and received. It was not in rituals, half pagan, whose meanings have long been forgotten. Christmas, for Ellen—and now for Noah— would always be in the warmth of family, in the hearts of loved ones, and of those who one cares about. It would always be in the drawing together against the world's cold to share the warmth that only family can give to each other, and, together, to dare hope for a time when the world won't be quite so lonely or cold.

The hurtling jet hit a pocket of turbulence causing the coffee in Noah's cup to spill onto the saucer, suddenly breaking his reverie. As the memory of that Christmas faded into the here and now, he wondered again if maybe he'd gotten off track and where his priorities truly were.

What do my actions actually say?

The Christmas event and so many others were gifts, he realized, that he had been given, and in his reflective mood he continued to turn and examine some of these gifts, these moments that were in whole or in part created or enabled by the woman he was speeding toward.

The coffee perfume rising from the steam off his cup reminded him of mornings and breakfast as a teenager. Coffee was and is a Lutheran's drink of choice. Noah's father preferred caffeinated Folgers and his mother, Sanka—decaffeinated. Every morning they would spoon their respective brands of freeze-dried, instant coffee into their cups, and Elmore Lindquist would pour in the boiling water. Boiling water was almost the complete extent of Elmore's cooking ability.

As he thought of the reason for this flight, Noah couldn't help himself from looking at his parents. Not only the life filled with Christmases and birthday parties and summers at the lake cabin, but he reflected on who his parents were and what they had taught him. He had absorbed their Midwestern straightforwardness and assumptions of trust and people's inherent goodness. He had internalized their conservatism, though politically he considered himself more middle of the road. He had taken on their tireless work ethic and willingness to sacrifice. In his reflections, he realized that all that he was proud to think of as good within him he had learned from the examples of his parents.

Noah had struggled with his identify, sense of nationality, and sense of race until he had had a revelation when he was eighteen. But his parents, especially his mother, had had to deal with his insecurities, his struggles of identity and belonging—or lack thereof—all throughout his teenage years. Their patience and unspoken understanding, Noah now could see, had been so critical to how he had turned out and who he was now. Even their Swedish stoicism and sense of duty, in hindsight, were crucial. They set an environment and an example that kept him from getting bogged down in endless self-analysis, self-pity, or self-focus. They kept him from drowning in unanswerable questions, but instead focused on actions and the present, rather than unhealable feelings and the unchangeable past. There were so many moments and events from which he had benefitted, from which he had learned, which had helped him grow despite of and beyond the pains of a distant childhood.

As he sipped his premium coffee from its very English, authentic bone china cup, Noah thought of one particular morning. He was sixteen, and his mother and he got into one of the stupidest fights of will—not unusual between a sixteen-year-old and his mother. The memory still pained him, but it also made Noah smile.

WHAT IN SAM HILL'S NAME is taking you so long to come down to breakfast, son?"

Noah's dad's voice boomed like the some Charlton Heston Moses invoking the Egyptians to "Let my people go!" It reverberated up the stairs from the kitchen of the Lindquist's split level home, overcoming yards of sound-sucking, gold shag carpeting—the height of 1979 Minnesota home fashion—to rattle around in Noah's small bedroom.

"On my way, Dad!"

Noah combed back his long hair, which was parted in the middle and feathered back, the perfect imitation of Keith Partridge's hair from the *Partridge Family*. At sixteen, Noah was very into his hair and wanted it to be perfectly in place.

There. Perfectly feathered back.

The teenager went down the five steps from the bedroom level to the kitchen split level in one leap. He bounded into the kitchen and its smell of toast and coffee. His sister, Carla, was already at her seat. As were his mom and dad. Carla always had amazingly perfectly curled and flowing translucent blonde hair. She gave him a closed-lipped smirk, and her blue eyes seemed to somehow each wag a finger at him. She was five months older than Noah, but a grade ahead of him at school. They had the usual teenage sibling relationship: indifference punctuated by moments of extreme annoyance with each other.

You're in trouble now! Smirk.

Noah took his seat.

The rest of the Lindquist children were away at college or graduate school, or were postcollege starting a career.

"Son, you've made all of us wait on you. You know we don't say grace until everyone's seated at the table!"

"Yes, Dad. Sorry, Dad."

As a typical teenage boy, it was Noah's most common statement to his parents.

"Let us pray."

They all sat around the same fake wood-grained, Formica-topped table that the family had sat around since before Noah was adopted. The Lindquists had moved across town to a bigger, split-level house a few years back. The house was Ellen's pride and joy, and she kept it immaculate and seasonally coordinated. Anyone who walked into Ellen Lindquist's home knew exactly what holiday season it was: Easter, Mother's Day, Father's Day, Memorial Day, Fourth of July, Thanksgiving—all the major and minor holidays and everyone's birthday—and especially Christmas.

Ellen loved knickknacks, and whole armies of Hummel figurines marched in and out of storage boxes, onto and off shelves and end tables and dressers. Every last one had a designated place and a designated time of year. The knickknacks marched to the precision of Ellen Lindquist's organization and energy and purpose. And the whole family was enlisted to deploy the little seasonal figures and larger items of decor. Especially to keep them clean, organized, and dusted in their respective countless locations throughout the house. Ellen's energy and organization permeated the Lindquist home. Elmore loved their home all the more for the "Ellen-ness" of it. His mother had been the complete opposite: a hardworking woman who never had time for house cleaning and order and planned armies of knickknacks. He had grown up with his mother's happy piles of disordered clutter that seemed to procreate and produce more offspring. His sister had inherited their mother's housekeeping genes.

Elmore adored his pretty blonde wife for many things, but maybe particularly for rescuing him from a world of domestic disarray and showing him that the world could be different. It appealed to the accountant in him—order, rules, seasons. Everything in its place; a place for everything. And he didn't have to put any mindshare into it. Ellen took care of it all, just like most everything in their day-to-day life. He loved the predictability of it all. And just like he followed the vagaries of the tax code, he happily followed the vagaries of Ellen's rules.

Elmore Lindquist folded his big hands, bowed his head, and led the family in saying the Lutheran grace, or prayer of thanksgiving, before starting a meal. It was really a trite rhyme rather than a heartfelt prayer. The family always said it very rapidly and ran all the sounds together as if it were all one word.

"Come-lord-jesus-be-our-guest-and-let-these-gifts-to-us-be-blessed-amen."

Noah reached over to the box of Raisin Bran on the table and was just about to grab it, when his mother fixed her sharp blue eyes on him.

"Noah, isn't that the same shirt that you wore yesterday?"

Noah drew his hand back from the cereal box.

"Yeah. So."

"So you need to go back upstairs and change your shirt, young man."

"Why?" Noah whined.

What? Really?

It was Noah's favorite shirt. It was long sleeved and he knew that he didn't have any other clean long-sleeved shirts available to wear. He liked long-sleeved shirts, especially this one. He had bought it himself using the money he earned from washing dishes at the local golf club, Shoreland Country Club. Usually he put up with his mother's rules, some of which seemed pretty arbitrary to a teenage boy. But something was different in his hormones today. His testosterone was up. And the shirt issue touched on something deeper.

"But it's not dirty, Mom . . ."

"I don't care. Go change your shirt."

Ellen's voice was getting "that tone," which meant she was in no mood to argue. Elmore had picked up the newspaper after leading the family in grace and had started to read the sports section. He didn't like where this seemed to be headed and lowered the paper enough to look at his wife and then look at his son. The shirt looked fine to him. He needed to leave for the office in five minutes. Just time enough to drink his coffee and catch the latest Minnesota Twins' score and game summary.

"But it's not dirty!"

"And I said, 'I don't care.' Do not talk back to me and do as you are told!"

"No! I am not going to change my shirt for no reason!"

"Well, no son of mine is going to leave this house wearing the same shirt two days in a row."

What in Sam Hill's name? The situation had escalated with lightning speed and it caught Elmore by surprise.

"So changing a stupid shirt is what makes me your *son*? It's good to know what makes me *fit* to be your son. I guess I won't be going to school then! If it's following stupid rules that makes me your son, then I guess I am NOT . . . since I am not changing my shirt!"

Noah didn't know what had come over him. He shouted these last words at his mother. On top of the whole deeper issue with this shirt, there also was something about the words "no son of mine" that tore something inside him and let out inner demons who now were screaming things through his mouth at his mother. Noah was shocked at himself and enraged at the same time. Every day he looked in the mirror he knew he wasn't her son. Every person who told him how "lucky" or "blessed" that he had been to be adopted by the Lindquists, nailed home in his marrow the fact that he was *not* their son, that he should be grateful to have been rescued, plucked by the hand of God and the generosity of the Lindquists out of his miserable, starving world.

But no one had asked him if he wanted to be "rescued."

No one ever seemed to point out how unlucky or how unblessed—cursed—he had been to have needed the luck and blessing of being adopted.

"You should thank God for such a blessing!" was what people often commented to Noah ever since he had arrived in America. And the boy had often wondered:

Really? Then what should I say to God for what my life was before this blessing?

Noah often had these thoughts and was afraid to answer them. He wanted to be a good person, to think the right thoughts, to be the Lindquists' son, but was so torn and confused at times. There was always a trickle of blood inside him from a wound that could never fully heal. And there simply existed too many questions he did not want to ask because the answers seemed to lead only to paths of pain and anguish—and stark loneliness of his inner bleeding that no one else could comprehend.

And his Asian face with its green eyes screamed at least one of the answers every day, an answer he did not want to hear.

"No son of mine."

It was a turn of phrase that hit the sixteen-year-old in a way Ellen could not have considered or never meant to be interpreted as Noah had. The teen pushed past his sister, Carla, who sat shocked at the sudden shouting and the clearly uncontrolled emotion that had expanded to crowd out the people in the small kitchen. Her smirk was gone.

The sixteen-year-old ran up the stairs and into his room, slamming the door behind him.

Ellen looked at Elmore. There was confusion and pain—and frustration—in her eyes.

Oh Lord! I did NOT mean anything of the sort!

I meant: It's BECAUSE he's my son that I expect him to live up to my standards!

The thoughts ranted defensively in Ellen Lindquist's head. She couldn't believe that her innocent words had been so twisted. She meant nothing like how Noah had taken them and felt anger and frustration at the sixteen-year-old. Yet she also felt distinct pangs of guilt, because she knew that she struggled inwardly, secretly, with her feelings toward Asians. She hated knowing that she had these feelings and hated even more that she was not alone. She knew that many of her generation likely held similar, secret—and maybe not so secret—racist feelings. And it angered her that they may have lumped her son into a racial category that held so many negative connotations for her peers.

She knew how much she emphasized Noah's American side—his white half—because she wanted others to see him as she wanted him seen. As white and American. She tended to act as if there were no other half. She did this because she wanted Noah to be as much as possible as she imagined her true son—William—who would not have been subjected to the hidden feelings that she herself had, along with most Americans of her age, about Noah's very un-William, Korean half. She wanted urgently to protect him from the biases, prejudices, and racism that existed, but also knew from experience that she was powerless to do so.

Chapter 22

Ellen and Noah

FALL 1970, ST. PETER

Noah was in first grade and the school year had started only the month before. The boy had made amazing progress with learning English since arriving in January. He was essentially fluent and was deemed ahead of his peers in his readiness to enter first grade. Noah's kindergarten progress report, dated June 1970, written by his teacher, Mrs. Witty, in her perfect teacher's penmanship, stated: "Noah has been an exciting addition to our classroom! He is active in all room activities and will be capable of doing above average work in first grade."

Ellen and Elmore had been so pleased and proud—and relieved. Their adopted son, who had spoken not one word of English when he arrived in St. Peter in January, had become fluent and deemed "capable of doing above average work" his next school year. Her hard work, faith, and dedication were showing. Elmore, more than anyone, was relieved. He had been so afraid of what might happen to his newly mission-oriented wife if the boy had turned out problematic. They had had a nasty little shock when he had first arrived. His burns and scars were much worse than what they had been led to believe. They had been assured that the boy would not need further medical procedures, to be treated differently, or need accommodation due to his injuries. This would turn out to be less than fully truthful. But the full extent of the impact that the boy's burns and scars and deformities would have were not evident to the Lindquists.

In terms of personality and intelligence, the boy seemed to be acceptable.

Thank God! Elmore thought. *Thank God.*

And on that bright, fall day in September, Ellen remembered how Noah had gotten off the yellow school bus that picked him up from his elementary school. There were two elementary schools in St. Peter, with a third under construction; imaginatively following the typical Swedish Lutheran utilitarianism, they were named North, Central, and South Elementary (under construction). Midwestern creativity at its height. Her boy was so tiny that he stepped off the bus taking gigantic hopping strides because the distance between the bus's steps were too great for him to navigate normally yet.

That evening, as the family sat around the little table in their fixed positions wedged in the small and cramped kitchen, conversation turned to various topics among the Lindquist children. Christina was now a twelfth grader; Karsten was in tenth grade, Karissa in sixth, and Carla in second. Karsten had reached six feet tall at the beginning of his tenth grade year, and Karissa was asking him if he would go out for the basketball team at St. Peter High School.

"No. Sports are mostly for stupid people, and I want to use my mind and go to space as a rocket scientist."

"Sports are not stupid. I like sports and I'm not stupid."

"Yes, you are."

"No. I'm not!"

"Are too."

"Am NOT! Mom, Karsten is calling me stupid."

Elmore was thinking how incredibly unwitty and predictable his children's conversations were. He was a professor at Gustavus Adolphus College in St. Peter, teaching business, finance, economics, and accounting. He concurrently was a licensed CPA with his own small firm. Compared to the business discussions he had with his clients and the academic discussions with his students, the contrast around his family dinner table was refreshing and simple. He loved his children and loved being a father. He looked over at his pert, blonde wife, and loved her most of all. She was so happy these days. After all those years when she would suddenly sink into depression and silence, Ellen Lindquist was back, and her blue eyes seemed brighter than ever.

"Karsten, don't call your sister stupid. You are all smart kids. You're Lindquists, after all." Despite making her voice sound stern, she couldn't help but let a smile slip past her lips.

"Besides, Karsten, if you did play basketball, we could nickname you Wilt Karsten!"

Karissa looked pleased with the nickname she'd thought of. She followed a number of sports, and she particularly liked Wilt Chamberlain, the 7 foot 1 inch star center for the Los Angeles Lakers, who had been traded from the Philadelphia 76ers in 1968. Karissa liked the Lakers because they used to be Minnesota's professional basketball team until 1958. Minnesota was "The Land of 10,000 Lakes," and so when the team was created in 1947, the owners called them The Lakers. Despite Los Angeles being in a Mediterranean, desert climate with no lakes to speak of, the team kept the name.

"What's a nickname?" Noah's first grader voice asked. He still spoke with a noticeable accent. Although he could speak English remarkably well, like any first grader there were words he didn't know or understand.

"It's a name that people call you that's not your real name, because it may describe something about you or something you're known for," Christina supplied the answer. She took her job as the oldest very seriously and liked being the knowledgeable and mature one, to Karsten's great annoyance and dislike.

"Karissa was comparing your brother, Karsten, to a famous basketball player whose name is Wilt Chamberlain. And Mr. Chamberlain has a nickname—Wilt the Stilt—because he is so tall!"

Christina enjoyed teaching little Noah things. She liked her new little brother very much, and Noah and she would always get along well, throughout their youth and their adult lives. For his part, Noah liked how she exuded intelligence and competency, what Karsten thought of as insufferable bossiness. Noah also thought she was beautiful. He thought all his sisters were beautiful with their blonde hair and blue or hazel eyes.

"I have a nickname!" Noah blurted out the new word that he'd just learned.

Ellen, Elmore, and all the kids turned and looked at Noah.

Even though he was seven years old, he was the size of a typical Minnesota three-year-old. Ellen had placed him at the foot of the table to her right, using the metal highchair that all the children had used when they had been toddlers. Noah fit in the highchair perfectly. He would not outgrow it for the next two years.

"Oh? What is it and who gave it to you?" Elmore's bass boomed the question, the sound bounding around the tiny kitchen. Elmore was smiling, to encourage the little boy to speak.

"Yeah, what is it?" A chorus of the family's voices chimed in.

"It's Joe Chink!"

Dead silence and blank stares.

Noah made his proclamation with a burst of pride. *He had a nickname! Like some famous basketball player!*

"Some of the bigger boys at school gave it to me. And they call me that all the time."

There was complete silence around the table. The smile had vanished from Elmore's face. Everyone just stared at Noah through a long, too-tight-in-the-collar silence. No one knew what to say. Little Carla wasn't quite sure what "Chink" meant, but had learned that it was sort of a naughty word among words that would get grownups mad at you.

Ellen's fears and her own sense of guilt at her own racial prejudices suddenly jabbed her in her spleen.

Oh my Lord . . .

Seven-year-old Noah was smiling and pleased at the news he was able to share. But all of a sudden, no one else was smiling, and he found the silence frightening. He shut off his smile immediately and thought that he was in trouble. He thought he'd done something very wrong. Just like when he and Carla had been spinning around to make each other dizzy and he had fallen, hitting his head against the living room lamp and shattering it. He still didn't understand all the American rules or the Lindquists' rules. He must have done something really, really wrong. The little boy felt a knot in his stomach, and he suddenly didn't feel very hungry.

I've done something bad now . . . look how unhappy I made everyone . . .

That September day was the day Ellen realized that her hard job might be harder than she had thought, in ways she had not thought about. She had never had to deal with racism against herself or anyone close to her. This boy was not going to be her dead son come to life. There were going to complications.

Oh my Lord! He's just a child . . . and it might get worse as he gets bigger and less cute and more Oriental looking. . . . He won't be my William . . . how do I protect him from such a thing? Especially when the feelings exist even inside me . . . Oh. My. Lord!

It dawned on Ellen that maybe there were things she didn't know about bringing a foreign, racially different child into her home, her life, and her family. Ellen started to doubt the adoption service's statement that love alone is enough.

How can it be enough to overcome ignorance and hate in others? He can never be William . . . People will never see him that way . . .

The future would prove her correct.

Ellen had been ten years old when planes from the Imperial Japanese Navy had attacked and bombed the US naval base at Pearl Harbor, Hawaii, on December 7, 1941. Until she was fifteen years old when the war ended, she was subjected to what today would be considered extreme brainwashing and indoctrination in overt racism, especially against the Japanese, "Japs," and exposure to appalling levels of racist propaganda.

When a sitting president of the United States openly expressed overt and blatant racist views of the Japanese and his views were based on public proclamations of noted scholars, how much more would an impressionable teenage girl growing up the Midwest internalize such sentiments after years of being subjected to anti-Japanese propaganda on the radio and at school? There were all sorts of propaganda associated with the Japanese that was pushed onto the American people during WWII. A leading technique used by WWII propagandists was to depict the Japanese as animals. The most common animal selected to represent the Japanese was the monkey. But monkeys wearing round Tojo-glasses with huge bucked teeth.

Ellen Lindquist, along with tens of thousands of teenagers just like her during the first half of the 1940s, was relentlessly subjected to the image of Japanese as subhuman primates. The US government specifically thought that part of what was required in the war effort was the undercutting of the humanity of the enemy. When less than human, the enemy was much easier to hate, despise, and ultimately, kill. Japanese were projected as peculiar objects of curiosity, to be treated and examined like lab rats, but also, the Japanese were depicted as a savage, inhuman beast that should be eradicated by any and all means. The United States was not alone or notably exceptional in such propaganda efforts. All nations conducted similar propaganda campaigns upon their citizens against their enemies, each portraying the enemy as subhuman, animalistic, barbarian, inferior, and bent on rape and pillage. All nations at war tend to manipulate racial, religious, or ethnic subthemes, fears, and animosities.

Ellen was deeply affected by all the propaganda and felt that she was more deeply affected compared to many of her peers, because her older brother, Andy, had enlisted in the US Navy at the age of seventeen. He was eventually sent to the Pacific to fight the Japanese. So during some of her most formative and impressionable years, Ellen prayed every night that God would keep her brother safe and that her adored brother would help kill as many of the Yellow Peril as possible so that the war would come to a speedier end.

There is a particularly graphic, racially charged, WWII propaganda poster that Ellen remembered seeing as a young teenage girl. It shows a background of flames, a city being pillaged with human figures hanging in front of the flames, and shadowy outlines of soldiers running with guns. In front of it all is a Japanese officer with the rising sun emblem on his uniform and cap, in a slight crouch, reminiscent of a monkey. His face looks like a caricature of General Hideki Tojo, then prime minister of Japan. He wears thick, round glasses through which one can see his highly slanted eyes. His face is extremely angular, highlighting its Orientalism, with his monkey-like nose showing nostril holes. The Japanese soldier sports an evil, buck-toothed smile under a scraggly mustache. In his left hand he holds a pistol.

Over his right shoulder he is carrying a completely naked white Western woman, who is draped pornographically backwards over the sinister Oriental pillager's shoulder, her breast clearly outlined against the burning city's flames with her hair falling and dragging on the ground. Her legs are splayed and bent over the front side of his shoulder and chest; his right hand is holding onto her left, naked leg, just above her ankle. He is carrying her like a sack of rice, but his face and evil smile are turned toward the poster's viewer, implying the violation that is imminent. His urine-yellow skin stands in contrast to the woman's milky whiteness. The words, in a large, bold font, state:

THIS
IS THE
ENEMY

The poster evoked young Ellen's—and white America's—deepest, racist horrors and fears, that some beastly, inferior Asiatic monkey-man would sexually defile the virtue of pristine white—human—feminine sanctity. The metaphor with Lady Liberty could not be mistaken. The one theme that propaganda of all countries share is that it is always the male enemy that is depicted. The monsters are always the enemy's men.

These themes did not simply end in America after WWII, but were perpetuated in more subtle ways as America fought other Asian enemies: the North Koreans and the Chinese in the 1950s and the Viet Cong and the North Vietnamese in the 1960s and into the '70s. More than three decades of Asian faces as enemy faces. Asians were perceived as some sort of endless horde, inscrutable, diametrically polar to American ideals, and expendable; they were never depicted as individuals or fully human. Their lives were seen as cheap, fungible, and disposable.

Asians in America were the perpetual foreigners. No matter how many generations, no matter their birthplace, an Asian face was a face of foreignness. Ellen's fears for her son would be supported by research and data that would confirm, even in the twenty-first century, that based on public government data, Asian American males would have the lowest probability of rising to a management level—lower than whites, blacks, Hispanics, and women of any race—despite having the highest education level of any race or ethnicity. Research would also show that people who were assertive in the work place were generally less popular than those who weren't, but that Americans *really* disliked East Asians, in particular, who showed *any* assertiveness or dominance. Many Americans, especially many white Americans, did not want some Asiatic monkey-man to be their boss. The years of official racist propaganda would spread its ripples far and wide and deep into the nation's subconsciousness.

Ellen knew this at a gut level. Like the vast majority of mainstream white Americans, she spent hardly any conscious thought upon such topics as race or racism, especially toward Asians—the "model" minority. But the knowledge and the feelings were there, buried in core assumptions and gut reactions. And this was the source of Ellen's guilt pangs. She knew that the gut reactions and deeply ingrained biases of Americans were counter to her intellect, her education, and her religion.

We are ALL created in his image.

This was the hard job that she had been called to. This was the challenge that *The Lutheran* magazine had issued that had moved her and reignited her faith and sense of life's mission. She would prove that she could take in and love any child of God that was in need of rescue, regardless of outer appearances. Especially if they were "American" by virtue of their fathers. But young Noah's words had taken her by surprise, cut her heart, and caused the inflammation of her guilt.

Oh my God! What if my secret feelings were visible to Noah? What if he sees and knows? What if he thinks . . . thinks something completely untrue . . . that I see him as some Asiatic monkey-boy who will become an Asiatic monkey-man?

Ellen's eyes were pleading with Elmore.

"Elmore. You have to do something. You know I meant nothing of the sort . . . go talk to him. Please!"

Elmore pushed his chair back from the Formica-covered table.

"Okay, Sweetheart. I'll do what I can."

He gave a deep sigh and started heading toward the stairway, his long legs striding slowly. He was chewing his tongue.

He was not a man of confrontation and emotions were in the realm of difficult to quantify, thus a realm he tended to avoid.

Carla looked at her father as he walked past and wondered.

As pesky and annoying as she found him at times, she never once thought of Noah as anything other than her brother. But she also knew that he had his struggles and difficulties. Not that he shared many details, but she'd seen and heard enough at school to know.

Noah sat on his bed in his small bedroom. The room's window sat above the front entryway, letting him have a view down upon anyone who was standing outside the front door of the Lindquist's home. He could also look down the curving driveway and up the suburban street on which the house sat. There was not a fence in sight, and every house had a perfectly manicured, mowed, and trimmed emerald green lawn. He knew every one of his neighbors. Every house up and down the street and every house on a cross street for blocks in every direction. He knew the names of the families that lived in each house. He had met every one of them at some point. Many had children who went to the same high school as Noah. Even more attended the church, First Lutheran Church, which Noah and his family attended. He knew the owners of nearly every store, gas station, shop, and business in St. Peter. And nearly everyone he ever met in St. Peter knew him.

"You're Ellen and Elmore's Korean boy, aren't you?" townspeople would often remark, a question that was telling in its own way.

Noah didn't think his knowing all his neighbors and a great number of his town's people and vice versa was odd. Approximately sixty percent of the state's population lives in a compact, eleven-county area in the central eastern edge of the state in and around the Twin Cities of Minneapolis and St. Paul. The rest of the forty percent is spread out over a huge area covering the other seventy-six counties to the north, west, and south of the Twin Cities. Minnesota is therefore a state that is sparsely populated throughout its rolling farmland in the southern half and wooded forests in the northern half, dotted throughout with small towns and with as many or more lakes.

St. Peter boasts a population of about ten thousand, but that's counting the seasonal students who attend Gustavus Adolphus

College, as well as the population of the large secure state hospital, also located within the city limits of St. Peter. The real residential population of the town is around 6,500. There are urban school districts in the United States that have nearly this number of students attending just one high school.

Not counting the foreign exchange students at the college and the one or two that were usually attending his high school, Noah was one of literally a handful of racially different people in the entire town. Everyone else was white, the majority of Scandinavian heritage, a minority of Germanic heritage. It was hard to find a truly nonblonde head in the bleachers at the local high school basketball games. For Noah, it was simply his normal to be the physically short and different, racial oddity among a sea of very white, very blonde, and very big people.

His town, like most towns and cities in America that were founded after the passage of the Northwest Ordinance of 1787, has its streets laid out in a grid pattern, running north/south, east/west. The Northwest Ordinance showed the influence of Thomas Jefferson, who would found the University of Virginia in 1819 that Noah Lindquist would attend and from which he would graduate 167 years later as an elite Echols Scholar. Jefferson insisted that the ordinance divide new territories into an orderly pattern for future settlement—leading to the familiar street patterns of most US towns and cities west of the Allegheny Mountains.

St. Peter's streets were wide, safe, and flat, and nearly the entire town was residential, except for along Main Street. There were only three traffic lights in all of St. Peter, all on Main Street. It had many more churches than bars and served as the county seat. Noah could easily ride his bicycle anywhere in the town, giving him and his peers great freedom and autonomy even before they had driver's licenses. The town's wide streets were lined with perfect sidewalks and big spreading elm trees, which made a cathedral-like arched canopy of branches and green shade in the summer until Dutch elm disease destroyed most elm trees in America in the late 1970s through the early 1990s.

The Green Giant Company had a number of canning plants along the Minnesota River Valley, and as one drove down from Minneapolis on State Highway 169, when entering the valley, one would—and still does—see a giant-sized Jolly Green Giant billboard, welcoming the traveler to the "Valley of the Jolly Green Giant."

At sixteen, Noah Lindquist grew up bicycling around wide, safe, tree-lined shady streets, living in the Valley of the Jolly Green Giant, where he knew nearly everyone, and nearly everyone knew him. His town had no serious crime, and parents didn't worry at all about their children walking to school, to get burgers, or return home from night football games.

The town's heartland beauty, its homogeneity and banality, underscored his differentness and made the youth feel intensely separate, insecure, and alien. Ellen Lindquist had just been scorched by that bubbling sense of alienation—fueled by extreme teenage insecurity—erupting, spewing his pyroclastic emotional cloud all over her innocent, unintended phrase.

Noah Lindquist sat on his bed, his sixteen-year-old green eyes looking out through his Asian featured lids at his neighborhood. He thought about how different his life and home had been in Korea. He thought how it was a human universe away from living in his Mayberry-esque town, where everybody knew Noah's name, and Noah's dad was president of the local Rotary Club and the Faculty Senate at the local college. But he was known mostly because he was different.

What are *you?*

Where are you from? . . . I mean, originally?

You're Ellen and Elmore's Korean boy, aren't you?

You should thank God! You are so blessed to be adopted by the Lindquists!

Listen you little Jap Fuck. I'll pound you if you talk to my girl-friend again in class!

The boy could hear the voices, the questions, the comments, and the high school threats of his teenage world, of life in beautiful, safe, heartland-of-America, St. Peter, Minnesota.

He felt horrible. He knew his mother hadn't meant her words the way he had accused. He knew he had hurt her, and that it had been unfair. He knew that it was just her being who she was, that she would not have let her husband wear the same shirt two days in a row either. But sometimes, his feelings inside, stoked by the questions, the comments, the stares, and threats, just came up.

And he was powerless to hold them in check.

Noah looked down at his crippled left hand. He usually wore long-sleeved shirts, never rolled up. He wanted to hide the scars. That was the reason he liked this shirt so much. It was the only long-sleeved shirt that he had that was in style, that he had picked and purchased, rather than one that had been picked out by his mom. She always bought shirts and pants that were slightly too big and never in fashion, because they were on deeply discounted sale.

"Don't want you to outgrow it too soon, you know," his mom would always say, holding up last year's fashion from the sales rack at J. C. Penney located at the mall in the "big" neighboring city of Mankato.

Noah hated gym class—what Minnesotans called "phy-ed"—when he would have to shower with all the other boys. All of them tall, blonde, and big, in the corn-fed-that's-how-we-grow-'em-down-on-the-farm, Midwest kind of way. It was the Korean public bath nightmare of his little boy's starving days in Korea, but on steroids. Nowhere to hide his deformities and scars at an age when he was excruciatingly aware of his body and how it did not measure up. He always got looks and stares from the other boys, even though by now they had all seen his Frankenstein scars and claw-like hand over the many years they had been his classmates. His hand looked even more like some reptilian claw than when he was younger, because it had only three fingers and the stub of his thumb. When he was in grade school, his parents, under the advice of doctors, invested in a series of operations to improve his left hand's dexterity and functionality. The operations mostly failed to deliver the promised miracle of normal function, though they did improve the hand's mobility somewhat. The last of the operations was to amputate his left little finger. It was too deformed and, after two operations failed to straighten it, surgeons recommended its removal, as it got in the way of many simple tasks such as grasping or dribbling a ball.

He felt he had the worst of two worlds: being both a shrimpy little Chink in the land of ten thousand tall blondes and also having a very visible and grotesque deformity. Faces and hands are the most used parts of the human body to support our words as we communicate as only humans can. Noah looked at his claw-like hand and he thought how it closely resembled the hand of a Sleestak, the lizard-like creatures in the TV series that ran from 1974 through 1976 and looked like cousins of the Creature from the Black Lagoon. He thought of the looks of repulsion and horror on the faces of girls who ended up with him as a partner for square dancing during gym class.

I have to touch that? No way I'm doing that. YEW!

Noah and his unfortunate square dance partner would do the hand-holding equivalent of an air kiss when the tape-recorded square dance caller's voice bellowed out to "dosey-doe!" Most girls—but not all, since some would air it fully like freshly-washed sheets drying in a summer breeze—would be embarrassed by their revulsion, and Noah could see it in their eyes. He could equally see the pleading in those eyes:

"Please don't try to touch me with that."

And he would pretend that he didn't notice the horrified look, the squeamish embarrassment, the pleading. And as naturally as possible, he would "accidentally" miss their hand while "dosey-doe-ing" or "Allemande lefting" his horrified, embarrassed partner.

His crippled, palsied left hand limited him not just socially, but in most physical activities. He couldn't take typing class, because what was the point of learning touch-type fingering when he didn't have the requisite digits and would need to teach himself all new fingering. Noah never would be able to touch type. He struggled every day to button his right shirt cuff or tie his shoes. And the only band instrument he could play was the trumpet. Not drums, flutes, saxophones, violins, guitars. The trumpet was the only thing that didn't require his left hand do anything except hold the instrument to his mouth while his right hand did all the work. Theoretically he could have played trombone, but he was too small, his arm too short to reach all the positions of the trombone slide.

The only sport in which his small size allowed Noah to have a possible chance in succeeding was wrestling. When he started in seventh grade, he wrestled in the lightest weight category, seventy-eight pounds. He actually weighed much less. His last year, as a junior, he wrestled in the lightest high school category: 112 pounds. His left hand didn't allow him to grasp fully missing that crucial opposable thumb—meaning he truly was handicapped in wrestling. He had losing records his first three years: 1 win and 22 losses his first year; 2 wins, 19 losses his second. Noah never learned how to lose well. Every loss hurt. A lot. And deep.

But the sport helped teach him not to quit.

Chapter 23

Hee Ae

Lee Hee Ae sat across the director's desk in his office at Korea Social Service, Inc. Seated in another chair next to Hee Ae was one of KSS's case managers, a young woman named Yang Man Hyung. The director, Mr. Paik, looked at Hee Ae and put the tips of his fingers and thumbs together, forming a triangular A-frame, resting his elbows on his desk. Mr. Paik was a deeply devout Presbyterian, as was the majority of the staff at KSS. A surprising percentage of Koreans were Christian, and the largest denomination was Presbyterian, almost nineteen percent of Korea's population today. Paik was in his fifties, with a white-walled hair cut, a comb-over, and the permanent downward frown of too many Korean men of his age and position. He radiated authoritarian, but gentle concern.

"So, Mrs. Lee"—even though she wasn't married, her being a mother made the title more natural—"I am to understand that you are following up on your first petition you made to this agency, which was in . . ."

"July of 1967," Miss Yang said, looking down at the file on her lap.

"Yes, that is correct, Mr. Paik."

Hee Ae spoke Korean in a course, country dialect, immediately revealing her as uneducated, agrarian, and poor.

"And you are currently working as a cook at a local restaurant in Munsan Village, Mrs. Lee?"

"Yes. Since November."

"And Mrs. Lee, pardon me for asking, but how much money do you make?"

Hee Ae gave Paik her monthly earnings in the Korean currency, Won. The amount equaled about seventeen dollars.

"I see," Paik said, talking past his touching fingertips. "And your son is living with you now, Mrs. Lee?"

"Yes. I rent a room in a village farmhouse, near Munsan."

During the follow-on questions and answers, Hee Ae explained that the room cost her about two dollars a month and there usually was not enough money to stretch the full month to cover all the expenses. She explained that she was able to bring home leftovers from the restaurant to help feed her and her son.

"Why do you want to put your son up for adoption abroad, Mrs. Lee?"

Paik could see how rough her hands were and that she looked older than her actual age, the sun, smoking, and hard drinking taking their toll. He could see the emotion churning inside the woman seated in front of him. She was clearly not washed and her clothes were tattered, her lips chapped and blistered from the winter cold. Suddenly, the emotions inside the tiny woman broke their confinement. Lee Hee Ae seemed to collapse as she started crying, her face melting into a tormented window into her agony. She buried that tortured face into her rough, heavily calloused hands and started weeping in shuddering sobs that she could not contain or control.

"I don't *want* to give him up!" Her voice broke and screeched.

"Mr. Paik! I don't want to give up my boy . . ." she blurted out between her sobs. "But what else can I do? What is there left for me to do? Mr. Paik . . . you know how it is for boys like him . . . and he's crippled . . ."

As Paik and Yang looked on, Hee Ae cried, taking several minutes to get herself back under emotional control. Yang and Paik were not unfamiliar with this scene. They had been witness to similar conversations and similar tears and the same searing pain of similar broken, destitute, desperate mothers facing a choice that was no choice at all.

With their American-fathered children having no legal rights in Korea, the majority of Korean mothers of mixed-race children came to believe that their children would be better off in the United States. Their children were not Korean citizens and therefore had no legal right to public education or healthcare. And as noncitizens, their employment prospects were extremely limited. Some Korean mothers of American-fathered children abandoned them in the belief that in abandoning their child they were giving that child access to some form of minimal security.

According to the Korean Nationality Law, a child found abandoned within the sovereign territory of the Republic of Korea automatically gained citizenship. Thus, prior to the changes adopted in 1998, which allowed Korean children born in Korea to a foreign father (or without a Korean father) to be considered citizens, under Korean law an orphan of any kind had more legal rights than a child of a Korean citizen mother, but not a Korean father.

Just like Hee Ae, single mothers felt they had no choice but to relinquish their children, out of love and the only possible hope for their child. There were many social workers, domestic and international, who facilitated and supported this heart-tearing decision made by these desperate, shunned, pariah women. Social workers at the time believed that they were doing the right thing for these stateless children. The norms and laws of the day made it crystal clear: There was no place and no future in Korean society for children of single Korean mothers—even more so if a foreigner had fathered the child.

Hee Ae looked up finally and said almost in a whisper.

"I love him too much. . . . What else can I do?"

"We understand, Mrs. Lee. We understand deeply and know very well that you have little choice. We know you do this out of love. But we have to ask and hear from you directly.

"And we'll do the best we can. But the likelihood of placing your son with an American family is very slim, because of his age, his handicaps, and his deformities. Also, most adoptive American families want girls. Westerners seem more comfortable with having adopted daughters if they are of a different race. But we'll do the best we can, Mrs. Lee."

"Thank you, Mr. Paik. . . . Thank you."

"Mrs. Lee, please come with me and I can start the additional paper work we'll need to complete for the next steps." Yang Man Hyun got up and gestured Hee Ae toward the door. Paik stood up as well, as the two women departed his office.

He would pray for this woman and her unfortunate son. Clearly, the sins of the mother were obvious, Paik thought. Koreans assumed that these military "camp town" women—women who had foreign-fathered children—were all prostitutes, therefore highly stigmatized, shunned, and treated almost as criminals. Even Paik, as part of his ingrained Korean perspective and judgment, could not help but hold these feelings. He was Christian, but he was Korean first. But he would pray to God to be merciful to her son; his Christianity let him see the innocence and tragedy in the child, where most Koreans only saw such a child as lumped into the stigma and status of the mother, something to be shunned, reviled, and criminalized. Prayer helped him cope with the emotionally draining aspects of his work, when the glaring destitution and desperation of these unfortunate women's and their socially, legally unacceptable children's fates ate too deep into his gut.

Miss Yang would eventually type up a report to put into the boy's file at KSS that read in part:

Young Nam is a child of racially mixed parents whose American father cannot be reached and whose Korean mother has released him for adoption abroad since she recognizes that she will not be able to provide proper care and education in [the] future. However, the possibility of overseas adoption is remote at the present time because of his physical deformity, and should [there be any possibility of] better care and education in the future [being] secured for him, he will need outside help.

Chapter 24

Elmore and Noah

Elmore Lindquist knocked on Noah's bedroom door.

"Mind if I come in, Son?"

There was a pause, before Elmore heard his son's voice coming muffled through the door.

"Whatever . . ."

Elmore turned the doorknob and stepped through the door into the small bedroom. Noah's slight back was to him as the boy kept staring out his window as he sat on his bed. Elmore came around and sat down next to him on the small twin bed. It sunk down noticeably under his weight. Elmore too stared out the room's window.

For Pete's sake . . . I am not good at this . . .

Elmore was not a man who handled emotions well and tended to avoid emotionally laden situations. Although highly intelligent and very well educated, he was not one for elegant words or eloquent phrasing. He didn't know what he would say or how. He feared that whatever he said he would say poorly, that he would make things worse. And though Elmore Lindquist would later completely forget this episode and this conversation, Noah Lindquist would not. The conversation would forever stick in Noah's mind and would repeat itself almost daily for the rest of his life.

For once, Elmore found his eloquence—at least this day, at this time.

"Son . . ."

Elmore almost never called Noah by his name, but nearly always addressed the boy as "Son." Elmore didn't know why, but he just did and it always felt right to do so. It would never have occurred to him how much that simple word always meant to Noah, coming from a man like Elmore. Noah had never had a man in his life until he was almost seven years old. Having been born and raised in such an overtly patriarchal culture, the absence of a father was a tangible, debilitating deficit in the little boy's life.

Like not having a leg.

Most of the men that Noah had met were through his mother, and there was always something off-putting, something not right. The small boy could feel that the men were there for some specific purpose related to his mother, that they were not interested or involved with him in any way. He grew up seeing men as either the remote, domineering, disapproving, and frightening figures represented by the Korean men in his life, like the soldiers who searched the buses he rode to Seoul, or as the foreign, giant creatures that were focused on his mother and caused her to sometimes go crazy and take out all her shame and pain on him.

Essentially, other than a general sense of gratitude toward American soldiers as a whole for their protection against North Korean violence, Noah had grown up with nothing positive being associated with men or being a man.

Until Elmore Lindquist.

Elmore was in many ways the typical father of his generation. He worked. His wife stayed home and raised the children. He was not "engaged" the way later generations of men and fathers would be expected to be, following a path blazed by Phil Donahue and Alan Alda. Elmore was more in the mold of Jim Anderson, played by Robert Young in the TV series *Father Knows Best*. The flesh and blood Elmore Lindquist was like the TV character: always thoughtful, very patient, never irritable, and always supportive and adoring of his children's mother. Elmore actually enjoyed the TV show, which ran from 1954 through 1960 and stayed on forever in reruns.

Elmore also liked the show *I Dream of Jeannie*. He would have been surprised to learn that the studio lot "house" front that served as Jim Anderson's home in *Father Knows Best* was also the same house front used for Major Nelson's home in *I Dream of Jeannie*.

Elmore was a new sort of creature to Noah when he first arrived in the United States. Elmore was a physical presence, but was never physical, except during yard work. He was a man, but seemed more a part of the fabric, structure, and framework of the house than some actual person. He never seemed to get sick or tired or impatient or demanding. He would drive endless hours along mind-numbing miles of highways during summer vacations, enduring countless hours of children squabbling about touching each other and whining for bathrooms. He could execute novel-length, unending honey-do lists and chores he would never have thought to invent.

He just was.

He was this constant, dependable, working, providing presence of strength and good humor. When Noah was first adjusting to his new St. Peter life, he didn't know what to make of Elmore and kept waiting for the proverbial other shoe to drop. It never did.

Elmore cleared his throat and realized that his tongue was bleeding from chewing it too hard as he'd climbed the stairs to confront the emotional roulette wheel of a sixteen-year-old boy who wrestled with his unique teenage harpies of differentness and deformity.

"Son, you're starting to become a young man now. . . . You're not a little kid anymore. And I know that it can be kind of hard doing things that grownups, like your mom and I, tell you. But I just want to share with you a little something I've learned. There are two people in this world that a man shouldn't argue with. One is his wife. If you want a successful, happy marriage, someday you'll know what I mean.

"The other is a man's mother. Just because.

"I know that sounds sort of lame, but it's that simple. A man just doesn't argue with his mother."

Elmore paused and glanced down at Noah, sitting to his left. The boy didn't look at him, but instead, kept staring out the window. No reaction. No comment.

Well, this is going well . . .

"Son . . . because . . . being a man is about . . . it's about . . . it's . . . it's NOT about how loud you can yell or how hard you can hit something or someone. You're going to learn that the hardest fights that a man will have in his life will be inside himself . . . with himself.

"Being a man is about winning against the pettiness of your ego. It means saying you were wrong, even when you know you were right; it's saying you are sorry, even though you're not . . .

"Because . . . it just doesn't matter.

"Of course, if it *does* matter, if you *truly* believe in your heart and soul that the world will be a better place, that the course of history and your corner of mankind will truly be better off, then of course, stand up and be a man.

"But if you *know* in your heart—deep down inside you—that it doesn't really matter, except to you and your ego, then be a *real* man. Say you are sorry, even when you're not. Say you were wrong, even though you are right. Because a man should only stand up for things that truly matter."

Still no reaction from the teen. Silence and staring.

"So . . . Son, if you really believe the world will be a better place because you wear that shirt, then by God, wear the shirt and make your mother unhappy. But if you know that it doesn't matter to the world at all—only to you—then be a man, Son. Be a man and wear something else. Tell your mother that you're sorry, even though you really aren't. And that you were wrong, even though you're not."

Elmore stopped talking. His big, bass voice stopped filling up the small bedroom, and he sat in silence with his adopted son. Just like real curse words didn't pop into Elmore's head, the word *adopted* never popped into his head as an adjective when thinking of Noah and the word *son*. It's just the sort of man he was. He followed rules. The rules said that Noah was his son because Ellen and he had decided to make him their son. And so he was.

The silence went on for minutes. Elmore finally stood up. He'd said what he had to say.

"Well, I have to get going to work now, Son. I'm late. Be the man I know that you are. I know you'll do the right thing . . .

"Be a man, Son."

With those words, Elmore turned and went out the bedroom door, closed it behind him, and went down the stairs into the kitchen. Ellen sat there by herself. Carla had finished breakfast and had left to walk the six blocks to the high school.

"Well, I talked to him. Don't know if anything got through."

"You know I didn't mean to imply that I don't consider him our son . . ."

"I know, Sweetheart. I know. I've got to get to the office. I'm late for a department faculty meeting."

Elmore leaned down to his seated wife and kissed her on the top of her blonde, perfectly curled hair.

"I'll come home for lunch, just to see how things are going."

Elmore picked up his briefcase from the floor where he always set it, next to the little kitchen desk that held the mustard-yellow, plastic phone. He paid extra to AT&T to have a colored telephone; it was a slim "banana swooped" one with push-button dialing rather than rotary. Ellen wanted everything perfect and matching in the house, and a black, standard phone just wouldn't go with the kitchen décor.

The breakup of AT&T, "Ma Bell," would not happen for another six years. AT&T held a monopoly on all local and long-distance telephone service, and all communications equipment for the entire country, thus allowing it to charge the Lindquists for a yellow phone versus a black phone. But after the 1984 breakup of the telecommunications monopoly, seven regional Bell operating companies would be formed to provide local phone service to their respective regions of the country. This allowed for competition in long-distance services and telecommunications equipment and led to the rise of companies like MCI and Sprint. And the disappearance of fees for color versus black telephones.

For all its flaws, only in an open society like America, that did not have castes or theocratic dictates, was it truly possible that the Lindquist's angry sixteen-year-old disfigured, mixed-race adoptive son could—and would—someday, some twenty years later, become an executive leading mergers and acquisitions deals worth hundreds of millions of dollars, even tens of billions of dollars, all over the world for one of those regional Bell companies. Or that he could become a senior vice president of AT&T's largest global venture in its history; that he would one day fly into Mankato Regional Airport on one of the company's corporate jets because his mother needed him.

Ellen looked up from her second cup of Sanka when she heard her son's steps coming down the stairs. She looked at him with her cup in her left hand, her right hand crushing the life out of another hapless napkin.

He was wearing a different shirt. One that she had gotten for him last year at a back-to-school sale at J. C. Penney in Mankato.

"Uh . . . hey Mom? I'm sorry for the things I said . . . you were right, I needed to change my shirt from yesterday."

Ellen felt relief and the release of more tension than she had been aware of. She realized her fears and guilt that Noah might have seen her secret struggles with racism was just that: her fears and sense of guilt. Noah only saw his mom being Mom.

"Thank you, Noah. You'd better hurry. You're already late for school."

Ellen wanted to say more, to say how sorry she was and to let him know that she loved him and worried for him. But couldn't and didn't say anything further. She always struggled to express her love and true feelings of affection toward her children. It was the legacy of the Linn family stoicism, the Småland derived, Swedish tradition: One should focus on what needed to be done and not on what one wanted to say. She hoped and prayed that her love showed in her everyday actions of devotion to her family.

Chapter 25

Noah

hat will she be like? The thought kept intruding into the sea swells and distant buoy-clanging that reached the ship as it trundled toward its ferry slip, still two hours away. The thought kept scratching at his consciousness. It was 8:00 a.m. and the ferry wasn't scheduled to dock until 10:00.

Brad Jackman had pulled off a minor miracle, locating Noah's Korean mother.

"Really, it wasn't that hard," Jackman had laughingly shared at the Blue Note.

"You would not have believed it! So I'm getting off this train from Seoul into Munsan Station . . . ya know? And I go up to the information or ticket window, and I pull out your little pendant thingy and show the man behind the glass. So . . . the guy looks at the pendant, then looks at me, then looks at the pendent, and says to me in really bad English, 'Young Nam. Please stay. I go get . . . I go get . . . please stay!'

"Next thing I know, like thirty minutes later, some kid your age shows up and says, 'You not him . . . you not Young Nam.' And he's shaking his head at me and there's this little crowd that's gathered, because I'm like the only pasty white guy . . . and I'm saying, 'No. No. I'm Brad. I'm Young Nam's friend . . . friend.' And I'm pointing at myself and they're all just looking at me."

Jackman was gesturing on his side of the coffee shop's table, recreating the scene.

"Then I accidentally slipped into Japanese, saying something like, 'Man! I wish I could speak Korean!' and one of the old guys in the little crowd says in Japanese, 'You can speak Japanese!'

"And I'm, like, 'Yea, I speak Japanese. Can you?'

"And it turns out that this guy does speak Japanese fluently. He grew up under the Japanese occupation. So I explain the whole situation to him. You know, your mom putting you up for adoption, that you lived at the address on your pendant, that you were now an exchange student in Japan, and I'm trying to find your mom for you.

"The old guy translated what I said to the kid. The kid turns out to be your cousin, your mom's brother's youngest son, I think . . . something like that. He said he remembers you, and that you two used to play together some."

Noah had sat there in his slightly too-short chair at the slightly too-short table holding his cup of green tea, listening to Jackman telling him all this in the little coffee shop. Noah remembered his cousin as a little boy who had been a year or so younger.

While reliving the conversation with Brad in the Blue Note *kissaten* in Kumamoto, Noah was suddenly chilled and realized he felt really damp from the misting sea water that had been spraying up at him from the ship's bow ploughing through the waves and swells. He needed to warm up and also get his bag and toilet kit out of the little locker below decks and prepare for debarkation in a couple of hours.

Jackman had not actually met his mother. Brad had shared that she lived in the city of Daegu, which is located inland in the southeastern part of the Korean peninsula. The city is the third largest metropolitan area in Korea, after Seoul and Busan. It was a full day's journey from Daegu to Munsan Village using coach class trains and buses. Jackman had given his mailing address at the dojo in Seoul, where he was staying with his friend, to Noah's cousin. Noah's mother had mailed a letter a couple of days later to Jackman at the dojo for him to take back to Noah.

That letter was now in Noah's coat pocket as he headed toward a doorway in the ferry's bulkhead that led inside to the main portside passageway.

What will she be like?

One of the inevitable facts of everyone's life is that you grow up and become an adult. And as adults, people can and do look back at people and events in their childhood. And people make judgments. The fairness and challenge of making such judgments involves the fact that what anyone remembers from their childhood is not only highly subjective, but the original evidence was collected by the mind, emotions, and limited perspective of the child who witnessed the evidence and who preceded the judging adult.

Noah realized how mixed his memories and feelings were about his Korean mother. He realized that how he perceived what she may be now could be highly influenced by how he chose to perceive and judge how she was in the past. How could he fairly judge her when, as a small child, he had known nothing about the complexities, the conflicting pressures, the wasted dreams of her adult world? The lesson that he had learned from his father, Elmore Lindquist, was that if something only mattered because it mattered to you, then maybe it should not matter at all, unless there was a broader reason beyond yourself. All his memories by definition only mattered to him from a small child's perspective and understanding. He only remembered them because they were imprinted on his brain. But how many other events left no lasting imprint because he lacked the understanding, hadn't grasped the importance or the true meaning? It dawned on Noah that he really had no basis for passing judgment on his Korean mother.

What will she be like? Certainly she will not be the woman I remember . . .

As he got out of the December winds coming off the Korea Strait, he could feel the warmth of the ferry's interior and he swayingly walked down the Haru Maru's passageway. Feeling the warmth around him and heading toward his steerage class accommodations, Noah pondered what, if any, broader point there might be to the things that had mattered to a destitute, crippled stateless boy so long ago.

Just as he was heading down the last ladder to the lower deck where he was berthed, a thought hit him.

What if she's not there waiting for me?

Chapter 26

Ellen

Ellen Lindquist had just collected the mail from her home's mailbox that hung outside the front door. Unlike many places where mailmen drove up to mailboxes at the end of each driveway, in St. Peter the mail boxes were right next to front doors for the convenience of the residents, especially given the long, cold, and snowy Minnesota winters.

It was a rainy day in mid-April with the barometer falling steadily throughout the day. But with a high of sixty-eight degrees, it was considered warm in Minnesota for mid-April. As she got to the top of the stairs that led up from the front door to her kitchen, Ellen saw that there was a letter from Lutheran Social Service of Minnesota, the adoption agency with which she and Elmore had been working. She dropped all the other mail onto the kitchen table and grabbed the letter opener sitting on her kitchen counter. Ellen would never have thought to tear a letter open with her fingers. She cut all her letters open with a carved imitation-ivory, bone letter opener that her brother Andy had brought back from Africa when his ship had made a port call in Morocco. Everything Ellen did was ordered and clean, even cast off, waste paper envelopes of letters.

April 11, 1969

Mr. & Mrs. Elmore Lindquist
138 Sunrise Ridge Drive
St. Peter, Minnesota

Dear Mr. & Mrs. Lindquist:

We have received word from Korea that one of the sponsorship children is definitely available for adoption so we are sending you background information on the boy and a slide to ask if you can consider him.

Miss Leslie Sandersson, of our staff, met Young Nam when she was in Korea in March (she took the slide of him). If you would like to discuss further the scars from the childhood accident, she would be happy to discuss this with you if you want to consider him.

He has been sponsored for several months by a Sunday school group in Borup, Minnesota.

We look forward to hearing about your reaction and will be happy to discuss this further with you.

Sincerely,

(Miss) Emily Iverson
Social Worker

Ellen reread the letter. She shook the envelope and out dropped a single slide projector photo-slide. It was too small for her to see what the picture actually was.

Sunday school children are sending money to this boy . . . he really is like those poster children I see in UNICEF ads . . . his poster photo is probably taped up in a Sunday school classroom in that church in Borup . . . Elmore can set up the slide projector when he comes home for lunch and we can take a look at the LSS picture . . .

Elmore had purchased a Kodak carousel slide projector the previous year so that the Lindquists could have friends over for slide show parties and share each other's summer vacations and other travel photos while eating brownies (what Minnesotans called "bars") with Sanka decaf coffee—because the parties would be in the evenings. Slide projectors for 35 mm slides began increasing in popularity in the 1950s, and by the late '60s everyone had one. And among the teetotalling crowd of the Lindquist's friends, Sanka was THE coffee to serve during evening slide shows. The brand name came from the French words *sans caféine*—without caffeine—although the brand was owned by a German company. Decaffeinated Sanka came in a bright orange coffee can and became so recognized by American consumers and associated with decaf coffee, that today coffee pots serving any brand of decaffeinated coffee have orange lids or handles.

Ellen took out the papers that contained a background report on this now confirmed, adoptable boy—this genuine poster child for international adoption. The report was written on the letterhead of Korea Social Service, Inc., with its emblem of a green circle containing the silhouette of a mother holding a baby. The paper of the report was onionskin, the especially thin, translucent paper that was commonly used in airmail of the day. The paper had a high cotton-fiber content, making it strong, despite its thinness and light weight.

Ellen read the five-page, typed report. It described the boy's father:

> An American soldier of Caucasian background, who has not
> been reached since Mrs. Lee was in 8th month of pregnancy
> of the child.

There was very little information otherwise about the biological father. Ellen couldn't help wondering and wanting to know more. Even though the prevailing mantra was that nurture mattered, not nature, she felt in her gut that nature still mattered. An old Swedish proverb that her grandmother used to say came to mind.

Dåligt material ger dåligt resultat.

Poor material yields poor results.

The boy's father hadn't been reached since the mother was eight months pregnant. But that implies that he was in contact and had knowledge of the mother's pregnancy, that he knew he had a child on the way.

What kind of man abandons an eight-month pregnant woman?

As she pondered what sort of man the boy's father might be, Ellen saw that the poster boy's birthday was listed as April 14, 1963. It occurred to Ellen that today was Monday, April 14. The nation's top hit song on this week's Billboard Top 40 would be "Aquarius/ Let the Sun Shine In" by the 5th Dimension. And the 41st Academy Awards would be held tonight in Los Angeles. *Oliver*, a movie about a poor, destitute, starving little boy in an orphanage, would win Best Picture.

Chapter 27

Hanlon

Hanlon was thinking about the conversation he had had in his tent with Tuck Riley last year as he watched his Korean live-in girlfriend—what the GIs called a "yobo"—cooking up dinner. Yobo was a word derived from Korean that meant something like "sweetheart," but as used by American GIs, the word was derisive and derogatory and usually meant a live-in maid and cook with "benefits." For the women who were the yobos, it meant being provided for, with a place to live and food to eat. They only had to interact with one man, rather than constantly get new "clients" if they worked in a club that serviced GIs. It meant stability, predictability, and less likelihood of contracting a disease. Some even found love and marriage.

They lived in a little apartment he rented off base. It was nice to have a place to go that was away from the Army regimentation. As an NCO, noncommissioned officer, he was older than the majority of enlisted men who were mostly junior ranking troops. He didn't like hanging out in local bars with all the drunk kids and the local hookers who were more than happy to get those drunk kids, fresh off the farm, to part with their GI money. His yobo's name was Lee Hee Ae.

What the fuck, Bobby."
The "F" word is a ubiquitous part of the lexicon of the US military—maybe all militaries have their version of the F word from their respective languages—and it is used in every grammatical

and nongrammatical function and role conceivable. It tends to be coupled with other terms and words to lend depth or breadth or for no reason at all.

Platoon Sergeant Tucker D. Riley was standing in the tent's entry. Sergeant Robert Hanlon, Jr. stood in the tent.

"How long you been here in Camp Page? Three months? You got here in March of this year, right?"

"That's right. March of '62. What's the problem Platoon Sergeant?" Robert "Bobby" Hanlon spoke in the slow chewy way that rural Alabama—way out on the state's western edge—had taught him, meaning he had a tendency to put too many syllables in one-syllable words and to talk at a maddeningly three-quarter speed.

"Then how the fuck is it that you ain't been off post yet?" Tucker "Tuck" Riley was also a Southern boy, as is eighty percent of the United States Army. But he was from South Carolina, not Alabama, and tended to speak at a more normal speed. Tuck's talk was all twang with a tinge of Army hooah. The twang was learned hanging onto his mama's skirts in Pontiac, SC, just off Highway 1.

"No reason to," Sergeant Hanlon said in his slow, almost retarded-sounding way. "Only a lot of thatched roofed, dusty Gook places which ain't got no running water and no toilets. Why the fuck would I want to go off post to that crap, Platoon Sergeant?"

"Because you're gonna go fucking loco, Bobby. TAD or no, you're one of the top NCOs I got. Need you to reset your safety valve once in a while. And you're sure as shit ain't gonna do that staying on post."

"So what you want me to do? Go and get me some off-post Gook pussy? Get shit faced at some Slope's slop house? Fuck that, Platoon Sergeant. The NCO club is just fine here on post at Camp fucking Page, the R-O-K."

"Bobby, Whisky. Tango. Foxtrot. Over! What The Fuck! I know you've been in the shit plenty."

Hanlon had been in the Korean War and had been a member of the 23rd Regimental Combat Team (RCT). The RCT had fought heroically in the Battle of Chipyong-ni, February 13–15, 1952. The battle has been called the "Gettysburg of the Korean War" because it represented the farthest point of advance of the Chinese People's Volunteer Army (PVA) during the war and because it was one of the most deadly and desperate battles of the war for American forces. The Battle of Chipyong-ni was studied for years at the US Army Command and General Staff College at Ft. Leavenworth as a textbook case of how to defeat a numerically superior enemy force.

The 23rd RCT was surrounded and cut off twelve miles behind enemy lines. The regiment also included a unit called the French Battalion, France's contribution to the UN forces in Korea. This 23rd RCT consisted of approximately 5,600 men. The Chinese threw at them the entire 3rd Army of the PVA plus additional units from two other armies, totaling approximately 25,500 men.

Sergeant Hanlon had fought off and survived some of the most fanatical, massed charges made by the Chinese PVA during that battle. He was a hardened combat veteran and had the medals and campaign ribbons to prove it. His experience at Chipyong-ni of fighting in desperate circumstances against a hugely outnumbering enemy force would serve him well thirteen years later in a country that Americans had not heard of in 1952: the Republic of South Vietnam.

"You ain't no green horn, Bobby. You're a goddamn war hero. So here's the deal. I've fixed it so that you get to do a TAD, Temporary Additional Duty, at Camp Dodge. Still meets your DMV duty obligations, but you're only twenty miles from Seoul!"

"You're shitting me, Platoon Sergeant."

"I shit you not. They need some A-sistance,"—Riley pronounced the "a" to rhyme with "hey"—"with post security and need a combat savvy shit like you to 'consult' with their staff. And your time there counts for my numbers for grunts on the fucking DMZ line.

So. Whisky. Tango. Foxtrot? Why ain't you packing your shit and getting your rebel ass on your way to Dodge!"

The one thing that Hanlon could say about the Army was that it sure took him to places far away from his hometown.

Rural Alabama was the environment and culture from which Sergeant Robert Hanlon, Jr., left to join the US Army in 1947. Although he had not finished high school, he'd taken to the Army, advancing up the enlisted ranks and would make it his career, until he retired in 1976.

He had met Hee Ae when he had been sent on that TAD to Camp Dodge. She was one of the many women who would get work around US military bases and camps. She had been working at the base laundry. Her English was better than most Koreans that he had met. Being a bit older than many of the bar girls, he clicked with her more and she was less flaky. She had been friendly at the base laundry where she worked, and he would chat her up whenever he went to pick up his clean laundry. One day he asked her out for drinks off base. She agreed. The night went better than he had anticipated, concluding with what GIs referred to as a "happy ending." Hanlon genuinely liked his yobo. But now he was going to have to tell her some bad news.

Generally, only the lowest class and the most economically or socially disenfranchised Korean women worked on or around US military installations. The immediate assumption by Koreans in general was that any woman who worked on or near such installations was a prostitute. Even if a majority of these women were employed in legitimate work as cooks, laundresses, cleaners, or in some other capacity, the taint and stigma of those who were prostitutes was equally applied to all the women. This was particularly true if any Korean woman had an identifiably mixed-race child.

Hanlon liked having a woman to come home to. He was, after all, a family man. He was married to a nice little Southern girl he'd met not long after he got to his first permanent posting at Fort Benning. Fort Benning is one of the Army's largest bases and is located just south of Columbus, Georgia, on the east side of the Chattahoochee River that is the western border of the State of Georgia, separating it from Alabama. Hanlon's wife grew up in Columbus and had been waitressing at a local joint popular with soldiers from the base. Once they started dating, things moved quickly, and he married his little Georgia Peach. They would have four children together, two sons and two daughters, and he would retire to his wife's hometown of Columbus, Georgia, where he would spend the rest of his life reliving his past.

Hanlon had been up front to his yobo and let her know that he had a wife and children. She seemed fine with it, so he didn't think anything more about it. The reality was that his yobo had few better alternatives. As a divorced, poor, and poorly educated outcast in Korean society, she had no real choices. What limited alternatives available to her tended to involve menial labor or poverty, and were unsavory. Being a married American's yobo was one of the best options she had.

The stigma of Korean women who work on US military installations, or even in the "camptowns" around them, continues to exist today. The clubs and bars and prostitution continue to thrive, with the prostitutes actually being licensed and regulated. And the yobo arrangement continues to exist in today's Korea.

Things get kind of surreal when one is deployed to some foreign land for months. One's real world and real life starts to feel like it is the fantasy and the current environment and one's current life is the real one. Somehow, his life with Hee Ae had taken on a life of its own, a sense of legitimacy and permanence. Real feelings had taken root and it had all been good. Until she told him she was packing one in the oven. This had been a major shock—Hanlon had been completely disciplined in his use of condoms. Getting his yobo pregnant was the last thing he needed. Also, initially, catching any sort of disease had been a concern.

You never know.

But, he'd worked it out. Even after his yobo had gotten pregnant, he was able to keep it between the lines.

Jesus, was that a major Charlie Foxtrot—a cluster fuck!

In 1962 abortions were illegal in Korea, and he wasn't going to risk having his yobo die on some butcher's table doing an illegal abortion. Besides, he was a good Southern Baptist. So he had said what he had to say.

"Listen Hee Ae."

Hanlon had pulled her to him, her small body fitting easily into his big arms.

"Listen, baby. I have buku love for you. Baby-san is OK-OK. When I go back America, I bye-bye my American wife and bring you and baby-san to America. I love you long time, Hee Ae. Long-time."

"You no bull shit me Bobby?"

There were tears dripping from her tiny chin, and her slanted Asian eyes were red and watery with more tears.

"I know buku GI go and no come back. Buku GI say bull shit! Bobby no say bull shit. Please! Maybe Bobby s'koshi love Lee Hee Ae. So . . . please no bull shit. No bull shit me!" She was gesturing hard and pointing at her heart.

"No bullshit, baby. I buku love you. Take you back to America . . . I shit you not."

Hanlon said all this in his three-quarter speed Alabama drawl. Her tiny form clung to him, and she buried her face into his chest. She was pregnant, and he had promised her that he would go back to The World—a term GIs used to refer to their real lives back in the States or the world outside of the military—when his orders expired and leave his real wife and his real American kids.

Whisky. Tango. Foxtrot!

What The Fuck!

In the surrealness of foreign deployment, Hanlon truly was confused and genuinely believed his words—sometimes. Other times he would see things as if suddenly waking from a dream and wonder how he had gotten himself into the situation he was in and how the hell was he going to get out of it?

If there even is a way out . . .

As the pregnancy progressed, she came to believe Hanlon's words. Maybe it was the hope of desperation. She couldn't imagine that he could tell the things he did, day after day, and not mean them in some way. *It must be true.*

And Hanlon continued to vacillate, trying to decide which of his worlds was the real one. But deep down, he knew.

And who the fuck knew? Maybe he would sneak her and his *Chink* kid back with him . . .

Yeah, right! November Foxtrot Whisky! Bobby, you are an A-number one, royal goddamn asshole. How the fuck did you get in the shit this deep? There's just no fucking way I'm gonna screw up my four kids back home.

Maybe I can figure a way to send her some money now and then.

Fuck! You can't just dump her ass and leave her to raise your kid . . . fuck!

. . . Hey. Wait a minute . . . how I do I know for certain it's my kid? I know some other guys' yobos who fuck around plenty when their Papa-san is away on maneuvers. How do I know mine didn't?

Plausible denial, however small, was worth grabbing hold of.

He had too much Canadian Mist whisky in him. And he was drinking even more now, smoking a Lucky Strike, thinking of that conversation with Tuck Riley and watching his heavily pregnant yobo through the haze of smoke. His Hee Ae and his unborn gook bastard kid.

Allegedly!

She looked up from the *bulgogi* that she was cooking for dinner and smiled, pulling a burning cigarette from her lips with her left hand and taking a gulp of her own whisky. She was very pregnant now, nearing eight months. Hanlon smiled back, raised his glass in a little, silent toast, and lifted the whisky to his lips and took a harsh, too-big gulp.

I'm going to have to tell her tomorrow that I'm heading off to maneuvers for a couple weeks.

Hanlon had actually received his transfer orders to go back to the States. He had thought it over for a long time. There was no good way to do this. A clean break would be the easiest way. Hanlon would tell Hee Ae that he was only going away for a couple weeks, when in reality, he would never come back and she would never hear from him again.

I'll leave some cash with Tuck for her. And I'll try to send money along to help her out. I hate to ask Tuck to do this for me, but I know that good old boy will. Damn! He's going to have one fucked up conversation . . . Shit happens.

As Hee Ae, with her belly straining with eight months of baby inside, was grilling the marinated beef, she looked over at her American man and took another drag on her cigarette. She'd come to love him. Maybe in the land of the blind, the one-eyed man truly is king.

Who knew? She thought.

She smiled and Bobby lifted his glass to her again. And smiled back.

Hee Ae didn't know it, but her world was going to end as she knew it and, in the words of Bobby Hanlon, things were really going to suck.

The day Tuck Riley told her that Hanlon had been transferred back to the United States shattered Hee Ae's world. She didn't cry or say anything as she listened to Platoon Sergeant Riley tell her the blunt truth as he held the wad of cash Hanlon had entrusted him to give to his former yobo. Riley explained that Hanlon had lied to her. He was not away on maneuvers. He was never coming back. But he did explain that Hanlon intended to keep sending support to her, to help her with raising their child. He tried to explain that Hanlon really had fallen for her, but ultimately, he just couldn't leave his American family. Like such information really mattered to Hee Ae.

Riley stood awkwardly in the small apartment that Hanlon had shared with his yobo. Hee Ae could only stare at him without really seeing anything. The room was feeling like it was tipping over. She was feeling sick and thought she might throw up and her baby felt huge and heavy inside her swollen, stretched belly. Her thoughts and heart had stopped at the word *lied*. He set the cash on the small table, turned, and left, closing the door to the apartment and slamming shut the phantom fantasy world that had been in Hee Ae's mind, fabricated by Bobby Hanlon's lies.

Everything was a lie!

She had known that the day would come when transfer orders would arrive. She had known that Hanlon was only in Korea on extended TAD orders, not a permanent change of station. But she had believed that she would be following Hanlon to America and to a new life. Their lives had been going along with a rhythm and a normalcy that had lulled her into a feeling they would go on together. As long as she was Hanlon's yobo, she was cared for and protected from the venom of Korean judgment. She had a home and food and someone to care for. And someday they would leave the scorn and judgment of Korea and she and Hanlon and their child would live freely in America. As far as she was concerned, she had a husband, a future, and a whole life ahead of her.

When she had gotten pregnant, she had offered to get an illegal abortion, but Hanlon had stopped her. He had told her everything she wanted to hear, that she had not dared to hope for.

Tuck Riley's visit and the terrible truth had been beyond numbing and heart crushing. She didn't know what would become of her. Hanlon had promised that, when transfer orders came, he would keep sending money so that she could stay in the apartment and support their child. He had promised that he would come back to take them to America as soon as he could. He had promised. And promised. And promised some more, assurance after assurance. And she had had no choice but to cling to the hope that his promises offered. After she learned the incomprehensible truth and Riley had shut the door behind him, Hee Ae had gotten physically ill, throwing up and intermittently, uncontrollably sobbing.

The lump sum of cash that Riley left on her table got her through her son's first year. But the money ran out and her work paid so little. Two more payments reached her, the last one in spring of 1965. But then nothing more, and they were not enough. She was told by one of Hanlon's former platoon members she ran into at the club she was working at in 1966, that there had been some sort of battle or maneuver or something where Hanlon had been seriously hurt. She didn't know what to believe.

All she knew was that in the end, all Hanlon's promises, all his assurances, all of it had been as hollow as the crater that he left in her heart and life. She had nothing from him or of him, except the pain, the memories, and the constant burden of his son, who looked so much like him.

Chapter 28

Hee Ae

JANUARY 1968, SEOUL/MUNSAN

Hee Ae had taken the bus up from Seoul that morning. The ride had taken double the normal time. There seemed to be endless security stops and extra-intense searches. She was glad that she had sold all her black market American cigarettes. There were rumors that North Korean infiltrators had tried to kill President Park and now there was a nationwide manhunt. With the traffic and security stops, the picking up and dropping off passengers at nearly every scheduled station, the trip had taken eight hours. She had stood in the aisle the whole time. Because of the rumors and speculation flying about fleeing infiltrators, gun battles in front of the presidential palace, and all out manhunts, she normally would have struck up conversations with the passengers around her—she was quite outgoing—and she fit in with her fellow passengers. When she didn't have her "American" son with her, she blended just fine with her fellow travelers. No stares, no judgment, no scarlet A. No one looked at her as a prostitute and whore for big, ugly, hairy foreigners with their huge noses and weird, big cow eyes that were pale and alien.

Nope. She was just another passenger riding the cheapest mode of transport other than walking, with others who shared her plight. There were raging conversations swapping theories and speculations, with each person adding another story of hearing from someone who knew someone who knew. There's something universal about the fact that lower levels of the social ladder tended to be friendlier, more gregarious, and definitely willing to share rumors and conspiracy theories.

Passengers who fly coach on airplanes readily chat with each other, lend magazines to total strangers, and say, "bless you" when anyone within a hundred feet sneezes. Sometimes you'll even see babies being passed around to be bounced on the lap of a stranger across the aisle.

But not in first class. No one talks to anyone, except for an occasional "excuse me" as a window passenger squeezes by an aisle passenger on his or her way to head toward the first class restroom. Everyone is too important and too damn busy—reading their newspapers, magazines, or legal briefs—to make any idle chatter. Why invest the time and energy talking to someone you'll never see again? If there was any conversation, typically it was between people traveling together—for work. Those married couples traveling together didn't talk.

Societies' elites don't readily strike up conversations with total strangers. It is just understood. Uppity elite social circle rule number one: keep a discreet, aloof silence. Besides, what if the guy next to you won't shut up? Why open *that* Pandora's box?

And so it was on the bus from Seoul to Munsan Village in late January 1968. Kids crying, chickens clucking, and people shouting their theories and I-heard-it-from-this-guy-who-heard-it-from-his-nephew-the-checkpoint-guard rumors . . . over the roar and leaking fumes of the bus's choking, grinding diesel engine. Normally, Hee Ae would be jumping in, sharing her observations on the topic at hand, enjoying the freedom of not being on the outside, of being welcomed inside this juicy conversation.

But not this trip. As fantastical as the rumors were, she had too many thoughts after her visit to Korea Social Service: her conversation with Mr. Paik and Miss Yang and signing preliminary papers.

She was on her way to legally and officially make her son available for adoption to anyone in America who would take him.

She was going to give her son away.

When and how am I going to tell him? How does a mommy tell her four-year-old that she won't be his mommy anymore?

There is general agreement among psychologists that one of the deepest, most enduring, and most basic human bonds and relationships is between a mother and her child. Outside of the extremely remote, rare occurrences of babies being accidentally switched at birth by a hospital, there's not one woman who is raising a child that is not her own who doesn't know it. As much as there is agreement among psychologists about the fundamental nature of the biological maternal bond, there is disagreement about what happens to children who either never had this bond or had it broken. But there is no one who presumes that such children benefit from an absence or breakage of this most basic human bond.

Hee Ae's gut kept retching and twisting with the thought that this would be very, very hard on her son. It had already been sickeningly painful for her. It was already rending her heart along fault lines that were new and uncharted, tearing the fiber of her emotional self in tortures that were new.

During the entire ride back from Seoul, the reason she did not talk to anyone was because she was too busy talking to herself. She talked to herself in her head through endless, circular, self-justifying arguments. She listed all that could—no would—be good for her son if she let him grow up in the United Sates. She lectured herself at length about the past and future of misery, hopelessness, and danger that would surely be his fate if she kept him with her. And Hee Ae pointed out to herself—even to the extent that she pictured herself wagging a finger in her own face—that she wasn't actually giving away her son. She did not agree to put him up for adoption to anyone, anywhere. She would be giving him a future that she could not offer on her own.

Koreans thought of her son as "American." And, ironically, being Korean, so did she. And she would only be putting him up for adoption to America, by Americans, to be raised by his people.

Oh no. Hee Ae, you are definitely NOT just going to give your son away . . . you would never do that. You are NOT that sort of self-centered, horror of a failed mother—a monster—to do such a thing! YOU are going to give him a LIFE and a FUTURE! You would be the ultimate monster of selfishness if you kept him, Hee Ae. There is no choice. This is your duty as his mother!

In her mind's-eye Hee Ae wagged and poked a commanding finger at her face.

This. Jab. *Is.* Jab. *Your.* Jab. *Duty.* Jab. *As his MOTHER!* Jab, jab, jab.

She was not worried that he wouldn't understand the implications and how all this adoption sort of thing would work—he always seemed to understand even complex, adult things—but in her gut's pit she was nauseated with the thought that he would be deeply wounded at some emotional level where it might not heal. She knew that her son loved her with an intensity that she did not see in other children, and that she was his only support in every way.

But this was for his sake. She would explain it clearly to him and he would understand.

He would understand because she needed so badly for him to understand. To know that this was for *his* sake, *his* future, bought by *her* self-loathing and hopelessness.

He would understand.

Plus, children forget their pain and get over things. And so will Young Nam.

The commanding finger jabbed the thought words at Hee Ae inside her head.

Like most parents about so many decisions that they make for their children, she had no real idea what this would actually do to the little boy's heart.

Most parents believe that when they make choices for their children, they do so with their child's best interests in mind. Most parents would take great exception at any suggestion that their child was not their top priority. Parents know that their child can't advocate for himself or herself. Therefore, the responsibility falls squarely on the shoulders of the parent. Most parents want to do things for their children that the children would do for themselves if they possessed the authority, the right, the maturity, and the wisdom.

Hee Ae was being forced to make one grotesque choice from among no good options. She would not know what price her choice would cost her or her son.

As she walked from the Munsan Village bus stop toward her tiny rented room on the village's outskirts, she'd run into a local shopkeeper who recognized her. She'd been walking down the rutted roadside along the main road running through Munsan. She had all of her clothes and baggage—she always traveled with trinkets and odds and ends that she would try to peddle, smuggle, and bargain for on street corners—wrapped in thin blankets into a large bundle. She balanced this bundle on her head. She was balancing this load and walking when the butcher, who Hee Ae sometimes bargained with for cast away meat cuts in exchange for some of her trinkets and junk, spotted her through his shop window as Hee Ae waddled past with her oversized load. He had a daughter who was Young Nam's age and the man was kind enough to let Young Nam and his daughter sometimes play together.

The butcher was one of the few people in the village who did not show any outward hostility or disdain for Hee Ae or her son. He felt sorry for the poor woman and her outcast boy and occasionally gave them a cast-off cutting of meat that he would have thrown away. He always did so as part of a bargain for a piece of junk that he didn't need or want, but did it to preserve Hee Ae's pride and to hide his charity.

There is a strong tradition of charity that runs throughout Korean culture and history, primarily driven by Buddhist influences. Although the charity in Korean folk tales does speak of helping the poor and the desperate, it tends to have a different focus than Western ideals of charity. Korean concepts of charity were often tied to beliefs in ethical behavior and of obtaining a desired level of ethical achievement with its rewards. Charity, defined as simply to give with no thought of return or ultimate reward, was not as strongly emphasized. Receiving the charity held a certain shame and burden, a debt of gratitude, which many wanted to avoid.

So the butcher hid his charity behind haggling over an old pot that Hee Ae had found in a trash heap and had mended its broken handle or some other equally unneeded item.

The butcher was a well-built man and fairly tall among Korean men of the day. He had a slight paunch and, in his early fifties, was mostly bald except for the fringe around his ears and around the back of his head. He had a scruffy mustache that was too sparse and too long; too many hairs hung over his lip and drooped down the corners of his mouth, which was set in a perpetual downward curl. He had very small, highly slanted slits for eyes. And the way his dark pupils were set in these slits, it made him look somewhat cross-eyed, even though he wasn't. However his exterior may have appeared, he had a heart that always made room for thoughts of others and a well of kindness that bubbled in a quiet, overflowing way.

Young Nam's memory of him would always be of his smell. He smelled of the fresh cut meat, the rich meaty aroma of lipids in the air, his nose detecting the fresh cut fat. It's the smell that gets on the hands of anyone who's ever trimmed the fat from a porterhouse in preparation for grilling out on a warm summer's evening. The butcher's daughter smelled of it as well. But he played with her anyway when invited. Beggars cannot be choosers.

The butcher stepped out of his shop door and, with his bloody, formerly white butcher's apron on, stood half way out into the road side and called after Hee Ae.

"Mrs. Lee! MRS. LEE!"

Hee Ae stopped and slowly turned her whole body because of the huge bundle she had balanced on her head, using her right hand to steady the load. Finally, she was turned enough to be looking at Shim Jin Ahn, the man who had called her name.

"What is it Mr. Shim? What do you want?"

"Has anyone told you yet about Young Nam and what happened?"

Memories of when her son had gotten burned raged back into her thoughts and emotions.

Oh God. No! Please . . .

"No, Mr. Shim. I haven't heard anything about what happened to Young Nam. I just got off the bus from Seoul and am heading home to get back to him."

Her head made little adjustment movements, quick and shifting, side-to-side and back-to-front, as she talked, unconsciously keeping the enormous bundle balanced on her head.

"Please tell me he's okay."

"Oh, yes, Mrs. Lee. He's fine . . . at least he's not hurt. But he had quite a fright yesterday."

Relief and still a continuing anxiety churned her bowels as she listened to Shim Jin Ahn tell her about her landlord, about how he had been murdered, and how little Young Nam had found the body. He explained how the boy had come running, screaming, and crying uncontrollably into the village. Mr. Shim elaborated how he had grabbed the running boy and had to fight the hysterically struggling, surprisingly strong child to the ground, pinning him there until he stopped screaming and kicking and flailing.

Hee Ae dropped the huge bundle she had been balancing on her head. Dropped it right there on the side of the road in front of Shim's butcher shop in an unruly heap of cheap junk and cheaper clothing.

"Where is Young Nam?"

"I had to keep him here yesterday while your landlord's daughter's family was notified and dealt with the body's recovery. He stayed with me last night, but I took him back to your place just an hour ago."

Hee Ae turned and started running up the road toward the thatch-roofed farmhouse at the edge of the village.

Shim Jin Ahn didn't tell Hee Ae, though, about how Young Nam had started shivering and shaking spastically and couldn't stop; that Jin Ahn had carried the boy quaking and jerking and shivering into his butcher shop and had to hold him.

He had held him tight to his chest with its big generous heart, which overflowed with his excess of sympathy for the boy.

"Daddy, what's wrong with him?" his daughter asked.

"I don't know, Princess . . . Young Nam-ya! Young Nam-ya! What's wrong?"

Jin Ahn raised his voice, holding the boy away from him now and trying to make eye contact. The boy never looked him in the eye, but haltingly, confusedly, he started to explain what he'd seen. He never stopped shaking, and Jin Ahn's generous heart started spilling ever more of its sympathy, so much so, it hurt the man to the point of tears as he listened to the shaking, shivering, terrified child.

Chapter 29

Noah

Noah set his coffee cup down on its bone china saucer. He looked at the video screen on the highly polished cherrywood-paneled bulkhead of the Citation V. It showed a map of the eastern half of the United States with the silhouette of a tiny airplane halfway along a curving line connecting Atlanta, Georgia, and Mankato, Minnesota. In the corner of the map the monitor displayed a rolling set of information: time to destination, time at destination, temperature at destination, speed over ground, and air speed as a decimal of Mach.

Mach is a ratio of the speed of an object through a fluid—in this case, air divided by the speed of sound through the fluid. At sea level and a temperature of 59 degrees Fahrenheit, the speed of sound is approximately 761 miles per hour.

The telescreen with the map was displaying speed through the air as Mach .99—Noah's Cessna Citation V Encore+ was traveling just shy of the speed of sound.

Pretty fast.

Noah thought about all the fluid mechanics calculations and formulas he had learned when studying nuclear engineering as an elite Rodman Scholar at the University of Virginia. But he'd hated engineering and had switched majors and graduated with a degree in economics. But he didn't escape engineering after all. He had been forced to do further studies and drilling in such formulas and more when he went through the Navy's Surface Warfare Officer's

School in Coronado, California, where he learned all about naval architecture, propulsion systems, naval weapons systems, and a whole lot more, starting with the underlying theory and the math supporting that theory. He'd never studied so hard as he had during his time at Coronado.

The map showed that he had an hour left on the flight. No matter how posh or comfortable the flight, the truth was that Noah was getting pretty tired of any flight. He'd just jumped on too many planes too often for too long to go to too many places. Delta Airlines had recently informed him that he was one of their top ten most frequent flyers—in the entire world. And he also had platinum or diamond or gold or whatever the top tier frequent flyer level was for a string of other airlines: United, American, British Air, Air France, Lufthansa, Japan Air, and Singapore Air. This year alone, Noah would do four around-the-world trips for his work.

Too much time stuck in long metal tubes, that's for sure.

But Noah was glad for the Citation and its Mach .99 airspeed. And that it would be landing at Mankato Regional Airport, just thirteen miles from his parents' home in St. Peter. This was one trip he knew he needed to make.

TWO YEARS AGO his dad, Elmore, had called Noah. It was unusual for Elmore to call Noah. Usually it was his mother who made calls and his dad would hop on the line for a brief bit. Elmore always said the same thing to Noah on those short phone call hop-ons.

"Hope you're not working too hard, Son."

But this time, it was Elmore who was on the line when Noah answered.

"Hi, Dad. It's good hearing from you. What's going on?"

"Son, I have some news to give you."

"Sure. What's up?"

"It's about your mother. She's going in for surgery tomorrow morning. It's exploratory."

"What? What's it for? Is she alright?"

"Well, you know how your mother has had her hip bothering her for some time. Well, it was getting worse and the cortisone shots weren't working anymore. So they did some X-rays. Dr. Larson thinks he can see some kind of mass in her colon. It might be colon cancer, so he's going to go in and do an exploratory and confirm and maybe remove whatever they find."

There was silence for some long seconds as Noah digested what his father has just said.

"How's Mom dealing with the situation, Dad?"

Another silence. Then Elmore cleared his throat, before his big rumbly bass voice resumed talking into the phone's mouthpiece.

"You know your mom. She's very clinical about the whole thing. She scheduled the surgery at the earliest date possible and is already packed for the hospital stay and has written down a reminder list of items I need to take care of while she is recovering."

Noah could picture his mother. She would be tight lipped with purpose, packing her overnight suitcase, making sure that all the right lipsticks were put inside the cosmetics container, organized by size and color. She wouldn't be doing any of her laughter, Noah was certain. No "Oh, dears" melodically ending her sentences. If there was a way to organize your way to victory over an illness, Ellen Lindquist would be that conquering general, deploying all the forces of efficiency, planning, and regimentation at her disposal.

"What is her prognosis, Dad?"

Elmore cleared his throat again.

"We won't know until after the surgery. The main point of the operation is to remove the mass that's in her colon and to biopsy it. The doctors will then make a recommendation of any other treatments that may be needed. At least that's what Dr. Larson has said. It all depends on what they find once they get in and see."

"You doing okay, Dad? Anything you need me to do?"

More throat clearing. Once. Twice. A third time.

"I'm fine, Son. Your sisters are here. Carla can come by every day after work, since she's so close. And Christina is down from Duluth and Karissa came up from Fairmont. I've already talked to your brother, Karsten, in California, so he knows. You were the last one I called, because I waited until you were back from your business trip to Germany."

"That's great that the girls are with you and Mom. And no sweat about calling me last. Just look after Mom, okay Dad?"

Another throat clearing.

"Sure, Son . . . well that's about all I have to say right now."

Three more harrumphing clearings.

"I'll call you with more news after the operation. Hope you aren't working too hard, Son."

"Don't worry about me, Dad. Talk to you soon."

Noah was glad that his sisters were there to be with his parents, especially his dad. It was particularly fortunate that Carla had married and settled in the next town down the road, only twelve miles from St. Peter. She still had the most perfect, beautiful translucent blonde hair, always flowing and curled just so. She'd married her high school boyfriend, whom she started dating the summer after ninth grade. After marrying, while she was still attending Gustavus Adolphus College, they had moved out to his parents' farm on the outskirts of St. Peter's neighboring town. Carla had graduated with a degree in accounting, taking after Elmore, and was now a bank administrative officer for a regional agricultural lending bank.

Noah was close to Carla, having survived each other through their adolescence; they had become good friends through their college years and as adults. He would often call her and catch up over lengthy phone conversations. Carla was as grounded and level headed as they came. And she was always a wonderful listener.

His oldest and second oldest sisters, Christina and Karissa, had both become teachers. Christina, who still clearly had the memory of that frightening and confusing June day in 1957, was now faculty at Fond du Lac Tribal and Community College outside of Duluth, Minnesota. The very things that she had found rewarding when she used to teach tiny Noah when he was new to America and its culture she had found in the work she now did, working with American Indian tribal students, although the school's student body is eighty percent non-Indian. She enjoyed not only teaching subject matter to them, but bridging the cultural gap between them and the broader American society. Just as she had done with Noah back in 1970.

Christina still liked to be in charge of her siblings, and Noah was certain that she was directing Karissa and Carla on all points of detail in the current situation.

Karissa was also a teacher, but on the other extreme. She had found her passion in working with special education students at the early elementary level. In some ways, both women resembled their mother in that each had gravitated toward hard jobs that many others would not have sought out. Noah's youngest sister, Carla, though looking so much like her mother, Ellen, as a child, had her father's temperament—fact oriented, unflappable, thriving on predictability.

Noah was always perplexed by the phenomenon of rivalries, including sibling rivalries. He couldn't understand how taking pride in one thing seemed to demand a derision of something else that was similar. Loyalties to professional sports teams mystified him; they were rotating groups of paid professionals, usually with no ties other than their employment contract to the local area. One might as well feel loyalty to and cheer on the construction crew repairing the state highway nearest one's town. At least that's how the logic appeared to Noah.

As he thought back to the day his father told him about his mother's cancer, he thought about his siblings. He had been incredibly lucky. He got on well with all of them. And though he could detect rivalries among them, he didn't feel any such rivalries between himself and any of them. It could have been so completely different, as he now knew from seeing the bitter and brutal sibling rivalries among his friends and others with whom he'd crossed paths.

It could have been so different, especially with Karsten.

Noah thought how it must have been for his older brother suddenly to have a foreign, Asian-looking boy thrust upon him. Karsten had pursued his dreams of space and buxom Earth women. He succeeded in the space part, and was now employed by NASA at its Pasadena, California, Jet Propulsion Laboratory, working on interplanetary space exploration missions. Losing your status as the only boy—during a time and era when boys were relatively more prized than girls by the prevailing American society—and being made by Ellen Lindquist to call a complete stranger—an Oriental— your brother, could not have been easy. But Noah could recall no instance of Karsten ever once showing any resentment or distance. None of them did. They had all taken to him, teaching him, explaining things to him, and supporting him when other kids were cruel. Always treating him as nothing different, nothing special, just their little brother. Nothing more and nothing less.

Which was everything.

The thought lingered as Noah stared at the map and the Mach reading, feeling the remote power of the Pratt & Whitney engines through his leather reclining seat, hurtling the Citation V at nearly the speed of sound 45,000 feet above the green fields of Ohio far below.

Chapter 30

Ellen

Ellen reread the letter she had just written. The words were written by hand, each letter and word in perfectly formed, textbook cursive. The lines of Ellen's letters never slanted up or fell sloping down on the pages of her letters. They were perfectly level, with the letters evenly tilted to the right.

Dear Miss Iverson,

Since talking to Miss Sandersson by phone yesterday, Elmore and I have been discussing the adoption of Young Nam Lee. I didn't think to ask if these scars in any way hindered his arm movements. She mentioned that he could close his hand normally, but since she had not actually seen the other scars we didn't go into this any further. She did mention a Dr. I believe could be contacted concerning this. The scars themselves are not of a great concern to us as long as they would not physically handicap him to the extent that he would have to be treated differently when with a group of children.

We noted that the information we received on Young Nam was written up March 19, 1968. Will there be any other report sent to you on his current physical condition, as to his height, weight and medical health? Is he still living with his Mother or released to KSS?

Ellen, as in all things, was a disciplined and diligent letter writer. No thank you note ever went unwritten and unsent. She had a list and schedule of all family and friends to whom she would write to, like clockwork. People on the receiving end of her written correspondence could set their calendars to the receipt of her letters. And they all marveled at her perfect cursive penmanship. Her letters were always written in ink with no misspellings, no cross outs. No mistakes. Textbook.

Years and a galaxy of personal journeys later, Ellen would send a letter every week to Noah when he was away, from the time he left for Japan as an exchange student. She only missed writing when ill, and then only rarely. She didn't know how much those letters would sustain Noah, especially during the days, weeks, months, and years of sea duty: four years of averaging more than three hundred days each year at sea. And at every port, at every mail call, there would be a bundle of Ellen's letters covered in that textbook perfect penmanship, telling him about the weather, his siblings, his grandparents—about births, illnesses, and deaths. And each letter would have a short scrawl at the end in Elmore's barely legible hand, "Hope you're not working too hard, Son."

The letter Ellen held now was a draft of a reply she was writing on the back of the letter she received from Miss Iverson a couple of days earlier. As she sat at her kitchen table on a Thursday morning, Ellen reread what she had just written.

I think that looks good. I don't want LSS to think we are hung up about physical appearances. We just need to know whether he's really handicapped . . . not that that's an issue on its own, but he's already going to be different enough, being Oriental. Lord, if he had to be treated differently because of a handicap, that could just be too much . . . But, Lord knows, we'd probably still take him. I just can't back out now. This is the mission the Lord called me to . . .

Ellen looked at a 3 x 2.5 inch color photograph that Elmore had made from the slide they'd received with the letter from Miss Iverson on Monday. It showed a boy with dark brown hair wearing a red, V-neck sweater over a blue, crew neck lighter sweater. He was wearing some sort of knitted pants that looked like bedtime attire. The photograph cut off above his feet, so Ellen did not know what sort of shoes the boy was wearing. He was holding something in his right hand, and his left hand was curled at the bottom of the red sweater, holding its seam. He was standing on what looked like packed gravel and in front of some sort of rock and mud wall. It was clear that someone had carefully combed his hair. It must have been a clear day, because the sun was obviously in the boy's eyes as he squinted up at the camera. He wasn't smiling at all, but seemed to have a wariness through the squinting expression, like he was sizing up the camera and who was behind it. There was only a short shadow, so it was probably taken near noon. And, the photographer, Miss Sandersson, had towered over the boy, making the photo seem like it could have been taken from a second story window. But it wasn't.

He looks so sad . . . maybe it's just squinting into the sun . . .

Ellen noted with more relief than she wanted to admit that the boy truly was cute and looked passably white—"American" to her mind—with only a slight Orientalism around his features, and his color was very Caucasian.

Oh, thank you, Lord! I don't mind a hard job, but I appreciate any breaks . . . Please let this picture be accurate . . . if I teach him to act as my boy, he could pass for being American and not at all Oriental . . .

Simultaneously, Ellen felt embarrassed and ashamed for having such thoughts and feelings. She tried to tell herself that it was not her feelings and biases, but those of others that she knew existed that might impact her possible future son. It was her drive for preparation and her pragmatism that drove these thoughts, not her prejudice.

But Ellen knew that it wasn't completely true.

Dear Lord, please help me and forgive me . . .

Later that day, after supper, Ellen showed Elmore her draft letter to the social worker at Lutheran Social Service. Elmore said he liked it and suggested she add some lines about having received the appropriate forms and their intent to fill them out and submit them to LSS.

Yes. They had thought about and discussed Miss Iverson's request to consider this new boy, and they would move forward.

Ellen still hurt from losing "her" first boy in the disrupted earlier adoption and was emotionally tender and afraid. But Elmore had pointed out that moving forward was what Ellen felt was God's mission for her. Ellen felt that this new boy was surely a sign of God's blessing and promise. She told herself that this boy's mother had been in contact with KSS for a couple of years and had confirmed and reconfirmed her intention to release him to adoption; that she had followed through with all the release papers. She and Elmore discussed how his scars and mixed race likely stigmatized the boy in Korea, that the boy's prospects for receiving an education were stated by Korea Social Service as limited and dim. And there were the words from Iverson's letter: "definitely available." LSS knew what the Lindquists had been through already and the definitive words of assurance were clearly purposeful.

"Elmore, let's hold a family meeting with the kids Friday evening, after supper. Like we did before, for our first Korean boy."

"Okay, Sweetheart."

Elmore looked at her bright blue eyes and saw the life and hope in them that he had seen the first time they had met, but also a hint of fear. He always liked looking at his wife's face, framed by her perfectly curled blonde hair and her expressive lips painted exactly correct with her favorite shade of red lipstick. He took her fine-boned hand in his big ones and felt their softness and smallness.

"It's going to be just fine, Sweetheart. It's all going to work out just fine."

Chapter 31

Hee Ae

JANUARY 1968, MUNSAN

It was night, and outside a clear, cold sky shown brilliant with stars and a waxing quarter moon just rising from behind the eastern distant mountains. A small glow of light wavered into the chilly dark night from one room of an otherwise completely dark thatch-roofed farmhouse.

Hee Ae had used some of the money she had made in Seoul unloading her black market goods to buy heating charcoal so that her room could be heated. The farmhouse was empty, except for Young Nam and her. The family of the landlord's daughter, who lived in the majority of the farmhouse, was gone to be with the murdered man's grieving extended family. The man's family was gathered at the home of his eldest son—the new patriarch—to mourn and bury their father.

The burning charcoal only warmed up the floor, not the room itself, and the January night air leaked into the room through its rice paper-covered window and sliding doors. There was a kerosene lamp that glowed from the single flame burning at the end of its soaked cotton wick as it stood on a low, mother-of-pearl inlaid table, very similar to the table that had held the boiling pot into which her infant son had fallen. Hee Ae had the bed mattress rolled out next to the table and its lamp, and she and her son were huddled together under the bed's blankets.

Lee Hee Ae had stopped sleeping under the same blankets recently, as her son was getting older, though their two bed roll mattresses would be right next to each other. But tonight, she had her son under the same blankets with her. He slept on her right side, with his head resting on her right shoulder and his body pressed and curled up next to her. He clung to her tight. She had found him huddled in the far corner of the room when she'd gotten home, clearly not yet recovered to normal. She had hugged him, talked to him, and fixed dinner for him, and now, she held him as he lay curled close against her right side. She was staring up at the dingy ceiling and sucked in on her half-burnt American cigarette. Smoke hazed the room and diffused the flickering kerosene-fed flame's light.

I can't tell him tonight, what I've been thinking about. Not now. Not with him being so frightened and still so shocked.

But the whole event of her son stumbling onto the grisly, horrifying, bloody, murdered body of the old man had strengthened Hee Ae's resolve about her decision to put her son up for adoption by Americans.

What a dangerous, fucked up place. What future is there for my boy in a place where there's so much violence and craziness. Korea is no place for him and a place like Munsan has nothing but misery for someone like Young Nam. He's not even a citizen in his own country. He doesn't qualify for education. If he stays and grows up here, he'll end up like that murdered old man.

You've done the only right thing. You must do your duty as his mother.

Her mental image loomed up again and poked its finger at her face, even as the ever-present submerged monsters of her guilt hissed and broached her consciousness with accusations.

Yes, but he suffers for YOUR sins . . .

"Mommy, can you sing to me?"

Young Nam's high-pitched voice cut through her thoughts and mental finger-jabbing images and hissing accusations. She also realized that she'd been smoking without thinking. She knew her son didn't like the smoke. So she pulled out the cigarette from her mouth with her left hand and snubbed out the glowing end into the ashtray she had on the floor to the left of her pillow.

"Sure Young Nam-ya. What do you want me to sing?"

Koreans love to sing. Especially when drinking. And especially maudlin, sad, pathetic, and sometimes, haunting, truly touching songs. Hee Ae knew many songs because she had learned them in the years she worked at the club for American soldiers. The foreign soldiers loved paying to have the bar girls take turns singing, even if it was in a language they didn't understand. Hee Ae was a popular singer at the club, because she actually had a striking voice. The name and comparison would have meant nothing to her, but some might have thought she sounded more than a little like Patsy Cline. She had the same soulful contralto with slight huskiness at the edges and a natural vibrato that textured the ends of long notes and musical phrases.

"Sing the song about the mom and her son, Mommy."

His words were muffled as he snuggled his face into her shoulder and the nape of her neck. There were many songs in Korea about mothers losing their sons or vice versa. Family was strong and the heartbreak of separation, of duty over desire and love, were common themes. But Hee Ae knew which song Young Nam meant.

"Okay, Young Nam-ya."

And she softly began to hum the melody in her husky Patsy Cline voice and sang the words of the song clear and soft to the smoke-filled ceiling.

> Before you're forever gone
> Smile for me and let me hold your warm little hand
> And let me run with you through your wonder play
> And let me hear your laughter peal through your childhood land
> Before you're forever gone from your toddler day . . .

And cry for me and let me hold you clinging closely tight
And let me fight your darkness demons and comfort your wounded
    heart
And let me tuck you in under your blankets in the wee little night
Before you're forever gone from your fragile, innocent part . . .

And sit warm for me so small and light upon my lap
And let me feel your patter pulse close 'gainst my breathing chest
And let me hold you far from the reaching world while you nod and nap
Before you're forever gone from your little boy nest . . .

Smile for me my little son and let me eternally hold you
And let me know a mother's infinite crazy pride
And let me have it wash over your life through all its shades, all its hue
Before you're forever gone from this time, this tide . . .
Before you're forever and ever gone.

She repeated the refrain several times and then let her voice trail away into its natural vibrato until it blended with the chill air of the tiny room. Hee Ae could hear that her son's breathing was deep and regular. She reached up with her left hand and turned out the kerosene flame. The room was completely black as she brought her arm back under the covers and stared into its darkness.

You must do your duty as his mother . . .

Tears were seeping down the corners of her eyes.

Oh my son, what have I done?

"Mommy, please don't leave me. I'm scared."

Young Nam whispered small and sleepy.

"I'm here, Young Nam-ya. Your Mommy's right here."

And she held him tighter and thought her endless circling thoughts. And she would not have the strength or the courage to tell him for over a year.

H ee Ae held the letter in her hand. Her stomach felt twisted and she could feel the old nausea returning. Time had run out for her. There would be no more pretending and putting off what she had to do.

Spring had come early in Munsan at the beginning of March 1969. There had been less snow this past year than Hee Ae had remembered in years, not that she was complaining. Time had seemingly healed the trauma that her son had gone through a little over a year ago, except that he was inordinately afraid of the night. He refused to sleep on his own bedding mattress, insisting on sleeping with her, snuggled under her right arm.

Things were starting to move forward with her adoption plans for her son. After her visit and petition a year ago, KSS had accepted and, as of last September, he was officially under their care, though he continued to live with her. Her son had been placed into a new sponsorship program connected with LSS and one of its churches located in Borup, Minnesota.

There would be those who would see the bizarre unlikeliness of linking Munsan, South Korea, with Borup, Minnesota, through one tiny, destitute boy—who himself was a member of a small population of mixed race children—as so improbable, so randomly unlikely, that it had to be proof of God's hand at work. Ellen Lindquist would express to Noah just such a belief years later.

Borup had a population of 128, according to the 1970 census, with its peak population reaching a whopping 160 in 1980. The population of the town is currently estimated at 107. It is located in Norman County, Minnesota, and borders North Dakota on the eastern side; the border is defined by the Red River, made famous by the song "Red River Valley" popularized by Gene Autry when he sang it in the 1936 film by the same name. The closest large city is Fargo, North Dakota.

The sponsorship by the Winchester Lutheran Sunday school in Borup and the support of LSS as well as the oversight of KSS had been a godsend; Hee Ae was more economically destitute than ever. It was getting harder and harder to procure black market cigarettes and other items from GIs based in the military camps around Munsan, and the money, clothing, food, and other items for Young Nam from this sponsorship was desperately needed.

But now, Hee Ae was holding a letter from KSS, written by a Mrs. Young Son Byon, whose title was "Social Worker." The letter said American representatives from Lutheran Social Service would be coming to visit Lee Hee Ae and her son in Munsan the second week of March, on Monday, March 10. This was part of the final process to try to match Young Nam to an American family who may be interested in adopting from Korea. Additionally the letter, typewritten in Korean Hangul, explained that Hee Ae would need to bring her son to Seoul to the KSS facility on Sangmoon-Dong (Sangmoon Street) for observation as well as for a full medical examination. Mrs. Young suggested that Hee Ae arrive with her son on the weekend because the medical examinations would take place from Monday, March 24 through Friday, March 28. Young Nam would need to stay at the facility without her for the entire week and through the end of the month.

Hee Ae read the letter a second time. It was signed by Mrs. Young in a neat, feminine hand that spoke of being well educated.

Hee Ae could put it off no longer. She had to tell him before the foreigners came to gawk at him and examine him like a pound puppy under consideration of being rescued. She felt sick.

How does a mommy tell her little boy she's not going to be his mommy anymore? I can't . . . I can't . . . I can't!

but . . .

You MUST do your duty. You must be his true mother and do this. It is your DUTY!

Her internal voices kept screaming at each other—and at the whole world—inside her head in an unending conflict between her sense of what she had to do and what her heart pleaded her not to do. Fueled by this irreconcilable conflict, her stomach started pumping out acid in a gush that burned and soured the pit of her gut. She stood frozen, holding the letter signed by the well-educated Mrs. Young Son Byong, Social Worker, and staring past its pages through eyes that were focused only on her inner world of conflict and anguish.

All of her actions and paper signing and trips to KSS and meeting with Mr. Paik had not truly sunk into her gut, her core understanding, her full comprehension of what the path she had set upon really meant. But it all had become very real today with the horror of knowing that she would have to tell her little son. Somehow, it wasn't really real, truly true, to her or the world, until her son knew. That's how it had been for Hee Ae. Like keeping your finger on the chess piece that you'd just moved; it wasn't truly moved until you took your finger off. Like when the coyote in the Road Runner cartoons still runs and stands on thin air until Road Runner points out to the coyote that he's no longer supported by anything; then he realizes his reality and then—only then—does gravity take over and the long fall with its diminishing whistle sound effect happens, ending with the sickening distant crunch as the coyote's reality literally hits. In the cartoons, the coyote, banged and bent with stars circling his head, always walks away. In the noncartoon world, Hee Ae could tell that the long fall would start to happen as soon as she told Young Nam.

Lee Hee Ae could not know how far that fall would be or how hard that reality would hit. And there would be no guarantee that she would survive intact.

Chapter 32

Noah

Y es, Mr. Lindquist?" Noah had pushed the attendant button on the arm of his chair.

"Hi, Mike. Could I have another scotch, please? The Balvenie."

"On its way."

Thinking back on the subsequent conversations and events from that first call from his dad had driven home the point of this flight. He was going to say goodbye to his mother for the last time.

Ever.

The exploratory surgery had revealed a horrible situation. The mass in Ellen's colon was not only bigger and more progressed than Dr. Larson had thought; it was well past Stage III as a colon cancer, having penetrated the tissue of the colon. But, worst of all, the cancer had spread—metastasized— to Ellen's liver. According to the National Institutes of Health, about one half of colorectal cancers metastasize to become liver cancers. Of these, something less than thirty percent, and maybe as few as ten percent, are deemed to have any possibility of a life expectancy beyond five years. Although there is improving data on survival rates recently, in 1998 Ellen's cancer was nearly a death sentence and almost incurable.

"Here's your scotch, Mr. Lindquist."

The copilot started setting the French cut crystal tumbler on the table in front of Noah, snapping Noah back to the here and now.

"Hey, Mike, can you make it a double?"

"Certainly."

With that, the tumbler never touched down on its intended table landing and was expertly piloted back to the galley where it would be appropriately increased. The copilot sensed that Lindquist would not object to a heavy pour and essentially made the drink a triple.

"Here you go, Mr. Lindquist."

"Thank you, Mike."

Noah took a long sip of the Balvenie 21-year-old single malt scotch whisky, finished in its last couple years in a port, rather than a bourbon oak barrel. This "double wood" treatment gave it a complexity not found in most scotches with fewer than thirty years of aging.

Noah thought through what he'd learned from reading up on his mother's cancer.

Ellen's exploratory surgery had resulted in the removal of a sizable part of her colon and the majority of her liver. The fact that the cancer had penetrated the wall of the colon and had spread to the liver already meant that it was a Stage IV cancer. There is no Stage V.

The liver is the only internal organ in the human body that can regenerate itself—even after removal of up to seventy-five percent of its mass—and has a remarkable capacity to regenerate after injury, disease, or surgery and to adjust its size to match its host. Changes within liver cells associated with regeneration can be observed within minutes of hepatic tissue removal. Within a week after a partial hepatectomy, the surgical removal of liver tissue, the liver's mass is back essentially to what it was prior to surgery. And it appears that liver cells have a practically unlimited capacity for regeneration, with full regeneration observed after as many as twelve sequential partial hepatectomies.

If anyone could beat the odds, Noah had been certain that it would be his mother. Indeed, she had wasted no time. She sought out her options and tackled every treatment head on: the surgery, the chemo, the radiation. Her courage and quiet fortitude had been amazing to Noah; she worried more that her terrible and deadly illness might interfere in the lives of her family and friends than worrying about herself. Her actions taught new lessons to Noah. They drove home the depth of her strength and the limitlessness of her sense of duty.

Of all the lessons he had learned that had helped him to become who he was, most of the important ones he had learned from Ellen Lindquist. She had a way of putting things in concrete, comprehensible ways that appealed to Noah's rationality and helped him better understand events and people around him. And how he needed to act and be. As Noah sipped the twenty-one year-old Balvenie, he thought back to one of most enduring and awakening things that she had taught him.

SIXTEEN-YEAR-OLD NOAH LINDQUIST was standing in front of Mr. Olson's desk in room 315 at St. Peter High School. The clock on the wall showed that it was 3:23 p.m. It was the day after school had finished for the year. The sixteen-year-old was furious.

It made no sense. And it was so unfair.

"Lindquist, that's my decision and it's final."

Frank Olson was a fire hydrant of a man: compact, solid through his chest with a waist that didn't exist, being the same circumference as his muscled chest, and with thick thighs and calves that made the comparison complete. On top of his fireplug body sat a head that looked like it had come to life off a robot from Rock'em Sock'em Robots, an iconic and popular toy of the time that actually made its debut in 1964. It said something about the times when children's game manufacturers could market a game whose point was to win by physically and graphically decapitating the head off your opponent. Frank Olson was the head coach of the St. Peter High School wrestling team and the school's advanced algebra teacher. He'd been teaching for nineteen years and had seen kids come and go. He could tell if a kid had promise or not, and he knew that Lindquist had promise . . . maybe.

But he might just piss it away through a laziness that relied too much on his intellect . . .

"But I got the high score on every quiz and test in the class. Mr.

Olson, how can you give me a C? A grade is supposed to let people know how well you learned the subject and the tests *prove* I learned advanced algebra at an A level."

Olson looked at Noah and saw a short, skinny kid with a Keith Partridge haircut, wearing a long-sleeved polyester shirt with the currently popular big collar with the top two buttons undone. Olson knew that Noah was adopted. Everybody in St. Peter knew he was Elmore and Ellen Lindquist's Oriental boy. He tried not to look at the kid's left hand. He'd been a teacher long enough to know that kids spotted such looks and glances a mile away.

He liked the kid. Noah never could make his varsity wrestling team, always being defeated in wrestle offs for the varsity spot because there was no way the kid could make up for the lack of strength and grip in his left hand. Not at a varsity level in high school wrestling. But the kid never quit and worked harder than nearly any-one of his wrestling team.

Kid's got real smarts . . . and heart, I'll give him that. But no sense. He needs to learn this lesson . . .

"Here, read this, Lindquist."

Olson held out a piece of mimeographed paper to the teen. Noah took it from his teacher's hand and brought it up to his eyes.

"Lindquist, what does it say about the final grade in my class?"

"It says that fifty percent is based on tests and quizzes and fifty percent is based on homework."

"And how many homework assignments did you turn in?"

There was silence as Noah looked at Mr. Olson. The wall clock's second hand kept sweeping around its face.

"Well, Lindquist? How many?"

"None."

"None. Exactly. That is an F in homework, is it not?"

"Uh . . . I guess . . ."

"Good guess, Lindquist. And what is halfway between an A and an F?"

Noah let the clock's hand continue sweeping in its circle, say-ing nothing. The seconds ticked by and the silence festered. Olson stopped waiting for Noah to provide the answer.

"A 'C' Lindquist! The average of an F and an A when weighted fifty-fifty is a C."

He let the statement soak in the silence between the teen and himself before continuing on.

"Noah, you always gave me a hundred percent during wrestling practice, every day this past season. But you know you have to work extra hard at wrestling because you know others are more gifted at it than you are. But in my math class, you gave almost nothing—zero percent effort—because you know you're smart and all of this comes easy to you.

"But being smart isn't going to be enough. You are going to be a failure in life if you think you can just be smart, but put out no effort. Noah, you need to learn that the world and those who make the rules in it will care more about how well you're following their rules than how smart you are. Failed geniuses are a dime a dozen, son.

"My class syllabus was perfectly clear. It didn't say you were graded on how well you may actually have learned just the topic of advanced algebra or on how smart you are. It clearly stated that your grade was based on a combination of elements: tests, quizzes, and homework. I teach more than algebra in my class, Lindquist. I teach timeliness, responsibility, accountability, fairness, persistence, effort, . . . and a little math. There's no question that with almost no effort you got the math. But you didn't demonstrate that you learned much of the other things I tried to teach.

"Lindquist, you are exceptionally smart. But you are *not* special—nobody is—and the rules will not be waived for you by me or anyone else in the world. And you will *never* be exceptional, unless you learn that your exceptional smarts will *never* be enough."

Noah stared down at his Adidas shoes. They were suede leather of navy blue with three yellow stripes down each side at a forty-five degree angle from the matching yellow laces slanting backward to the soles. His fury was mounting higher, and the rage in him was nearly uncontrollable.

What did this idiot know? He's just jealous of my intelligence and pissed off that I aced all of his tests without even trying. What did Olson know about the world? He'd spent his whole life here in St. Peter. The world only cares about the final result. Screw this!

"Lindquist, you got the grade you earned. That's my decision, and it's final."

As the sixteen-year-old left the classroom, his eyes were wet with tears of rage.

This isn't fair!

That evening, after supper, Noah cleared the table and loaded the dishwasher with Ellen's beloved Corningware plates. That was his job. Carla set the table and helped get supper plated, and Noah cleared. Tonight he also volunteered to help his mother and dry the dishes, pots, and other items that Ellen forbade from going in the dishwasher. Normally, his mother would wash these items by hand and his father would dry and put them away in their designated posts inside drawers and cupboard shelves. A place for everything; everything in its place—the Ellen Lindquist mantra.

Noah wanted to explain what happened today with Mr. Olson. He wanted to explain and show that he really got an A in the class, but that he was being unfairly treated. Noah needed to get his version of the story out there to his mother. He was thinking of how to start the conversation as Ellen started washing and rinsing the dishes and handing them to Noah for drying.

"Did you go by school and pick up your grades today?"

"Uh . . . yeah. I did."

"Well, how'd you do?"

"Pretty good. I got four As, two B+s, a B, and . . ."

Ellen looked over at her son, turning her head to her right.

"And what?"

". . . and a C in math. But the grade's not fair. I went and talked to Mr. Olson and he was unfair."

Noah went on to explain how he'd gotten all As on the tests and quizzes, but that Mr. Olson had unfairly penalized him for not doing the homework.

"But I didn't *need* to do the homework. That's why it's so unfair! It's like not giving Mark Spitz a gold medal even though he came in first because he didn't eat his Wheaties!"

Ellen went back to washing and rinsing the dishes, pots, and pans in the sink and didn't say anything for a while.

"Noah, Mr. Olson was not being unfair, and he's right. This situation isn't like your example about eating Wheaties. It's about the requirements of the race, not just who finishes first."

Most of the time when his mother said things to him, which was usually about picking up his room or taking out the trash or mowing the lawn, Noah tended to tune his mother's words and voice out. He'd learned that he could get her to stop talking to him with the universal magic phrase, "Okay, Mom. I'll get to it."

But something about what had happened today and the way she said what she just said, made him tune in. Noah suddenly realized the reason he had been brought to an almost-uncontrollable fury at Olson. The teacher had minimized the one thing that Noah took pride in, that was his refuge from a world where he didn't measure up, was always on the outside looking in, always the perpetual foreigner. It was the one thing that he thought he had that others did not. In a world where everyone you know is blonde, tall, "All-American," where every male was stronger, faster, bigger, and more attractive to the girls who all ignored you, even as, and maybe because, they towered over you, Noah's intelligence was the one thing that stood out. And he liked proving the reality of it by intentionally not working at things like math, then showing that he could still figure it out faster and better than all those big, beautiful, blonde, blue-eyed All-Americans who, unlike him, had to work so hard and struggled and tried.

Unfairly, in his defensiveness, Noah had interpreted his teacher's words as a put-down of his intellect. Noah thought that Mr. Olson, rather than celebrating his talent, instead had told him that it would be the root of his failure; that he would forever be the un-American runt on the outside looking in. Noah realized just how much he wanted to prove wrong what he thought Olson had implied and how incredibly much the teacher's wrongly perceived belittling of Noah's intellect had enraged him.

"Your exceptional smarts will never be enough . . ."

Noah could still hear the words spat out by Mr. Olson's emphatic voice in his mind's ear. But now, his mother was saying that Olson was right? That somehow Noah's outrage and anger were wrong?

What the hell!

"Noah, look around you. How do you know what exists and what the world is like?"

"Uh . . . because I can see it and touch it and stuff like that?"

"Exactly. You know a chair or a table or a tree exists because it reflects light that your eyes can detect. Because it has mass and momentum so that if you walk into it, it doesn't move, and you can feel it because it has atoms that resist the atoms of your fingers. Everything you know about the world around you is because of what the world around you does.

"But you're different. You're real to you because you can 'see' your thoughts and feel your emotions. You know what you're capable of and what you intend to do. So you're real to you not just because of the things you do, like eat and run, but because of what you think, feel, and intend."

Ellen put the stainless steel pan she had been washing back into the soapy water in the sink and looked directly into Noah's green eyes.

"But that reality of who you are is only real to you. No one else can see your thoughts, feel your emotions, or know your potential or your intentions. The only thing that makes you real to every other human being in the world and that makes you, YOU to them, is what you do. Your existence and reality to others is solely based on what they can see, hear, touch, smell, and taste. And everybody does this. Everybody judges and values themselves based on their thoughts and intentions, but can—and do—only judge others by their actions.

"So, you may truly be grateful when someone has given you a present for your birthday. And you may truly intend to send a thank you note. Therefore you know you are a person who feels gratitude and indebtedness. But if you never send that thank you note, the other person *will never know and will judge you as an ingrate and a loser.* Because just as chairs and tables and trees are real, and are what they are because of what they do and don't do, so to all other people in the world you are real, and you are you, based only on what you do."

Ellen paused and looked to see if any of this was sinking in.

"You are what you do. Noah, do you understand?"

He understood.

Holy crap!

It felt like the first time Noah had seen the *Wizard of Oz* on TV when he was seven years old and it came to the part when Toto, Dorothy's dog, had pulled the curtain back to reveal the little man behind it, showing the reality behind the façade of the great and powerful Wizard of Oz. What his mother had just said was so rational, so logical, so . . . simple. *So right!* It was like a curtain was pulled back, revealing a simple, clear reality.

You are what you do.

"And there's one more thing you need to understand about how people will see you . . . remember this, Noah:

"As you do any one thing, so people assume you will do all things.

"I know; it's not fair. But I know that you already know very well that the world is not fair."

Ellen's last remark was the closest she could bring herself to tell Noah that the world will also judge him in other ways, based on deep biases, ignorances, and prejudices. But she knew he was very experienced in this particular truth, even at sixteen. And that tore at her heart. She wanted the world to see him as she had come to see him—simply as her son.

Noah looked into his mother's intense, bright blue eyes and he could see the earnestness in them.

Wow. This all makes sense, Mom . . .

And Ellen could see Noah's eyes literally grow wide with comprehension. The "a-ha" moment was clear to see, somewhat to her surprise. Although she had hoped she'd get through to her son, she hadn't expected such an overt reaction on his face and in his eyes. Noah's eyes were his most striking feature, Ellen thought, and as she fixed on them now, she remembered when she saw them for the first time, very late on a cold January night a decade ago . . . and what had happened inside of her at the sight of them.

Chapter 33

Noah

W hat are you thinking, Noah?" Rusty Carlisle asked, looking sidelong at the youth.

Kinuko turned to look as well. Noah was still sitting at the dinner table with Kinuko and Rusty. Brad had excused himself earlier and left for the evening. His day at his aikido dojo always started at 4:00 a.m. so he needed to close out the evening and get himself back to the dojo and his futon. Rusty and Kinuko would be driving Noah back to his homestay family's house, but tomorrow wasn't a school day so Noah could stay for a while.

Maybe because of the fact that there were so few foreigners or maybe because Noah was headed on the path to being a Navy officer, he and Rusty, despite the age difference—eighteen and forty—had formed an unusually close, intimate bond in the few months that Noah had known Rusty. In Rusty, Noah found something between a big brother and a father. Rusty was worldly, broadly traveled, deeply perceptive, and radiated an energy and a self-assuredness that Noah had never seen before. To Noah, Rusty Carlisle seemed to have it all. He was everything that Noah felt he himself was not. In addition to being tall, athletic, a doppelgänger for Sean Connery, and a combat fighter pilot, Rusty just always seemed at home, accepted, and comfortable anywhere, while Noah felt self-conscious, never truly accepted, and never felt at home anywhere, even in his parent's house in St. Peter. Noah had none of the easy confidence that glowed from Rusty's every movement.

Noah reached out and picked up the sake cup in front of him. In Japan, the legal drinking age is twenty. In fact the legal age for everything was twenty: getting your driver's license, voting, being an adult, being allowed to marry. One simple, easy, nice round number. But, because back then in Minnesota and most states the legal drinking age was eighteen, and it was the age of legal maturity in the United States, Rusty and Kinuko offered the traditional Japanese sake that would accompany a dinner like this.

Sake is often referred to as rice wine by Westerners. But sake is made differently from wine or beer. The rice from which sake is made is first "polished," which takes off the outer layer of the grain of that makes rice white; otherwise it's brown, its natural color. White rice cannot sprout, and it is almost pure starch. The Japanese discovered that if they add a special mold to steamed rice, it converts starch in rice to simple sugars, which yeast can now eat and throw off alcohol and carbon dioxide. Therefore, sake is not directly fermented like wine is, nor is it malted—sprouted—to get the sugars to feed the yeast.

This sake was having an effect on Noah, who had rarely had any type or amount of alcoholic beverage before coming to Japan and Rusty's home. He lifted the sake to his lips and tossed it back in one gulp, as was traditional in Japan, at least among businessmen. He was feeling the sake's warmth spread in his stomach and the buzz of the alcohol in his head.

"I was thinking that I'm not sure I should have given Brad my pendant and asked him to look for my Korean mother."

"Why is that?" Kinuko inquired in her Bond girl Japanese accent.

"What if he finds her? What do I do then? What do I owe her and what would it do to my parents in Minnesota? What will it do to my relationship with my family? Whose son would I be? Who would my family really be?

"What kind of crap have I gotten myself into? It's bad enough that I feel like a foreigner in my own hometown and sometimes even in my own household. If I now have a living, breathing Korean mother that I drag into the mix, how does that help make me fit in better?

"I shouldn't have done it. I'm going to tell Brad to forget the whole thing."

Noah spewed out the string of questions and doubts that had been swirling in his head, now mixed with the buzz of the sake. He sat in the silence that had sprung up after his rant of questions. Rusty and Kinuko looked at each other.

"Noah, in a certain, important sense, you don't owe your mother anything. Nor do your owe your American parents anything." Rusty leaned in, toward Noah as he continued to speak.

"I want to explain something called *agency*. It's kind of a legal as well as a sociological concept. I was taught something about it at the academy, in relation to what officers owe the men under their command. I think the concept fits in your situation as well."

Noah looked at Rusty, and behind his cleft chin, square-jawed good looks, there was a genuine look of concern and empathy in his eyes. Noah listened.

"Agency is a term that applies to a person who has the power of free will and the ability and authority to exercise it. So, legally, for instance, if two people who have full agency enter into a contract, it is binding. They each had the free will, the authority to act, and the ability to act in their own interests. Sociologically, agency refers to those people in a society who have the actual freedom to act on their own behalf and to be able to fully make choices. Therefore, some argue that certain members of a society may not have agency because they don't have real choices, like slaves, or women before they had the vote, or people without enough education. The concept also applies to people who may be disadvantaged, like the mentally-impaired, or those who suffer from an illness or injury that impairs their cognition."

Noah eyes must have indicated that he wasn't quite with Rusty.

"Okay, Noah, think of it this way. If someone was in a coma and you put a pen in their hand and signed their name to a contract, most anyone would agree that the person in the coma really did not agree to the contract and has no obligation to be bound by it. That person had no agency. So somewhere between that sort of situation and the situation of two fully informed and trained lawyers signing a contract, there is a range of agency. There's not always a bright line.

"But one thing I believe is that children—especially young children—do not have agency: not legally, not physically, not mentally, and not emotionally.

"Noah, *you* were a small child. You were the passive object of your life when you were adopted. Your Korean and American mothers were the active subjects. They had agency. *You* did not. Your Korean mother did what she did as an adult, fully informed. She had agency. Your American parents did what they did as adults, fully informed. They had agency. You had no information; you were incapable of being fully informed, even if all the information was provided and explained, because you were too young to truly comprehend the information. *You* had no agency. You were like the guy in the coma. You cannot be bound to obligations you didn't choose or understand, even if others bound themselves to obligations that benefitted you.

"So, you were not a party—an acting agent within the situation—to your adoption. Therefore, you owe neither side anything. All of the adults in your life acted for their own reasons, their own purposes, their own needs. Yes, they may have been motivated by their perceived understanding of your needs and what they thought was in your best interest."

It was all connecting now for Noah. He felt the way he did at one of those amusement park mazes, where he could only see up to the next turn and didn't have any sense of the overall path, until suddenly he would do a final turn and reach the exit—and there he was, able to see the path in its completeness.

"But . . ."

Rusty Carlisle pointed his index finger and thumped it on the table, poking the table top with each word to emphasize it.

"But, it was *their* interpretations of your interests, seen through *their* biases and the filters of *their* own needs. Each adult involved was an 'interested party.' Meaning they were not a disinterested, uninvolved person, with no personal bias or desires of their own."

Noah was nodding now, the enlightenment feeling like X-ray vision.

Carlisle continued, "By this rationale, I might argue that no child owes his or her parents anything until after they reach adulthood and accept help and support from their parents. Then, yes. There is an obligation. But no child had a choice in being born. They had no choice in being made dependent on their parents or the adults in their life. If I broke your legs and therefore made you dependent on me and my care, do you owe me for that care? Not if I was the one who knowingly and willfully put you in that dependent position in the first place."

Rusty stopped talking and fixed Noah with his gaze.

"But don't I owe them gratitude?"

"Sure, Noah. Feeling grateful to people who have shown you kindness or helped you or sacrificed for you . . . that's a normal and healthy human reaction. But *feeling* it toward your parents is different from you *owing* it to them."

"But doesn't a kid owe something to his or her parents? I mean, parents give their children the gift of life! There must be something that is owed for that!"

"But, Noah, you just said the key word: *gift*. The very definition of a gift is something that is given with no expectation or implication of it being repaid or reciprocated. A gift cannot, if it truly is a gift, create an obligation on the person who received the gift. If an obligation is intended or created, then it's not a gift. It's an exchange—a transaction, a deal—that then requires that both sides in the exchange are informed, have the free will, and the authority—the agency—to enter into the deal and for the exchange to be valid and the obligations to be binding.

"But, you're right, Noah. Children do, I believe, have a great obligation to their parents. But it is a moral obligation that comes with receiving a gift. If you look at what a parent has given to a child as a gift, then the child has a moral obligation to appreciate that gift, to treasure it, and to make the most of it."

"Noah, it says a lot about you that you are asking these questions and that you feel gratitude and a sense of obligation," Kinuko interjected. "But what Rusty is saying is that the best way you can show your gratitude is to appreciate the life you've been given and to make the most of it."

"Exactly, Kinuko," agreed Carlisle. "You have every right to find your Korean mother, to learn more about yourself by doing so. Because the better you know who you are, the better you will be able to share yourself with, and on behalf of, others."

Noah thought about what the older man had just said and the points that Kinuko had emphasized. He reached over and took another gulp of sake, Kinuko having refilled his cup. And the buzz and warmth it was creating made him open up as he rarely did. Noah had learned a long time ago not to share much of his past, except in a broad, hazy way. It was too disturbing to and disconnected from anyone else's normalcy that he would just get uncomfortable stares in return.

What is the polite response to hearing that someone's mother was a third world prostitute? That she'd been strung along, lied to, used, and dumped, and Noah was the result? That he'd grown up in a war zone and knew violence and death graphically up close and the sex trade even more intimately? He remembered the awkward conversations with parents of his friends.

"So Noah, it's good to have you over for dinner since you and Johnny have become friends. You're so blessed to have been adopted by the Lindquists. You are a lucky young man. They are such nice people. Y'know, I served on the church council with your dad and Johnny's mom does Meals on Wheels with Mrs. Lindquist . . . say . . . do you remember much about Korea?"

And Noah would want to blurt out something like . . .

"Gee, thanks for having me over, Mr. Larson. Yes, I remember *everything*. I remember watching strange men fuck my mother for cash five feet from me. And how drunk she would get. And how she would beat me. I remember starving and seeing worms crawling around in my shit and pulling them out of my ass when I took a dump at the communal outhouse. I remember getting the shit kicked out of me for looking different and being a cripple— but that part's really not that different than here in St. Peter, is it Johnny? And you're right. I *am* very blessed to have been adopted, because clearly I was living one very huge fucking curse and goddamn *unlucky* before that. Please pass the peas, Mrs. Larson; they're very good."

But instead, Noah would usually just say something vague about not really remembering much, just that things were different in Korea. And, yes, he knew how blessed he was. And everyone would smile and usually make some comment about how much they admired Orientals for their hard work and being good with their hands and how a cousin had served in the Army with an Oriental boy and said good things about him. And the conversation would move on to other things closer and more normal to life in the American Midwest.

It's just that I've always felt that my parents' acceptance of me was conditional . . . like they could void the contract and declare me not their son . . . unless I met their expectations."

"Well, a lot of children feel that way, regardless of not being adopted, especially here in Japan," Kinuko said.

"I guess . . . but when you're a different race than either parent . . . I guess . . . I just feel like, that they might see it, like . . . like they rescued this aboriginal kid from some third world backwater hellhole. That they gave him a home and cleaned him up and taught him to act like he wasn't some aboriginal throwback; that they'd given him a first world existence and made him American. They might think they had given him—me—their name and their history and their world, their identity, and . . . and what if they think my searching for my Korean mom is a rejection of what they've given me? What if they think I'm reverting to my aboriginal roots, turning Oriental rather than being white and American? What if they think I'm rejecting *them?*"

"Have they ever said anything remotely like this?" Carlisle pointedly asked Noah.

"No. Of course not."

"Then it's all in *your* head, Noah. From all that you've told me about them, the things you're worried about just aren't in them. These are your fears and insecurities that you're projecting onto them. I think you are the one who doesn't think you measure up to being white and American. Not them.

"Noah, you've told me plenty of times that you were rejected as not being Korean; that you yourself never saw yourself as Korean. Now you've been living in Japan, do you think you fit in here?"

"No. Not by a long shot."

Kinuko was nodding her agreement with Noah's statement.

"Exactly, Noah. The point is: you are American and you are a Lindquist and you are your parents' son. Do you know what is so unique about America?"

"Uh . . . that it was the first democracy?"

"No. What do you think the Greeks had? There have been other democracies in history before America. It's this . . ." Carlisle paused and reached over and poured more sake into his, Kinuko's, and Noah's cups and set the sake bottle back down on the table in front of him.

"Noah, for all of human history, for millions of years, starting from even before we were exactly fully 'human,' a number of things were very tightly linked with each other. Location—call it geography—physical appearance or attributes—call it race—language and culture—all these things—were very closely linked and tied to each other. People were born, lived, and died within a very small, fixed area. So, if someone looked a certain way or talked a certain language or was from a certain area, then by knowing just that one fact, you could deduce almost everything about them. This was true until very recently in human history. In fact until the United States of America occurred. We were the first nation that was made up of *everyone* coming from somewhere else originally.

"Therefore, in America, you can't tell based upon someone's physical appearance, like race, or by their historical culture or preferred language, like Japanese, or by their location of birth, or their religion whether or not someone is American. In fact, even as early as 1750, one-third of the population of Pennsylvania spoke only German, and in 1795, Congress debated and almost voted to publish federal laws in English and German. The point being, from the very beginning, Americans knew and acknowledged that there were many fellow citizens—all equally citizens of the United States of America—who looked different, talked different, worshiped different, ate different foods, and came from different places. But all were Americans.

"Being American isn't being white or Western. It is about freely embracing a set of ideals and beliefs. And it is these shared ideals and beliefs, which are not coerced, and the shared efforts in striving to perfect their realization that binds us as a people and as a nation. Of course there are plenty of arguments and disagreements among Americans. But what was drilled into me at the Naval Academy was that I don't have to agree with what someone else says. Hell! I don't even have to like it! I have the freedom to even hate what someone says and maybe even hate the person for saying and thinking it. But what makes us American is that we are willing to die defending the *right* of that person to think and say that which we may disagree with or even hate."

I've never thought of it this way before . . .

Noah could see that Rusty really believed in what he was saying. He could see it in Carlisle's eyes, the way there was a light in them as he said these words and by the way his body was leaning toward Noah and his finger was occasionally poking the table, making small thumps of punctuation.

"And, Noah, this sort of thinking does not exist in Japan. Here, and in most places, you are expected to say and think only certain things and in certain ways; that what you say and how you think is part of how people believe you must talk and believe to be truly Japanese," Carlisle's wife added, looking equally earnest.

"Noah, you're already accepted at UVA, right?" Carlisle asked.

"Yes. I went early decision. The University of Virginia was the only college I applied to."

"You know that Thomas Jefferson founded it, right?"

"Duh . . . Everyone at UVA makes sure you know that."

"Did you visit Jefferson's home, Monticello, and see his headstone where he is buried?"

"Yes."

"Well, I went there too a few times, because when I was a midshipman at Annapolis, I was dating a Virginia gal who was a student at Randolph Macon Women's College."

Kinuko gave Carlisle a look of reproach, skewing her beautiful face into a parody of shock.

"It was a long time before I even you knew you existed, Babe," Carlisle quickly interjected, before going back to what he was saying to Noah.

"I'm sure she was a cow."

"Babe, *everyone* is a cow compared to you."

Kinuko smiled, lighting up her perfect porcelain china doll looks.

"So. Noah. Jefferson wanted to be remembered for only three things."

Carlisle raised his index finger.

"Being the author of the Declaration of Independence."

Carlisle raised his middle finger next to his index finger to hold up two fingers.

"Being the author of the Virginia Statute for Religious Freedom."

Carlisle raised his ring finger to join the first two, showing three fingers.

"And being the Father of the University of Virginia."

He waived his three fingers in front of his face toward Noah.

"Those are the three things, in that order, that he himself wrote for his epitaph on the headstone he personally designed.

"Jefferson wanting to be remembered for authoring the Virginia Statute for Religious Freedom was very important. Religion was a *huge* deal in Jefferson's time and the majority of wars that had been fought for centuries were overtly fueled by religion or had religious undercurrents. What Jefferson's epitaph demonstrates is that America was *not* founded on the idea that society would force conformity in thinking or beliefs. The exact opposite. People were free to think and believe whatever they chose. What citizens were constrained in was only their actions. Actions that were contrary to mutual safety, respect, and social functioning—like theft and assault—were prohibited. But not any sort of offensive beliefs and thinking . . . and believe me, Noah, people were *highly* offended by differing religious beliefs in Jefferson's day!"

How did Rusty know all this?

"But what made America a nation—a united people, then and still does today—is the voluntary embrace, the united willingness, and shouldering of the duty to defend each citizen's right to hold beliefs that may be repugnant or offensive to any one of us."

"Well, I guess that makes sense . . . but people still think I'm not American and ask me where I'm from and stuff like that."

"So what? Most of what you're talking about is all just stuff kids have said. Kids say all sorts of mean stuff to each other. So. What? What's it matter?

"You, Noah Lindquist, need to make a decision. Either you can keep obsessing about your past and what people said and did to make you feel bad or . . ."

Rusty tossed back the cup of sake that had been in front of him and thudded the small cup on the table, adding emphasis to what he said next.

"Or . . . you can decide to focus on your future and how you are going to define who you are and who you will become. This is the obligation you have to all of your parents. To appreciate the gift that you have been given and make the most of it.

"You can't change what people think of you or say about you . . . in fact, you're going to take an oath someday, after you finish up all your Navy ROTC training, to protect and defend their right to think and say those things! The *only* thing you can change is yourself and the *only* way that people can know who you are—that you're as American as they are—will be through your actions."

Suddenly Noah remembered his mother's—Ellen Lindquist's—words.

You are what you DO.

Noah could still see his mother's penetrating blue eyes as she had fixed them on him when she had taught him this lesson.

There was one other very good thing that came out of his experience with Mr. Olson, and it would occur a year and a half later.

Early mornings in his little farmhouse room in Munsan, he would hear in the distance the chanting of male voices and rhythmic thudding of boots. This was the sound of the American soldiers who were stationed in the nearby camps doing their morning run, singing out their cadences—what the soldiers called "jodies." When he was that small Korean boy in that far away village, he would hear that chanting and the drum beat thudding of the many men, jogging in perfect unison. As a little boy, Noah had known that it was these men who kept him safe from men like the North Korean commandos who had killed his landlord.

The chanting male voices and the thud beat of their boots made him feel safe. America had been a fabled and remote magical land, sending these strong big men to protect little starving boys, just like what Noah had once been. His past made him understand the enormous opportunities and benefits that came with being an American, with being the son of Ellen and Elmore Lindquist.

Of the lessons that she taught him, Ellen Lindquist had drilled home to Noah not only that one is what one does, but that what one does must be driven by duty and not merely personal gain. If one benefitted from society, then one needed to step up and bear the burdens of that society.

"Societies grow and flourish only so long as there are those who are willing to sacrifice on their behalf," Noah remembered her telling him.

The harder the burden, the more a Lindquist should look at bearing that burden. And she and Elmore lived these words. Each volunteered for all the tough, thankless community projects and organizations. Elmore served as treasurer of the church council forever, along with countless other community volunteer positions, while Ellen volunteered with Red Cross, the local hospice, Meals on Wheels—a never ending list of volunteer charities and seeming drudgery to many. Elmore would eventually serve two terms as mayor of St. Peter.

So, with the example of service and having deep feelings of gratitude to the American military men who had jogged through his early boyhood mornings making him feel safe, Noah had determined in his junior year of high school that he would serve in his country's military.

His uncle Andy, who had become a career Navy man, eventually rising from the lowest enlisted rank to a field grade officer before retiring, had explained the differences between an officer and an enlisted man.

"Go the officer track, if you can."

That had been the advice of Andrew G. Swenson, Lieutenant Commander, United States Navy (Retired).

When he had applied for a Navy four-year scholarship, based on his being named a National Merit Finalist, which meant that he had scored in the top one percent in both his preliminary scholastic aptitude test (PSAT) and his SAT, he thought he was guaranteed. For all the insecurities and issues that his unique circumstances caused (and that his parents quietly endured), Noah looked pretty good on paper. He was ranked seventh in his high school class and was first trumpet in the Jazz Band, the Concert Band, and the orchestra. He was an Eagle Scout and sang tenor in his school's Chamber Singers and Concert Choir. He was a star on his speech and debate team. And he had been on the wrestling team, losing record and all, for five years. Noah thought he was a shoo-in, completing all interviews with strong marks and the Armed Forces Vocational Aptitude Battery with a perfect score. Until he got his decision letter and the results of his physical examination.

It had said something to the effect that although he was an outstanding applicant, he did not meet the minimum physical requirements. No new officer candidate could have permanent joint injuries that limited movement and must have all digits of both hands.

"Physically Disqualified" was stamped across the rejection letter.

So Noah had put his lessons learned about not quitting into action and mounted an appeals process. He got letters from his doctors and from his Boy Scout troop leaders. And most importantly, from his wrestling coach, Frank Olson. By the time that Noah asked him to write an appeals recommendation letter, Olson felt that Noah had learned some of the lessons he had tried to teach the youth, both as a coach and as his math teacher.

Olson's letter spoke of Noah's tenacity, of his unwillingness to give up. To keep trying even when the match is clearly lost.

"I never had a kid who would literally do whatever I asked him to do. No matter how much extra, how many more laps, no matter what. He always said, 'sure coach' and did it," Olson wrote.

The appeals package worked its way up the Navy's bureaucracy, being recommended for denial at each and every step, until it reached the desk of Captain Scott Davis, US Navy Medical Corps and head of medical evaluations for Navy officer ascension programs. He read the full file. He looked at the photos. And he read the letter from Mr. Frank Olson, high school math teacher and head wrestling coach at St. Peter High School.

Captain Davis was an amateur historian, especially of US naval history. He often found himself linking things in his present with events that he'd read in history books. When he was reviewing Lindquist's appeals request and original application file and came across Frank Olson's letter, it triggered one of those present/past links in his mind. Something in Olson's words and description of the Lindquist kid made Captain Davis think of the "Father of the American Navy," John Paul Jones. The captain especially recalled, that in the desperate Battle of Flamborough Head, in August of 1779, when Jones's ship, the *Bonhomme Richard*, was sinking and the British captain of the HMS *Serapis* had asked Jones to strike his colors—to surrender—the words that John Paul Jones had screamed to his enemy.

"Surrender? No Sir! I have not yet begun to fight!"

With those brave and reckless words, Jones had ordered his ship to be lashed to his enemy's, keeping it from sinking, and then led a boarding party and took over the British vessel and won the battle. This sea battle and Jones's words and actions set the example for the fledgling US Navy that would guide its traditions, expectations, and conduct for the next two and a quarter centuries.

In the file before him, and in the words of Frank Olson's letter, Captain Davis sensed a spirit in the Lindquist kid that just might be in line with the traditions that Jones had established that fateful day in August 1779. This kid clearly hated to lose and did not quit. Maybe he too had not yet begun to fight. He stamped the application: WAIVED.

And added these words in his own hand:

> Although the applicant clearly does not meet the physical requirements pursuant to the naval regulations, in all other aspects, he appears to be an outstanding candidate. His appeals file is compelling and may indicate his ability to succeed as a midshipman in the US naval training program and succeed in the four-year scholarship officer ascension program. A physical waiver is granted.

Captain Davis would not have been surprised—and certainly very pleased—to learn that his gamble paid off. Noah would receive the First Class Award from his Midshipmen Battalion upon commissioning, and he would graduate number three in his class of six hundred in his Surface Warfare Officer's School. And he would go on to be recommended for early promotion by every commanding officer under whom he served, and each of those exacting, driving men would rank him number one compared to his peers in officer performance evaluations.

Noah realized that Rusty was completely validating what his mother had told him over a sink full of dirty dishes in her perfectly neat kitchen in St. Peter, Minnesota.

"Have I told you my 'Pile of Shit Theory of Life' Noah?"

Carlisle's wife rolled her eyes.

"Oh God. Better pour the poor kid another shot of sake if you're going to throw that crap at him . . . all puns intended!" Kinuko reached for the sake bottle and discovered that it was empty and got up from the table to fetch a new bottle from the kitchen.

"No, Rusty. You haven't told me your 'Pile of Shit Theory of Life.' "

Carlisle ignored his wife's comment and proceeded.

"Good. Okay . . . listen up, Lindquist. I've spent years perfecting this theory and it's brilliant, even if I say so myself.

"Now, Noah. I concede that you've had some real shit to deal with in your young life. But everybody has some shit they have to deal with. Because of that, a lot of people go around carrying their little pile of shit in their hands and wailing and bitching and complaining.

"'Eeew! My life stinks! My life is a pile of shit!'

"And the shit is running all through their fingers and making them miserable. And right next to them—metaphorically, you understand . . ."

Noah nodded as Kinuko returned to the table and poured more sake into Noah's and Rusty's cups before seating herself on her seat cushion.

"So, right next them, is a table with a big, juicy steak dinner. With *all* the trimmings!"

Carlisle who had had his hands cupped in front of him, carrying his make-believe pile of shit, now waved his right hand grandly toward his metaphorical table and steaming steak dinner and gestured emphatically.

"It's right there, Noah . . . right there! All they have to do is drop their pile of shit and reach over and take the plate holding the steak dinner!"

Rusty Carlisle stopped and paused, looking at Noah fixedly with his cleft chin and Ringo Starr mustache jutting a bit toward Noah.

"But they don't take the steak dinner. Do you know why, Noah?"

"Uh, uh, no. . . .why?"

"Because Noah . . . They. Are. Afraid. Of. The. Moment. When. They. Have. Dropped. Their. Pile. Of. Shit. And. Have. Nothing."

Each word was separately said to give the sentence complete emphasis.

"Noah, people are terrified of having nothing and having the steak dinner suddenly vanish while they're reaching for it. They would rather keep holding onto their pile of shit than risk having nothing. The stupid thing is, if the steak dinner were suddenly to disappear, they can *always* stoop down and pick up their pile of shit again . . . or another pile of shit that stinks just as bad!

"Life is full of shit! Piles and piles of it. In fact, there's so much shit in this world that most of us have trouble not stepping in a pile of it nearly every day, because shit is all around us!

"You just have to get over the fact that it may not be the *same* pile of shit, but you can always get another pile that stinks just as bad and is just as crappy.

"That's it. That's my 'Pile of Shit Theory of Life.'

"So Noah, you need to decide what defines your steak dinner and drop your pile of shit, which is all about the past, and start reaching for the steak. That is the *only* thing you owe your folks.

"But, you may have to work to get that steak dinner, and it may not always be glamorous work, but the dinner is within your reach. Go for it. Reaching for the steak is what you owe your parents and your Korean mom. Nothing else. And Noah, the truly wonder-ful part of the gift, the life and future you have been given by the actions and love of both of your mothers, is that you will have so many potential steak dinners to choose from."

With that, Carlisle drank up another shot of sake. Noah followed the older man's example and his head buzzed with the drink and the words and concepts that Rusty had just shared.

The concepts exactly matched the lessons his mother had drilled into him, but somehow put his mother's words into a new light. Ellen Lindquist's often repeated words now felt like a challenge to aim high, a formula for pursuing Rusty's metaphorical "steak dinner," rather than as a simple devotion to duty as he had always thought of them before.

Step up and take on the hard jobs that no one wants and do them well, Noah . . . and do the things you hate about them as well or better than the things you love about them.

But most of all, Noah's head swirled with the dawning realization of the amazing promise and potential of the life and future he had been given, as the real American he now saw that he was. Noah would be forever grateful to Rusty and Kinuko.

Chapter 34

Noah

A s he packed up his few personal toiletries from his steerage accommodation's storage locker, Noah was thinking of that night at Rusty and Kinuko's home and the conversations that had opened his mind to whole new ways of thinking about himself, his life, and his future. He could feel the trundling vibration of the engines and rolling and pitching of the vessel. He had not gotten seasick, but the movement while he was below decks was less than comfortable.

That night had been an epiphany and perfectly meshed with the flash of insight that had struck him when his mother had set him straight about his anger toward his math teacher and his algebra grade. The warmth of the ship below decks was welcome. Even though the motion without any visual reference was uncomfortable, Noah decided that he needed to soak up the warmth a bit more. He lay on his bunk and thought.

What if she isn't waiting for me?

What if she is?

Noah couldn't decide which was causing him more anxiety. He thought back to the night she had finally told him about her decision and explained what adoption was. He remembered that night as clearly now as it was then. Physical pain was one thing, but he had never felt the sort of absolute, sheer, stark, and blinding pain in his soul, and what that brutal pain had driven him to do.

That sort of tearing, ripping wound to your soul never truly heals . . . you just learn to live with it.

Lee Hee Ae was lying in her bedding on the warm floor of her room. Her son was lying snuggled under her right arm, close against her. Her breath could be seen in white, steaming puffs in the light of the kerosene lamp that was next to her left side, on the low table that was never put away—there was no "away" in which to put it. On the table was also a bottle of *soju,* the Korean version of sake on steroids. It was the drink of choice among Koreans and is essentially sake that has been distilled into a spirit. Usually about half the alcohol strength of whisky, but Koreans tended to make up for that with the amount consumed. Hee Ae was not going to get through tonight without some liquid courage to steel her nerves and dampen her guilt, as well as to settle the cramps in her bowels. She'd finished one bottle and was half through the one sitting on the little table. The soju was dutifully dulling the raging voices in her head. But they were still there, maybe not raging now, but still plenty shrill. She was agonizing over what she had to do. The same sickness and nausea she'd been feeling every time she confronted this issue swept over her now, making her swallow hard to keep from retching. She didn't know exactly what time it was. She had no watch, but she knew it was getting later with each moment she said nothing to her son, while debating endlessly in her head with herself, her doubts, and her ever-hissing guilt. And her crushing loneliness. She raised the glass of soju that she held in her left hand to her lips and let the clear liquor slide into her mouth, which immediately tossed it down the back of her throat with a practiced gulp. She no longer felt the burn of it down her esophagus.

Lying in her cold little room, she felt just as hollow, just as sick as the day Tuck Riley had told her the truth about Hanlon, and even more torn with uncertainty.

Do your duty!

Her voice kept repeating in her head.

Young Nam was sleeping cuddled against her side. She shook him with her right arm on which he was resting. She set the glass of soju down on the table, next to the half-full bottle. She reached over with her now free hand and shook her tiny son.

"Young Nam-ya . . . wake up . . . Young Nam-ya."

She shook him for a longer time and he stirred, blinking his eyes and looking up at her.

"What Mommy? Is it time to get up? It's so dark; is it morning?"

"No, Young Nam. It's still night, but I need to tell you some good news."

That's a good lie, Hee Ae. Can't wait to hear how you're going to spin this!

"What is it Mommy?"

"Well . . . you know how you've been getting money and presents from an American church? Remember what I told you about how some people believe in a god—a super powerful magical person—and the stories about that god? And how people who all share the same belief about the same god and the same stories are called a church?"

"Uh huh. I remember, Mommy."

"There are many Koreans who believe in this kind of god too, and the same stories about that god here in Korea. They also belong to this church . . . well, the people of this church believe that their god tells them to share and be kind to poor people . . . and you know how poor we are, right Young Nam?"

The boy didn't know quite where his mother was going with this explanation, and he certainly didn't know why he and mother were poor. He just accepted it. It didn't cross his mind that there was an alternative, that under different circumstances he and his mother could have been wealthy.

Nearly all children at his age have yet to develop the capacity to think hypothetically. A French cognitive developmental theorist named Jean Piaget postulated that children of Young Nam's age cannot think hypothetically; despite starting to ask unending "why" and "how" questions, they can only accept something that matches a concrete situation. So Young Nam knew that he and his mother were very poor. If you asked him why, he would likely provide an answer such as, "Because we don't have money." But Hee Ae knew that her son surprised her and other adults by how often he was able to demonstrate deductive reasoning: the type of reasoning where one applies a general principle to predict a specific outcome, such as realizing that doing tasks take time, and therefore, Santa Claus can't possibly go to every house in one night. So Hee Ae was confident that her son would understand what she was telling him.

Young Nam answered his mother, providing an explanation of her leavings as a way to please her, to show that he understood and wanted her to be proud of him for understanding.

"Uh huh. That's why sometimes you have to go away, because we're poor and you have to go make some money by selling stuff."

"That's right, Little One."

The words were coming out slowly. Each word seemed to cling to her insides, clawing to stay in, leaving blood trails of guilt across her heart. She was choking up and fighting tears.

You can't cry! Not now! Remember, this is good news . . .

More words were forced out, fighting all the way until each was pushed out against its will—which was really Hee Ae's conflicted will—to add to the spin that she was trying to keep going.

"So . . . some people . . . who are members of this church in America, with the . . . help . . . the . . . help of some . . . of their . . . Korean members . . . here in Korea, have been the ones . . . the people . . . who . . . who . . . have been . . . sending us the money and things. . . . Well, some of these . . . American . . . people . . . are going to come . . . come by . . . here in Munsan . . . to see you . . . "

Didn't do such a good job of making it sound like good news. . . . Come on Hee Ae, get on with telling him . . . wait! What if I ask him if he WANTS to go to America and live there? . . . and he says yes?

"Little One," she only used this term very infrequently and almost never since he had turned five.

"You know that your father is American . . . so that makes you American, right?"

The words were coming out easier—Hee Ae had a plan now.

"Uh huh. Everybody calls me American and that I should go away to America, because I'm not Korean and don't belong here . . . "

"Well, would you like to go to America and live there with Americans?"

Hee Ae waited for a response. And waited. The minutes stretched one after another, but there was no response from her small son. She looked down at him, tucked under her arm. He was not looking at her, but staring at the far wall.

"Well, Young Nam-ya? What if that could happen?"

Part of the reason that her boy wasn't answering was because her question required hypothetical thinking. The question made no sense to the boy.

But I can't go to America . . . I live here in Munsan . . .

Finally, he answered.

"Would I still live here in Munsan with you?"

"No, Young Nam. It wouldn't be like going to Seoul for a trip. I'm asking if you would want to live in America, not just go for a visit."

"But you'd be coming with me, right Mommy? We'd live together in America?"

Hee Ae stared up at the ceiling and watched the clouds of her breath drift upward with each exhale she did. Puff . . . puff . . . puff . . . puff . . . her breathing and the silence stretched longer than she had intended.

This is it . . .

"No, Little One. I would not be going with you. But there would be nice American people who would be waiting for you and to take care of you . . ."

"No! I don't want to *not* live with you, Mommy. I *don't* want to go to America if I can't live with you!"

Young Nam's little stick arms gripped tighter onto his mother's body, where he had been loosely hugging her before. Her hope that maybe he would express a desire to live in America wasn't going to be realized. Hee Ae was going to have to do this the hard way.

Crap!

"Well . . . Young Nam-ya, these people from the American church are . . . are coming to visit . . . next week . . . because . . . because . . . I made a decision. . . . It's to help you. . . . I talked with some very educated people who know best about how to help little boys like you . . . who have American fathers. . . . You'll be going to America to live and become part of an American family . . . "

Young Nam's shrill preschool voice cut her off.

"No! Mommy, no! I don't *want* to live in America without you! I want to stay with *you*! You're my *mommy* and a mommy's son lives with his mommy! I'm your son . . . so I'm supposed to only live with you, because you're my mommy!"

There it was. A five-year-old's logic, simple and circular. Little boys lived with their real mommies because mommies were their mommies. And therefore little boys should live with their mommies. And what the boy didn't say was how much he loved and needed *his* mommy. He had no one else in his world. She had been the only constant, the only adult, the only fixture in his life. Child abandonment was not rare in Korea in the 1960s, especially in urban areas like Seoul. The boy had seen homeless, abandoned children, begging on the streets of Seoul. His baleful eyes had met their hard gazes as he walked past them, holding tightly to his mother's hand. They were the only people that were more destitute than he and his mother. He did not want to become one of those children. He knew that the only way they survived was to join into a gang of other homeless, parentless children and that it was the law of the gang that ruled over their lives. A mixed-race boy like him—especially a crippled, deformed one—would not be welcome into any gang. He would be alone and completely vulnerable. And he would not survive. A lone homeless boy without a protective gang would starve, be beaten, get sick, and die on the streets. Young Nam knew that his mommy was the only protection he had.

And he craved and needed her love beyond anything in his world.

"Young Nam-ya, I made this decision for *you*."

Hee Ae squeezed back in reply to her son's increased clasping of her body—and to give emphasis to the word *you*.

"You know that, without the money and gifts from the foreign church, I would not be able to afford to feed both of us and pay for a place to live and for charcoal . . . and everything . . . you should be starting school already, but . . . you're not Korean . . . so . . . I can't even give you an education. . . . Little One, I have no choice! I'm making this decision because I love you so very, very much! But my love alone is not enough. I want you to have a good life, a good education, a good home, and a good family . . . here, in Korea, you know that people will always see you as not Korean. In America, you can be with people who are American like *you*!"

Her tiny son had his face buried in her shoulder and was crying and kept repeating the word *no*, muffled and sobbing. His tiny body was shaking as he clung desperately to Hee Ae's body. Hee Ae kept talking through her son's sobs and "nos," through her nausea and heart-tearing pain. If she stopped now, she was afraid that she would not be able to go through with what she knew she had to do: her duty as a mother. She was fighting to keep her own tears that kept threatening, from bursting their dam inside her.

I must not cry! I have to make this real! . . . I have to finish telling him . . .

"Little One, the American church people won't—can't—support you living here in Korea forever. They're supporting you because

I made this decision. The people who are coming to visit you are going to find an American family for you . . . so that you can grow up with an education and become a rich American man someday. And when you do, you can come back to Korea and bring me back to America, and we can be together again. That would be great, wouldn't it Young Nam-ya?"

"Rich American" was almost one word. It certainly was a single, unified concept in the minds of Koreans who were in Hee Ae's circumstance. To be American meant to be rich—beyond imagining. Hee Ae put a cheeriness in her voice that was founded on nothing but her desperation. She felt like a lying fraud, selling her five-year-old son on the benefits of selling him off to unknown foreigners on the other side of the planet, geographically and metaphorically. Her son was still not buying it and was continuing to repeat his sobbing "nos" as he hugged her, buried his face into her, and cried his shaking, convulsing little-boy tears. Her shoulder and right side were wet with them, and Hee Ae could feel the tears running down and pooling onto the bedroll under her right armpit.

The soft, caring approach with her fake cheeriness wasn't working. Maybe a different approach was needed. Korean culture emphasized duty and loyalty to one's elders, nearly to the exclusion of all other obligations one has in life. It is *the* moral imperative among Koreans, and it is drilled in starting in the crib and permeates the fables, tales, laws, ethics, movies, textbooks, TV, music, work, and social behaviors of all Koreans. Doing one's duty and acting one's role and place in society and one's family was strictly enforced. Those, like Hee Ae, who had broken this highest of Korean morals and expected behaviors suffered the consequences of social ostracism. Lee Hee Ae's poverty was a direct consequence of her breaking the rules of subordinating her desires to her family, her parents, and her husband, and for not keeping to her role and place in Korean society.

But even at his age, her tiny son would have internalized these norms and she had instilled some of them—the expected stoicism of Korean males—through the sting of her lashings. She would use the specter of her son's duty to Hee Ae, as his mother, to gain his cooperation and to mitigate her own bleeding guilt.

"Young Nam-ya. Do you want me to live poor my whole life?"

Hee Ae shook the crying, tiny boy.

"Look at me Young Nam. And stop your crying! You are a boy! Boys, if they want to become men, don't cry. It's shameful for a man to be weak like this! Look. At. Me!"

The boy raised his face, wet with tears that he was trying to stop, and focused his eyes onto his mother's face.

"Do you? Do you want your mother to live all her life so poor?"

"No, Mommy . . ."

"Then it is your duty to help me—your mother—by going to America, going to school, becoming a rich American, and coming back to take care of me . . . do you understand? I can't support you. You are too much of a burden to me and will make me even more poor. I have found a solution . . . because if you stay here in Korea with me, you will *not* get educated, you will *not* be able to find work, and you will be too poor to take care of *me*, your mother. If you truly love me and want to do your duty as my son, you will go to America and be a good son to an American family, you will work hard and become rich and come back for me.

"That is your duty as my son and a future man. . . . Do not be so selfish to only think of yourself and what you want! Do you understand, Young Nam?"

The boy looked at his mother and did not understand. All he really understood was that his crying had made her angry, and that he had displeased her. He knew that the word *duty* was very important among Korean people and that somehow he was supposed to do this word to make his mother not angry. He understood her words to mean that he was the reason his mother was so poor, and that if she got rid of him, she could be better off. The little boy wanted to do this word *duty* but he desperately did not want to leave his mother. He knew this deeper than he knew any other truth in his short and limited life. No one made him feel safe, cherished, and loved except his mother. Being incapable of thinking in hypotheticals at his age, he could not imagine an alternative. His mother was his mother. No one else can be his mother.

It's my fault! If I had never been born, Mommy wouldn't be poor! . . . It's all my fault! No wonder she sometimes gets so angry at me. I deserve it! I'm sorry Mommy! I'm sorry for being born!

This revelation seared his young little world and tore his spirit. The twin realizations that he could not imagine a world without his mother, and that he was the cause of all her suffering and misery, grabbed hold of his heart and gashed his young, limited cognition through to its inner soul.

I should never have been born!

The intensity of the thought was almost blinding, and its implications sucked dry the boy's will. He found he had no desire to cry. He had no desire other than to do his duty, as *he* saw it and understood it. He was starting to feel a numbness come over him. He knew what he had to do. He finally answered his mother's question.

"Yes, Mommy. I understand. . . . I'll do my duty. I'm sorry for being selfish and making you mad . . . "

Hee Ae could see the intensity of her son's contriteness and his imploring for her affection in his always attention-catching green eyes. She hugged him tight.

"I'm not angry, Little One. Remember, I love you and made my decision because of *you* and *your* future. When you go to America, you will have a new mother and you'll also have a father. You must be a good son to them. You must do your duty to them and obey them. And, someday, when you have studied hard and become a rich American man, you can come back for me, because I will always be Mommy—your Mommy. That is my dream and hope for you—for us—my good son."

She kissed him on his forehead and reached over to the glass of soju on the table. She drained the glass, feeling its burn and needing its warmth and alcoholic fuzziness.

It's done. It's now real . . .

"I'm sorry I made us poor, Mommy . . . I promise; I'll do my duty . . . I love you, Mommy."

Young Nam's small soprano voice whispered.

"Can you sing the song to me, Mommy?"

"Young Nam-ya, Little One, you didn't make us poor, but thank you for being brave—you're already such a little man—and understanding and being willing to do your duty for me—for us."

She started humming the song's melody, soft and slow and sad. And sang the song's words quietly into the cold night.

". . . Before you're forever gone . . ."

Hee Ae sang the song twice to ensure that her son fell asleep. She gently moved her arm from under his head, holding it up with her left hand while sliding out her right arm and setting his head down on her pillow. She wanted to be free to sit up. She reached over to the soju bottle and poured the rest of it into the now empty glass. Hee Ae reached under the left pillow and pulled out her pack of American cigarettes and tamped one out. She lifted the kerosene lamp's glass off and put the tip of the cigarette into the lamp's flame, took a few quick puffs to get it lit and replaced the lamp's glass. She took a long, deep drag and held the smoke deep in her lungs. The tobacco tasted wonderful and the ritual movements and the nicotine were soothing. She slowly blew out the smoke in her habitual left-sided "who" shaped lip funnel. The nausea retreated and her gut started to settle.

Wow! That was awful . . . but at least he understands from a duty perspective . . . and now he knows. It truly is going to happen. It'll be a new life for him . . . and for me . . .

She grabbed the glass of soju off the low table, refilled it from the bottle, and took a big slug. She liked drinking soju in winter because it tasted so much better when chilled. With no electricity, she had no refrigeration. But in winter, her room was plenty cold to keep soju nicely chilled and drinkable. Hee Ae sat with her burning cigarette in her right hand and her drink in her left hand and stared at the opposite wall in the dim, flickering glow of the kerosene lamp's one small flame. She was strolling down new corridors in her mind, far behind the vacant stare of her Asian eyes, with their black pupils and slanted lids. The corridors led into unexplored rooms labeled "adoption," "new life," and "second chance," but sometimes they also led through some mental wormhole instantly into old familiar rooms labeled "loneliness," "self-loathing," and "fear." As she mentally walked through this new territory and wormhole-popped back into familiar psychic and emotional places, she unconsciously sipped the soju dry and smoked the cigarette to its filter. She snubbed out the cigarette, turned down the lamp flame until it was extinguished, and sank into her pillow, further under the blankets and succumbed to her alcohol-assisted sleep.

The moon was out and approaching its half-moon phase from being a full moon several days ago, known as a waning gibbous moon. It was sending a soft, pale silvery glow through the rice-paper covered window of Lee Hee Ae's room as she dropped off to sleep.

Something woke her.

Was it a noise? Something . . .

She slowly came to consciousness, and as she opened her eyes, she realized she could dimly see in the silvery glow of rice paper filtered moonlight. Then she noticed that she was alone in her bed. Young Nam wasn't there. Where his small body had been lying next to her on her right side, there was only an empty space under the blankets. Suddenly, Hee Ae was fully awake as her right hand groped vainly to feel for her son next to her.

Where is he?

She sat up and looked around the room, and she noticed a small shadow in the far corner.

"Young Nam-ya! Is that you? Are you there?"

There was no reply, but she thought she heard a whimper. She fumbled for the small box of short wooden matches that were next to the lamp; found it. She slid the outer cover back and pulled out a match and struck it, and a flame burst forth and settled down to its flickering burning glow. Hee Ae waved the match toward the far corner in front of her and could see that it was her son.

Oh my fucking God! NO!

Her one large cutting knife glinted in the match flame as it was held in her son's small hand. There was blood on the blade and blood on the floor all around him. His eyes were wide and staring at her as his breaths pushed out steam in front of him. The match flame seemed like a flash bulb, freezing the scene in its flame burst and putting it into shadow as it slowly burned down. The boy's right leg was bent and naked in front of him, and she could see a bloody gash just above the inside front part of his ankle on the shinbone. And in the dying match flame, she saw her boy raise the knife that looked far too big in his hand and bring it down onto the gash. She heard the knife thwack into blood and bone with a sickening "thuck" sound.

No! No! No! NO!

Simultaneously, as the knife started to descend, Hee Ae screamed.

"No, Young Nam! Stop it! What are you *doing*?"

The match burned out as she shrieked these words. She threw back the blankets from her and scampered over to her bloody, tiny boy. She went to grab the knife out of his hand, but it stuck in his leg bone. She had to give a quick jerk to free it, and Young Nam gave a squeal of pain. She could see the dark shadow of more blood freely oozing out of the wound. Hee Ae didn't know it, but her little boy had severed a minor artery, the anterior medial malleolar artery that runs just in front of the inside ankle joint. Clearly, it had been bleeding for several minutes or more. There was a large and growing pool of blood around her son's foot and lower leg, and it was pooling and running into dimples in the uneven floor around where the boy sat in the room's corner. She threw the knife across the room to the opposite side where it landed on the bedding, smearing blood onto the blanket where it touched and slid to a stop.

Hee Ae tore a piece of fabric from the bedsheet and tied it around Young Nam's right lower leg, wrapping it around multiple times and tying it tightly. While tearing the sheet and binding his leg, she frantically was questioning her bloody boy.

"What were you *thinking*? What the hell is this about? Why would you try to hack your foot off? What is *wrong* with you?"

But the cramping, gripping nausea in the pit of her gut was already answering her questions for her. Her slithery, broaching, raging guilt monsters were frothing violently, hissing their accusations.

You know why he did this . . . it's your fault . . . you drove him to this!
She had to choke down her bile.

And then she heard her tiny, bleeding son speak and it confirmed all her hissing, frothing guilt.

The boy sobbed out his answer. "Mommy, you don't want me because I'm too much trouble for you . . . and it's my fault that you're so poor. . . . It's all my fault . . . and I wish that I had never been born, because then you would never have become poor and had to work to take care of me . . .

"I was trying to do my duty, Mommy . . . to not be trouble for you anymore. You wanted me to go away, Mommy, so if I was dead, I'd be gone and you wouldn't stay poor . . . "

Young Nam was in agony. Not just that his leg throbbed and burned with pain, but his soul felt cut and bleeding far beyond his leg. He wanted to be a good son. To do the "duty" word. His mommy wanted him to go away, but he felt he could not live without her. He could not imagine life without her. Who would love him? Who could ever replace her? She was an element of nature for him. She was his air, his water, his sun. The thought of the world without her would leave him gasping and dying as if the air had been sucked away from his life.

He didn't want to go away, and he knew his mommy didn't want him to stay . . . and it was all his fault that she had to smuggle things, to sell herself, why she drank so much, and hated herself and sometimes him. His five-year-old logic and grasp of his mother's words led him to no other conclusion. He was more torn and in agony than the time when he had been certain that his mother had died. He knew the duty he had to do.

He needed to kill himself.

But he hadn't been sure how to do it. He didn't know enough about how living things worked to know how to most effectively end life. The boy had waited for his mother to fall asleep, thinking of how he should kill himself. He'd mostly seen chickens being killed and butchered. The thing that stood out most about butchered chickens—or butchered anything—to Young Nam, was the visibility of bones. With anything that was living, he never saw bones. With all butchered, dead things, he saw bones.

So maybe that was the answer. Cut through to the bone and then you die.

The little boy looked for where it may be easiest to reach bone and knew that he could feel his bones best around his shin and ankle. He slipped out from under the covers into the cold March night, seeing dimly by the light of the waning gibbous moon. In his numbed state of soul-torn agony, he found it easy to overcome his usually uncontrollable fear of the dark and the night. If something was hiding in the dark to kill him, well, that was just fine with the tiny boy. It would save him the trouble of finishing what he was about to do.

He quietly pulled the sliding door to the kitchen pit and crawled out to the earthen-floored, semi-exposed enclosure. The big cutting knife that his mother used to chop up napa cabbage to make kimchee was out in the open on a small wooden ledge. The boy grasped it and crawled back into the room. The thought of killing himself in the cooking pit somehow didn't appeal to the boy. It didn't dawn on him that dead was dead, and it wouldn't matter where he was when dead. But the boy didn't want to get soiled from the dusty, dirt floor. He silently slid closed the door and crawled to the far corner of the room, as far from his sleeping mother as he could. He looked down at his right leg and put the blade of the big knife against his shin, just above his ankle and slightly to the inside.

And started cutting.

The boy suddenly was eager to die, to have the heart-numbing pain inside him stop, to do his duty for his mother. He was surprised by the amount of blood that started coming out, but there was no sign of or feeling that he was dying, only a searing intense pain from the wound. But it paled compared to the pain he was feeling in his chest.

I wonder what dying feels like? Maybe I need to chop through the bone to die . . .

As he raised the knife to chop into the bone of his leg, convinced that would end his life and internal gushing, consuming agony, his mother suddenly stirred.

"Young Nam-ya! Is that you? Are you there?"

He almost replied and a small whimper escaped his lips. She then struck a match and suddenly screamed, disrupting the force with which he was about to chop off his foot above the ankle.

"No, Young Nam! Stop it! What are you *doing*?"

I'm going to die for you, Mommy . . .

He swung. The knife cut through the thin layer of flesh where he had been cutting already and thwacked into his tibia.

Chapter 35

Noah

JULY 2000, JET TO ST. PETER

Mr. Lindquist, this is Captain Nelson, coming in on final approach to Mankato Regional Airport, out fifty miles. Wheels touch down in fifteen minutes. ETA at the gate in twenty minutes."

Noah heard the captain's voice over the muted speakers in the Cessna Citation V's softly glowing interior. He took out his Motorola tri-band phone and speed dialed his executive assistant, Debbie McKinsey.

"Hey Boss, how was the flight? Everything as you ordered? The Crab Louie salad, the scotch, the Jamaican Blue Mountain?"

"Yeah, Debbie. All good, thank you."

"You are welcome . . . how are you doing? I know it's hard for you."

"It's okay, Debbie. As a better man—my mother—once told me, it's not about me and don't go on . . . Hey, I just called to check in on the . . ."

". . . the ground transportation, way ahead of you, Boss. All taken care of. BLS Limo services will meet you at Mankato Regional's GAT and be ready to take you to St. Peter. Don't worry, I didn't get you a big white stretch; it's a Ford Explorer. Should fit in better. . . . Is that good with you?"

"Debbie, you read my mind . . ."

"And the driver should already have the flowers from Mary's in the car . . . your mom's favorites: lilies and red roses. There's a box of peanut brittle for your dad, as well."

"You're sort of okay to average Debbie . . . I'm sure that I could replace you in a heartbeat . . ."

"Yes, Boss . . . good luck with that, but I guess I should say, 'You're welcome.' You really need to get better at expressing your gratitude."

Noah and Debbie had a good understanding of each other and enjoyed a certain banter. He had hired her from a temp company (after he had gone through eight assistants before her in two weeks). He had tasked her on a Friday to put together a PowerPoint presentation that he'd handwritten and demanded she have it to him finished and polished on Monday morning. Debbie didn't know PowerPoint at all, but she had gone out and gotten a manual for MS PowerPoint, taught herself on a Saturday, and completed the presentation and delivered it Sunday. He had hired her away from the temp agency on the following Monday.

As the plane descended, Noah's ears popped and he made yawning movements to equalize the pressure on his eardrums. He felt and heard the aircraft's wheels drop and lock. Despite the whisky, he felt the chorded snake of his bowels twist and churn, and the cold, numb feeling in his chest seemed to expand. He would be saying goodbye—forever—to his mother. He clicked closed his seat belt and as the plane descended through the bright Minnesota sky toward a small runway among the fields of waving emerald corn and soybeans, he thought about his mother's—Ellen Lindquist's—recent decision.

"SHE'S DOING WHAT?" Noah was on the phone with his father, Elmore Lindquist, who had called him at work at BellSouth—Noah was always at work. He'd stepped out of one of BellSouth's corporate headquarters' boardrooms where he was conducting a conference call with his lawyers from the firm of Fried, Frank, Harris, Shriver & Jacobson and investment bankers from Goldman Sachs and Merrill Lynch. There were people on the call who were physically in New York City, London, Amsterdam, and Atlanta. It was

October 1999 and Noah was in the midst of the largest merger and acquisition deal he would complete. When it finally closed and was publicly announced at the end of the year, at nearly $20 billion in value, it would represent the largest cellular company deal outside the United States for BellSouth Corporation in its history. The deal would end up creating the largest wireless company in Europe at the time and thwart the expansion plans and aspirations of France Telecom and play off those same aspirations shared by Telecom Italia, Spain's Telefonica, Finland's Sonera, Sweden's Telia, Norway's Telenor, U.K.-based Orange, and KPN Royal Dutch Telecom.

"Your mom is going to the Mayo Clinic in Rochester to be a part of a clinical trial for gene therapy."

Elmore's booming bass came over loudly through Noah's cell phone, such that anyone standing within twenty feet of Noah would have been able to hear his words clearly. Noah walked swiftly past his secretary's desk and went into his large, plushly appointed, over-sized office and closed the door. He wanted to keep his private life private.

"Dad, is she still doing the chemo?"

"No. Apparently none of the chemo treatments had any positive effect. Her cancer is continuing to grow, after it came back since the original surgery to remove the tumor. So this may be something that can help."

Noah couldn't believe what he had just heard from his father, normally a very factual, conservative man in most all things, but particularly in assumptions of untested outcomes. But, he also had learned to never take another person's hope.

I understand, Dad . . .

"Okay. Sure, Dad. I appreciate the call and letting me know. Let me know if I can help in some way."

"You bet, Son. Hope you're not working too hard . . . oh . . . sure Sweetheart. . . . Son, your mom would like to have a few words with you. Here she is . . ."

"Noah? This is Mom."

Ellen's voice was as smooth and efficient as she ever sounded despite her cancer. She had decided to take on another hard job, maybe her last, and needed to explain it to each of her children—differently—in her own way and in a way that each would best understand. She knew that God had a plan for her life, and her cancer must therefore be a part of that plan. And she would make every part of her life meaningful. Even at its end, she would take on yet another thankless job in the service of others. To the end, she would define herself by her actions and devotion to the calling she heard in her faith.

"Hi, Mom. How are you feeling?"

"I'm feeling pretty good today, thank goodness."

She gave a short version of her musical laugh, ending in her signature "Ohhhh deeaaarrrrr."

"Noah, I wanted to tell you a little more about the treatments I'll be starting at the Mayo Clinic next week, because I know that you'll be worried and probably have some questions."

"Well . . . Mom, you're the important one. This is all about you and how to get you better, but . . . yes, I guess . . . I do have some concerns for you. I'm not quite sure what the point of the treatment is. From what I know about gene therapy, I'm concerned about the side effects and other issues."

Noah had read that gene therapy is the term used to describe a set of procedures where doctors attempt to replace a portion of the DNA or a gene in living cells within a person. For certain genetic diseases, like hemophilia, where a particular gene is not functioning because it was inherited from parents that way, gene therapy potentially could replace the defective gene with a functioning gene, curing the person of the genetic disease. With cancer, the concept has some variations. One approach is to replace a gene or genes in the cancerous tumor making it die, stop growing, or become susceptible to chemical or radiation treatments. Alternatively, genes could be replaced in noncancerous cells to make them resistant or destructive of the particular cancer. Recently, this latter approach has been successful in fighting certain types of leukemia.

However, there are no approved gene therapies, and all such procedures are only available as a clinical trial, meaning that these are all experiments. Especially in 1999, when Ellen Lindquist was starting her gene therapy, there was no track record of any success with any gene therapy trials, particularly for cancers. The difficulty in implementing this potentially very promising treatment lay in successfully inserting a gene into a living person, and then into that person's living cells and the particular cells that needed to be targeted for the insertion of the gene.

The theory of gene therapy involves a lot of moving parts and the use of special viruses as gene insertion tools. A lot of "first this, then that." And then there are the risks. The virus may not target the desired cells. The genes may not express as wanted or sustain in replication. The human body may react with inflammation and other reactions that can cause anything from mild discomfort to tissue death to organ shut down to death of the whole person. And the virus could revert to its original condition and cause a viral infection, actually giving the infected person a viral disease. The clinical trial participation was often invasive and painful for participants, requiring needle injections, blood draws, and other intrusive or uncomfortable tests multiple times per week, in some cases, and over a period of time which could be weeks to months.

Noah knew that the treatments for his mother's liver cancer had not been successful. His mother was a trained nurse. She would know and understand that gene therapy was mostly a theory at this point and had little hope of curing or helping her. Why would she sign up for the pain, the inconvenience, the intrusions, and the risks in what might be the last year of her life on a procedure that offered only pain and suffering with no hope of benefit?

Mom, why do this?

"Noah, you know that my treatments have not been successful. My liver cancer is not likely to be cured, and now it's not responding to any chemicals that might cause remission. I know that it is now most likely simply a matter of time for me. But one's life should always have meaning and purpose, Noah. We've talked about this many times. . . . It is not enough to simply be . . . one must also do. Noah this is true when we are young, when we grow up, and even at the end of our life."

"But, Mom, haven't you suffered enough through all the treatments already? Can't you find something to do—to keep giving you purpose and meaning—that doesn't involve so much pain and potential for more suffering?"

Doesn't she know that it hurts us to see her suffer?

"You want me to know that other people are willing to participate in these trials, to suffer and take risks, but then somehow excuse myself from participating? Noah, haven't I taught you better? I have had a wonderful life. The Lord has blessed me with so many things, and I have benefitted from the sacrifice, not just of Christ, but of so many who have contributed to make the society that I have had the good blessing to live in and to have my children grow and succeed in . . .

"I just wanted to have this conversation, Noah, so that you know and understand that I am doing this intentionally and not out of some unrealistic hope. My nursing training allows me to understand the procedures, but also the potential of gene therapies. And, of course, our faith calls us to bear the cross as our Lord showed us. He gave each of us the gift of life. What each of us owe in return is to make the most of it, by following his example of service, faith in God, and actions that bear witness to our faith."

Noah shared his mother's faith in a general sense. He thought of himself as Lutheran and belonged to a church. But he had never had the intensity, the complete acceptance of religious faith as a constant, always visible aspect of his life. But his mother did and always had. Those not knowing her might find what she had just said as not truly credible. But Noah knew that Ellen Lindquist's words and her blatant faith were as real and a part of her as her blue eyes and her Swedish heritage.

Noah was reminded of a conversation that had a similar theme, about what one owes for the gift of one's life, a conversation he had had a long time ago with a philosophical former fighter pilot on the other side of the planet when he was a much younger man.

Truth has a way of repeatedly finding its voice . . .

"Mom, you always amaze me."

Noah was truly in wonder of Ellen Lindquist. His love for her—for all that she was, in all her actions, in all her courage, and especially in all her humility—was impossible for him actually to put into words, even in his own head. He just felt it, like an ache deep in his core. It had started when she had made him feel safe as a scared little boy, and it had only grown through seeing the perfect unity of her words with her actions—actions that spoke of and for the emotions inside her that she rarely ever expressed.

"You know that I don't have quite the same level of faith that you do, Mom, and . . ."

Ellen interrupted him, in a voice that was just shy of a rebuke and words that came out rapidly.

"Noah, stop it. It's not about me . . . don't be going on . . . and . . . and your faith is between God and you. . . . I just wanted to share with you directly that this is what I want to do, because I know it's what I believe is right, and that it's a part of what I was placed on this earth to do."

"Okay, Mom, okay. I understand. Just let me know if you need anything from me."

"You bet . . . your dad and I were thinking we might come to visit you in Atlanta. Can you make some time for us? I know you're pretty busy with your job and all, but that's something you can do for me."

"No problem, Mom. Just let me know the dates."

"As soon as I know more about the schedule of the clinical trial, we'll let you know . . . in the meantime, take good care of yourself and make sure you're making enough time for yourself now and then."

"I will, Mom."

"Well, that's about all we have. Thanks for talking to us. Know your dad and I love you."

"Love you too, Mom."

"Good-bye, Noah."

"'Bye, Mom."

His mother had started saying the "love" word since her cancer diagnosis. It still seemed awkward and out of place. In the Lindquist home, Swedish reserve had always dictated that love was something that was shown in what one did for each other, not in words that were spoken.

Noah stood gazing out his tenth floor window that looked out over Atlanta's famed Peachtree Street and the city's very upscale Buckhead neighborhood.

Oh God! It finally feels real . . . Oh Christ! Shit! Mom's handled all her cancer treatments without really showing any of us what she's been going through . . . but now . . . now that she admitted in her own words that the end may only be a matter of time . . . Shit, it truly is real . . . and horrible . . .

Noah felt a growing constriction in his chest and a cold lump in his throat. She had been such a force of nature in his life that Noah couldn't imagine a world where Ellen Lindquist didn't exist. He remembered when he had first met this towering—but outwardly normal, unremarkable—force that was Ellen Lindquist.

Chapter 36

Ellen

The door to the Jetway leading from the just-arrived jetliner had been opened, and the first passengers were just stepping out. Ellen's heart felt like it was trying to crawl up her throat and yank her tongue back from her mouth. She stood off to the side in front of the arrival gate door with a small picture in her hand. She and Elmore, Christina, Karsten, Karissa, and Carla had all been waiting in the Minneapolis-St. Paul International Airport, MSP, international arrivals gate area for a couple of hours. The Cathay Pacific flight had been delayed in taking off after stopping for refueling, debarking, and embarking passengers at Vancouver International Airport.

Twenty minutes ago there had been an announcement that Cathay Pacific flight CX883 inbound from Vancouver had just landed on Runway 11 Right, more than an hour late. It took the plane about fifteen minutes to arrive at its changed gate, now Gate 24 on the Red Concourse. MSP used color to designate its concourses, of which there were only two: Red and Blue. The disaster movie *Airport*, released in 1970, was partially filmed at MSP, and the fictional airport in the movie used colors to designate its concourses. MSP would change its use of colors for concourse names to letter designations in 2000, being one of the last to shift to this global standard.

The day had finally arrived, and Ellen's heart had been racing since she woke up. It was Friday, January 9, 1970. The day would forever be etched into Ellen's memories, as she would learn a great truth about herself. Standing outside the Jetway door, she knew that she would face the true beginning of answering God's call to take on a job that would turn out harder and more transforming than she could have ever imagined. For being such an impactful day, the "day" was surprisingly short. Official weather services would report that the sun was only above the horizon for nine out of the day's twenty-four hours. The sun had not risen on this Friday until just before 8:00 a.m. and would set before 5:00 p.m.

This particular Friday was only the second Friday of the 1970s, a decade that would be one of the most pivotal social and cultural watersheds in American history. The '60s tend to get most of the credit as the decade of change, but through most of that decade, American society was much like the '50s. Only the last couple years of the '60s signaled the radical changes to come. But it was the 1970s when all the social and cultural changes would go viral and society wide, when the radical parts of the late '60s would become the new normal for America, even in its grassroots, small town core: the Midwest.

This Friday started out windy in St. Peter, with winds blowing at nearly twenty miles per hour, though they would die down to almost nothing by the time Ellen would finally go to bed in the wee hours of the following day. And it was a clear, cold day with not a cloud in the sky, its blueness vaulting over the snow-covered farmlands around and in the Valley of the Jolly Green Giant. The trees were bare and stretched their leafless ice-covered branches toward that vaulted crystal blue sky, reaching towards a sun too distant and small to offer any meaningful warmth.

Ellen had been busy all day making preparations for her new son and getting her family ready to go to Minneapolis to meet the boy she had only read about, seen in pictures, and in her dreams. She'd fixed a quick supper and had gotten everyone loaded into the family car, and she had sat in the front passenger seat of their 1969 "frost green" Chevy Impala Kingswood station wagon. Elmore, behind the wheel, had turned onto Highway 169 north toward Minneapolis. Seven-year-old Carla, with her perfect blonde hair in two long braids and front bangs had been sitting in between Ellen and Elmore on the front bench seat of the car. The older kids had taken the backseat, sitting on the cold vinyl seat surface huddled in their winter coats, waiting for the heat to fully warm up the frost green interior of the station wagon. Karsten and Christina liked being seated as far apart as possible, claiming the window seats, leaving the younger Karissa relegated to the middle. Rare for the period, everyone had worn their seatbelts, though they were only lap belts. Ellen Lindquist knew that an ounce of prevention was worth a pound of cure and insisted that safety always come first. She had read convincing statistics in a recent *Reader's Digest* piece about the amazing power of seatbelts to save lives. Ellen read the *Reader's Digest* from cover to cover every month, and especially enjoyed the humorous reader-submitted stories in the sections called, "Humor in Uniform," "All in a Day's Work," and "Laughter, the Best Medicine."

Being on her way to meet her new son had been simultaneously exhilarating and starkly frightening for Ellen, all through the ride to the airport.

Just a few more hours . . . Ellen had thought on the ride, among a host of other thoughts and anxieties that had whirled around inside the confines of her perfectly set blonde hair and red lipstick.

Can I love a boy who isn't William? Can I love a foreign Oriental boy? . . . and can he love me?

LSS had conducted some orientation visits with the Lindquists, but mostly the social workers, like Miss Iverson, kept stressing the mantra "love is enough." The thinking at the time, when intellectuals believed that all human differences could be attributed to nurture rather than nature, was that any child can be successfully raised by any family. What mattered was the environment and the most important factor: parental love for the child. "Love is enough" had a ring of simplicity, fit well with the prevailing sentiments like "make love not war," and—for the Lutheran church—meshed well with the words of Jesus Christ as quoted in the King James Bible, John 13, verse 34: "A new commandment I give unto you, That ye love one another; as I have loved you . . . "

Love is enough . . . if I can love enough . . .

Ellen had held in her hands a typed, written document that was the last full, descriptive report on the boy that was to be her new son, as well as the photo that was made from the slide that had been sent last spring. The report was date stamped in red: 1969. 8. 5. Earlier today, she had reread the part of the report titled "Description of the Child."

> Young Nam is a child of well developed and balanced physique, who looks handsome and bright. His complexion is fair and he has Caucasian-shaped green large eyes with dark-brown hair, and his mother feels that he has a strong resemblance to his father in his appearance and coloring. At the present time, he is 40 inches tall with weighting of 33 pounds.

> In many ways, he is closely related to his mother and his relationship with her is considered to be very normal for his age. He is fully aware of the fact of being an Amerasian child and does express verbally that his father is an American who is now living in America.

> According to Miss Park, his housemother while he was in the Reception Home for his medical examination, from the first day of his entry into the Home he was able to get along well with other children, housemothers and the daily routine of the Home as if he has been there previously, and did not show any sign of newness or home-sickness. While he was in the Home, any particular care problem or feeding or medical problem has not been observed on him.

In the worker's opinion, it would seem that he has been thrived and developed properly even under such limited circumstances and condition, and he will be quite capable in making adjustment to any Western adoptive home, if he would be properly assisted in his first step adjustment to the new environment and to the new customs.

As she thought through the words in the report, Ellen's blue eyes had shone bright and reflective in the light of the oncoming headlights.

"He is closely related to his mother and his relationship with her is considered very normal for his age." *Will he ever feel "closely related" to me? Will he develop a normal relationship with me? Can this boy love? And can he love me? Please Lord, let love be enough . . . and let there be enough love for it to be enough . . .*

Ellen's heart had continued to race and beat loudly within her all through the drive. If she had had access to a napkin, it would have been strangled and crushed into a dense ball of bleached wood pulp. Her eyes had stared unfocused into the dark beyond the windshield as the Impala had droned into the darkness beyond its headlight beams. Ellen would recall almost all details of this drive, how the sun had set over an hour ago when Elmore had gunned the car up to highway speeds and the twilight had grown to full-on night. Venus had shown like a jewel—bright and sparkling—low in the southwestern night sky, drowning out the nearby stars next to it in the star scattered darkness. The outside temperature had been below zero, headed to its low of minus eight degrees Fahrenheit.

"A strong resemblance to his father" . . . *I wonder who he was and what's become of him.* Ellen thought as part of the jumble of other thoughts, and still had the instinctive belief that nature mattered.

Dåligt material ger dåligt resultat.

Poor materials yields poor results.

Sergeant Robert Hanlon felt the heavy machine gun bullet tear into his right arm and blow apart his M-16A1 assault rifle. An instant later he was violently thrown to the ground, and his helmet was ripped from his head as another heavy automatic machine gun round hit his helmet, shattering it with enough force to make Hanlon think he'd broken his neck. When he finally was able to get up, he found that all that was left of his weapon was the plastic stock. The force that had thrown him down had also stripped him of all his ammunition and grenades. The battle was still raging all around him and it was only a little after 8:00 a.m. It was the third time he had been hit by bullets today, Monday, November 15, 1965, in the Ia Drang Valley of the highlands of South Vietnam.

Hanlon was a Platoon Sergeant in the 1st Battalion, 7th Cavalry. He had arrived into Landing Zone X-Ray—LZ X-Ray to the men who would fight and die there—the day before as part of a mission to seek and engage a suspected North Vietnamese Army, NVA, force operating in the vicinity of the Ia Drang River. Bobby Hanlon had been dropped, along with four hundred and fifty men of the 1st Battalion, into the small clearing that was LZ X-Ray shortly after noon on Sunday, November 14. Immediately upon getting out of their Bell UH-1 Iroquois "Huey" helicopters, Hanlon's platoon had been hit by enemy fire as they ran to form a perimeter around the LZ. Two of his men were hit, one of whom died at the LZ in the first minutes of a battle that would rage for four days.

Hanlon's battalion was quickly surrounded by more than two thousand NVA troops and fought desperately to repel wave after assault wave of NVA soldiers throughout that Sunday and into the night. His experience during the Korean War at the Battle of Chipyong-ni served him well. He knew what it was like to be surrounded by a vastly larger enemy force, what it was like to fight desperately to beat back human wave attacks. Just keep shooting, keep firing, keep the ammo coming.

After a tense night of vigil and collecting the dead and wounded, predawn patrols had been sent out to scout the area in front of their lines. This probably saved the battalion. The patrol discovered the NVA massing to overrun the lightly dug in American troops.

An hour and a half into the second day's battle, Hanlon's platoon commander was shot through the head and died instantly, and in the ensuing hail of enemy fire, Bobby Hanlon felt a bullet hit his gut and go clean through. The pain was blinding, but he overrode it and kept firing his M-16 and directing his troops. Thirty minutes more into the savage fighting and Hueys were inbound to drop off supplies and remove the wounded. The order came at 7:55 a.m. for each platoon to throw colored smoke grenades to mark their perimeter so that the helicopters could see where the LZ was and the location of friendly forces. As the platoon made ready for the choppers, Hanlon was shot through his left shoulder and thrown to the ground like a spiked football. This was the second bullet to hit him in a span of thirty minutes. The pain left him shocked and breathless, but he tried to ignore it, knowing that the only hope of survival was to keep putting rounds down range, toward the enemy. He got up again, but much slower than when shot in his stomach. He was bleeding profusely, but he started firing again, adding his fire to the fire of his troops to slow and stop the NVA assault. It was another thirty minutes when he was shot a third and last time. As he lay in his blood and the red dirt of the Ia Drang Valley, he thought he was likely not going to survive the day or the battle. As he stared into the morning sky of the South Vietnamese Highlands, with the horrific roar, rage, and deafening noise of the largest battle that US forces had been in since the end of the Korean War, Bobby Hanlon had many thoughts and fears go through his mind.

Hanlon would survive the day and the battle—a battle that claimed 234 American men of the 7th Cavalry Regiment, more than any Confederate or Union regiment lost in the Battle of

Gettysburg—and be carried out to safety. He would endure almost three years of surgeries and therapies in Army hospitals, but never fully recover from the wounds or the battle or the Vietnam War. Through all the time that he had to think back over his life, he would think of the Ia Drang Valley and his troops that died in that horrific battle. And . . . he would sometimes think of what he had been doing when called to join the 7th Cavalry and wonder what became of his yobo's baby—his baby—in Korea. He had truly intended to keep sending support, but during his long recovery and three years of hospitalization, he had not been able to fulfill his intention. Once he left the hospital, he had no way of knowing where Hee Ae was or how to reach her and trying seemed pointless. He didn't like to think about it, because he didn't like how it made him feel.

It's a fucked up world . . .

Hanlon often told himself, and he knew this truth first hand, up close, and intimately: He had been in some of the most brutal, savage, and raw fucked-upness of it. But like a scab that wouldn't heal in his conscience, he knew he had added his part to making it a little more fucked up, and he would mentally touch that scab, powerless to stop it from crossing his mind at the most inconvenient times. Hanlon would die in 2003, never knowing the answer to the question that voiced itself in his uncomfortable scabbed-over conscience, as he lived out his disabled days after leaving the Army and working as a hobbling part-time night watchman in Columbus, Georgia.

I wonder what ever became of my bastard Gook kid . . .

Chapter 37

Young Nam

There was a group of about a dozen children, ranging in ages from infants to a nine-year-old girl. There were three women who were standing among the children, each holding an infant. Two of the women were Korean; one was American and white. Her light brown hair and height made her literally stand out from the small crowd. They were standing in front of the brick and stone Georgian-style structure that was the main administrative building for Korea Social Service. All of the children were heavily bundled in brand new winter coats, hats, and mittens. They all wore new shoes and clothes under their new winter coats. In the predawn darkness the white steam of their breath was visible.

Standing just off to the side of this group was another group of about equal size. This group was composed of all adults, and all were women except for one man. That man was Mr. Paik, the director of KSS. Most of these women were the mothers of the children who were bundled up in spotless new coats, along with a few more of the KSS staff. Mrs. Young Son Byon, who had written up the final report on Lee Young Nam that Ellen Lindquist would be holding in her hands several hours later—on the other side of the globe—was among this group. Both groups were looking down the drive leading to the KSS main building, toward a small bus that was backing up toward them.

It was a cold, dark Friday morning on January 9, 1970, in Seoul, South Korea. The bus, which was creeping backward toward the

children and the women, would be taking the waiting children forever away from the women who waited with Mr. Paik. It would soon
load these children and set off down the KSS driveway and through
the out-of-place, Southern plantation-style brick gate posts, turn right
onto Sangmoon-dong to speed toward Gimpo International Airport
on the opposite, far side of Seoul, on the other side of the Han River.

Lee Young Nam stood with his hands in his pockets and, unlike
the other children, was not watching the backing bus. His eyes
were fixed on one of the women in the group around Mr. Paik. He
was looking at his mother. And she was looking at him. Some of
the children around him were crying, mostly the girls. The oldest
child in the group was a nine-year-old girl—all the kids called her
"Elder Sister"—who was crying the most. Young Nam felt a pain
and loss—a loneliness, a feeling that his soul had been cut out of
him and he was a small mortal shell in a vast darkness of separateness—that he could not have put into words, even if he had possessed the vocabulary to do so. But he was proud that he was able
to hold his tears. He was in public, and a boy was not supposed
to cry. He did not want to shame his mother and cry in public in
front of her, in front of Mr. Paik.

After he had failed in his attempt to kill himself, mainly because of
his lack of any knowledge of biology, his mother had been both furious and openly—if there was a word that was light years more intense,
it would have fit—deeply saddened. She had cried, hugged him, yet
rebuked him. She had insisted that he had been selfish and a coward
to try to do such a dishonorable thing, to run away from his real duty.
She had ranted that he must never do such a thing ever again. She
had made him promise that he would live—for her—and that only in
living and growing and succeeding and coming back for her, could
Young Nam fulfill his duty to his mother. She had made him promise
over and again. In the months since that night and this cold morning,
she had drilled this lesson and sense of duty into him.

"Young Nam, if you love me, then you must never do anything cowardly and selfish like you tried. . . . *Promise me!* You must do your *duty* and fulfill my *dream* for you . . . and for me. You must become a good American son to your American family. *Promise me!* You must *not* cause trouble! You must *obey* your American mother and father. You must study and learn and succeed . . . and become a rich American. Only if you do all that can you call yourself my *true* son . . . and a *real* man someday! And when you are a man, you can come back to me. That is my dream. . . . I will be waiting—always. That is *my* dream, and that is your *duty*. Do you understand, Young Nam-ya?"

"Yes, Mommy . . . I promise. . . . I'll become a real man and someday come back for you."

I promise, Mommy . . . I want to be your true son . . .

A few months before this cold January morning, Young Nam's mother had brought him here, to the KSS Reception Home. It was policy that all children placed for adoption would start living at the KSS Home, away from their birth mothers, to start the process of separation. In the official KSS literature that was sent to Ellen and Elmore Lindquist, it states that the purpose of the KSS Reception Home is to provide a variety of services for children who are to be adopted abroad and in need of short-term care before placement. At the time when Young Nam lived there, the Home, as Korea Social Service referred to its temporary living facility, consisted of four buildings:

> The buildings are on grounds that are pleasantly land-
> scaped, covering approximately one and a half acres. The
> main building houses an office, an interview room, an
> indoor playroom, a medical examination and treatment
> room, and an isolation room for new resident intakes and
> for patients. There are two buildings that house up to six

groups consisting of three to four children in each group. There is another building that serves as staff housing, which has an attached kitchen and storage. The outdoor play areas are extensive.

The staff consists of the superintendent and seven house-mothers and three housekeepers. The housemother is the staff person who provides day-to-day care for the children. A housemother is with the children during meals, at nighttime, through all routines, and provides physical care, affection, and discipline. At any time, there are four housemothers on duty who are responsible for the direct care of the children. Additionally, a medical consultant and a senior caseworker make weekly visits and supervise the housemothers through individual and group meetings. Community volunteers help with leisure activities and teach Western customs as well as English language for children of preschool age.

The daily schedule of activities at the Home is fully planned and executed according to a written, daily plan, starting from wake up at 6:30 a.m. until lights out at 8:30 p.m. Changes may be made if a staff member feels a modification may be in the interests of the children, but only after consultation with and approval by the superintendent.

This had been Young Nam's world for the last few months, until today. The boy never took his eyes off his mother as the bus pulled to a stop beside the children's group. The three women, including the American, would accompany the children as chaperones all the way to the final American destination for each child. All but a couple would end their journey some twenty-seven hours later at Gate 24, Red Concourse, Minneapolis-St. Paul International Airport, where they would meet their new mothers, fathers, and siblings who were from a racial, cultural, and social world that was a half a planet's distance away.

The children had no luggage.

Whatever they had on their bodies would be all that they would have as physical evidence of their lives in Korea. Everything else would only be the memories that would forever haunt them and the torn souls within their hearts that would never fully be made whole—ever.

As the children were herded onto the bus, Young Nam kept his eyes locked on his mother. In the bus's headlights, the boy could see that his mother's face was streaked with tears and that she was shaking slightly as she hugged her crossed arms in front of her body. She never stopped looking at her son, and the boy never took his eyes off his mother. As the bus driver closed the door behind the American woman who was the last one to climb on board, the interior lights were turned off and the bus lurched into motion, its tires crunching the frozen gravel of the driveway. Young Nam watched his mother recede and felt an absolute loneliness—an abandoned isolation and separateness—that was so crystal clear, pure, and intense, that he would always remember it and always keep a piece of it in his deepest core. The boy could feel the weight of the silver chain around his neck and pendant that hung from it. It was the last thing his mother had given him, and the pendant pressed cold against his chest above his heart.

Goodbye, Mommy . . . I promise . . . and I will not cry . . .

Dropping from number two to number three on the Billboard Top 100 list for the week ending January 10, 1970, was Peter, Paul & Mary's *Leaving on a Jet Plane*. Years later, even as he grew older, the words would always have a resonance with the little boy who was staring after his disappearing mother, whom he thought he would never see again.

Young Nam was tired, but strangely not really sleepy. He didn't understand that his body's biological clock was fifteen hours ahead of the local time. Most living creatures—animals, plants, and even some single celled organisms—have a set of physical, mental, or behavioral changes that follow a roughly twenty-four-hour cycle, responding primarily to light and darkness in an environment. This cycle is called the circadian rhythm, and it's driven by the organism's biological clock. The mismatch between a person's biological clock and the local time is what causes jet lag. Young Nam felt exhausted, tired, sleepy, and wide-awake all at the same time.

His ears hurt and sounds around him had gotten muffled and remote. It was dark outside the windows, and he could feel the jetliner descending. He had gone through this a few times already as he and his group had changed planes or had stops for refueling. He wasn't sure if this was one more such stop or not. In his tiredness, he yawned, and suddenly his ears opened up, the sounds around him popped into normal volume and distinction and the pain in his inner ears stopped. The boy had just discovered how to "pop" his ears. It would be a skill that he would employ beyond count in the years of his distant future.

He had never been on an airplane before, and the modernness and "Westernness" of it was shocking, thrilling, and bewildering. Other than American soldiers running in formation or handing out food through the barbed wire fencing around their bases, the boy had never seen so many Westerners. He thought of all Westerners as "American," because white Caucasian equaled "American" in his mind and understanding. The airplane speakers rang out with announcements every now and then. He only understood the announcements in Korean. He could hear that these announcements were repeated in at least two other languages, but they sounded like garbled noise to him.

Cathay Pacific is based in Hong Kong and therefore did all its announcements in the version of spoken Chinese native to Hong Kong, Cantonese, then would follow with one or more other languages, depending on the immediate departure and destination of a flight. The second language was always English, because the airline was founded by an Englishman and an Australian in 1946. On this flight, because of the departure from Seoul's Gimpo International Airport, the third language used for announcements was Korean.

What really was new for the little boy—among endless new things on the technological and creature comfort marvel that is a jetliner—was the number of American women. He had never before seen so many of these odd-looking people. They looked so very different from the big, hulking American soldiers that he was used to. But they were also so very different from the Korean girls and women he had known. They all had elaborate hair and all different colors. They wore a bewildering range of clothing, most of it very bright. And he noticed they had more jewelry than he knew could exist on a person: rings, bracelets, necklaces, earrings, brooches, pins, hair clips, and pendants—it didn't seem to end. They were all so obviously *rich*.

Rich Americans.

But they towered over Korean women and had pale painted faces with red-painted shallow cheeks. And weird large, staring eyes — Koreans rarely made eye contact; it was considered impolite— that were too round and painted with blue on the upper lid. And their noses were enormous and pointed, making the shape of their faces seem hatchet like to the boy, unlike the pleasant round normal features of Koreans that he was used to. And all of them, men and women, smelled of odd perfumes, colognes, and body odors. And all were very hairy to Young Nam, sporting masses of arm hair and knuckle hair and facial hair. Even some of the women had fuzzy hair on their upper lip.

All the Americans stared at the children when they had gotten on the plane to take their seats all together in a section toward the back of the plane. And they would keep taking staring glances at the children throughout the duration of each flight leg. Many of the older children had continued to cry, even after boarding the first airplane. Young Nam took great pride in the fact that he did not cry. He kept telling himself that he had a duty to his mother, and he needed to start fulfilling it now. He crammed down his feelings. He found that he had an ability to focus on the present. He had developed this as a way to deal with the taunts and attacks and isolation that he'd known all his life in Korea. It would prove to be a key component of his inner self that stayed and deepened through the years and would let him live with unseen wounds that many would never guess he carried.

An announcement had told everyone to buckle their seat belts and prepare for landing. The boy complied and waited in his seat. He had put his coat back on and had his hat—a Charlie Brown sort of one with earflaps that were fuzzy and could be folded up or worn down for extra warmth—in his hands. He had the strap of a little red bag across his chest. He had picked out the bag when the KSS housemothers had taken the children to shop for clothes and items in preparation for this trip. The boy's favorite color was blue, so it was odd that he had been attracted to this red bag. But it had an *anime*-like picture on it that had drawn him and captured his eye. The picture was of a girl in profile with blonde hair, big expressive *anime*-drawn eyes that sparkled, and elfin, fine features. He had picked it out and brought it to a housemother for purchase, and now he wore it on his shoulder. Inside were the only toys he had ever had: two Korean tops and the string to wrap around them to make them spin.

The big jet thumped and bounced as its wheels touched down on Runway 11 Right at Minneapolis-St. Paul International Airport. Local time was a bit before midnight, January 9. Because of the international date line, Young Nam had "gained" a day, allowing him to land at his destination the night of the "same" day in which he had departed. The temperature was minus eight degrees Fahrenheit. The night was crystal clear and the winds had died down to only a light breeze. The plane taxied to the terminal at MSP and pulled into gate 24, Red Concourse.

The little boy followed up the aisle of the plane behind some of his group, the American chaperone leading the way, other children following behind Young Nam. Some of the children were speculating on whether they would be getting onto yet another plane. Young Nam was so small that his world right now was just a forest of legs. But something in the way that the American chaperone was carrying herself and gesturing gave the boy the gut feeling that this was the final stop.

And suddenly he was frightened. At least the chaperones had been familiar: two of them were part of the KSS staff. He realized that somewhere outside of this plane waited complete strangers who would have total power over him. He would be alone with no one whom he knew to turn to, in a land that was strange beyond his understanding, where he spoke not one word of the language. As he shuffled along up the airplane's aisle among the forest of moving legs, surrounded by strange, hulking, hairy people, their odd, sometimes gag-inducing smells and their growing volume of gibberish, his fear at the truth of his reality closed its fist around his heart and squeezed it, shooting up his blood pressure and his runaway fear. He reached the plane's door and stepped into the enclosed, but unheated Jetway and the January air hit him. He put on his Charlie Brown hat and walked with leaden legs up the Jetway ramp, jostled and pushed by the other children around him.

Without warning, the little boy came to an open set of aluminum-framed, glass double doors that were clipped open and walked through.

There were bright flashes and popping sounds and a throng of people and a tremendous volume of unintelligible vocalizations. Young Nam's fear escalated further and his heart was pounding in his ears. The line of children disintegrated in front of him and broke into groups of big Americans who pushed their way forward and took by the hand or lifted up the children in front of him.

He stood all alone, it seemed, when someone loomed up in front of him. He looked up and saw an American woman with blonde hair and blue eyes, a long high nose, and perfectly shaped lips that were painted red. He could see the earnestness and intentness in those eyes. And something else.

Ellen had talked with some of the other expectant, adoptive mothers while waiting the long hours for the plane's delayed arrival. But somehow, the conversations seemed almost inappropriate. There was a puppy-pound feel to the whole scene that seemed wrong because they were here not to pick up their puppies, but to pick up human beings. As the time went on, the conversations tapered off as each waiting, pending parent grappled with his or her own anxieties and mixed emotions.

It seemed to take forever for the first passengers to file out of the plane. Body after body, people with jet lag and tired faces and dragging gaits shuffled past Ellen and the other waiting families.

Suddenly, a momentary hush went through the waiting group as a woman with an LSS emblem on her collar stepped through the concourse gate door carrying an infant. Immediately following her was a small Asian child—and another, and another, and more. The hush passed when someone shouted.

"That's him!"

"There she is!"

"There's Hyun Jun!"

"Oh my goodness. She's right over there!"

And people pushed forward as flashcubes popped and splattered blinding moments of light at the children. Ellen's pulse was coursing and her adrenalin was quickening her breathing.

This is it. This is real! Please, Lord, let my love be enough . . . let there be enough love in my heart for it to be enough . . . please Lord!

Then she saw a tiny boy who looked frightened and lost with a bright red bag hanging across his little shoulder. Ellen had looked and studied the only one, colored photo that she had of Young Nam. She had stared at and worried and wondered what was behind the squinting, unsmiling eyes in the photo. The boy's face was carved in Ellen's visual nerves, and she knew that it was him.

She heard Elmore's big bass voice.

"Ellen, I think that's him."

And it was.

Ellen stepped forward in front of the boy. She knelt down and reached forward and touched the boy's two shoulders with her hands. The boy looked up at her with striking green eyes.

Ellen Lindquist then knew.

She could feel the rush of it inside her, like an explosion. It expanded and filled her whole being. It made her flushed and red cheeked. She felt a joy and a sense of life that she had not known since the birth of her Carla, but somehow different and more surprising. She felt that her heart would burst, and that she would splatter this tsunami of emotion in a flooding gush all around her.

She could see the fright in those green innocent eyes, the confusion, the terror. It twisted something inside her to see the look in this tiny boy's eyes as she felt the great welling up of warmth within her. It was a desire so strong that it shocked her. This was truly a love beyond all understanding and surely a gift from God.

I can do this!

She knew then that she had more than enough love. She made a promise to herself as she pulled the small boy, now looking down and not meeting her gaze, to her and lifted him up and kissed him on his cheek. Just then, a flash popped off over her left shoulder. Elmore had taken a photo.

It would show a boy being held in the arms of a woman who was looking at him intently. The boy wore a Charlie Brown hat and was looking down with a wary and uncertain expression on his face. And in the moment that was captured in the flash of a Kodak instamatic, Ellen was promising in her heart and before her God, that she would love this boy—that would be easy—and that she would do whatever it took to take away that fear, that terror she saw in the soul of this tiny lost boy and banish it from his eyes. She promised that he would be her son in every way and in all ways and for always.

Lord, let him be all that William might have been . . . and thank you, Lord, for choosing me for this task . . .and for the love you've filled within me . . .

What the photo could not show was what the little boy was feeling inside. It could not show that the fear and confusion that had been mounting in his little heart as he had walked up a cold Jetway and into a crowded concourse had suddenly retreated when his eyes had met the bright blue eyes of Ellen Lindquist and he was lifted up and held and kissed. The boy saw tears that were making those eyes seem brighter and sparklier and somehow, those tears made this woman who was holding him human and real. His feelings, which the photo could not show, planted a seed that would grow into a love and awe for the woman who held him and kissed his cheek.

And he felt safe. Finally.

Chapter 38

Noah

DECEMBER 1981, BUSAN

Noah listened to the announcement over the ship's PA system. "Attention, please. Passengers should collect all of their belongings and move to the disembarkation points. The ship will be docking in fifteen minutes. Disembarkation will commence in thirty minutes. Attention, please. Passengers . . ."

As the announcement repeated itself, Noah zipped up his duffle bag and headed down the passageway that led to the ladders to take him to the main deck and the disembarkation point. Noah had been thinking about the last time he had seen his Korean mother shrinking into the predawn darkness with tears streaming down her face and the desolation of his loneliness as he rode away on a bus never to return to the life he had known. As he walked, his thoughts kept churning over many memories and old, scabbed-over wounds. The ache of that day's lonely desolation throbbed back into his heart.

What if she isn't there waiting for me? I promised to come back for her when I became a man, but I'm not yet . . . I can't take her back to America with me now . . . but what if she's poor and destitute? What do I owe her? What is my duty now?

The thoughts and anxieties chased each other like a cat chasing its tail in endless, pointless circles. There were no answers for these questions yet he was powerless not to keep asking them. Noah reached the main deck and got in line behind the queuing passengers waiting for the ship to complete its docking at the ferry terminal in Busan. Other passengers filed in behind Noah and they could all feel the shudders of the vessel as it was brought alongside the commercial ferry pier. Line handlers could be seen through the main deck windows pulling mooring lines to place over docking bollards on the pier.

Noah watched the mooring and gazed around the queued passengers surrounding him. His eye focused on a woman holding a child's hand, waiting a few feet ahead of him in line. He had been about the child's age when he had last seen his mother. He thought about how his mother had told him that he had been cowardly to try to take his life when he was five.

But it occurred to Noah that where he had failed, his mother had succeeded in killing the child he had been. Whoever that long ago little boy was, he had been mortally wounded on a jetliner over the Pacific Ocean, and his rapid, final death was consummated during a midnight drive through a Minnesota winter to a small town in the Minnesota River Valley. While the boy who had boarded that airplane was unknowingly dying, someone new and undefined had begun to emerge as the boy had walked through a Jetway gate to the blinding flashes of photos that would be taped into scrapbooks. When he had met Ellen Lindquist's gaze and felt the energy of her presence, he had felt that all that he had been, all that had been his life, would soon be forever dead and gone. A new life and a new identity stretched out ahead of him, and it started with being picked up and kissed by Ellen Lindquist and then being surrounded by the Lindquist family.

Time is change . . . the movement of a clock's hand . . . but some change is far more profound . . . I wonder, is it a different measure of time if the change is more drastic and irreversible?

Noah pondered this as the line started moving and he started walking toward a mother who no longer was and a meeting for which he'd longed . . . and feared.

And what had happened to her after I was taken away on a bus that dark, cold January morning? What has been her life since and what is she like now?

H ee Ae knew that she was going insane. She welcomed the cold and the dark and embraced their hold.

She had not eaten anything in nearly two weeks. She was unwashed and didn't care. All she did was sit alone in her room, at times crying uncontrollably. She sat all day and stared at nothing and did nothing, other than chain-smoke her black market, American cigarettes. And now she was down to her last pack. And down to her last couple of bottles of soju. Hee Ae had used up all her meager reserves of cash on buying the liquor to keep herself numb.

But it wasn't numbing enough. Nothing seemed to dull the wrenching ache in her chest, her stomach, her head, her feet, her limbs—the pain of her agony was all pervasive.

Young Nam-ya! Oh my little boy! What have I done? What was I thinking? It hurts so much. Oh God, it hurts so bad! I want him back! Oh, God . . .

She sat and hugged herself and rocked back and forth mumbling in her inebriation and manifest insanity. Hee Ae sometimes could see her son, right there in the room with her. Sometimes she could see him so clearly and talk to him and he would smile his smile and flash his green eyes. Then suddenly he would vanish and she would remember that she no longer had a small son. That she was alone. That she had, for all practical purposes, killed her boy. She couldn't bear the pain of knowing that she would never see him again, never know what would become of him. And she would drink more.

She had been drunk for two weeks straight. She had repeatedly vomited and passed out, only to reawaken to the unbearable pain of her soul and the pounding pain of too much alcohol.

She had watched the taillights of the bus drive away into the dawning morning through the blurring tears that she could not contain. She was not alone. All the women were crying, even the KSS staff. Once the bus had turned out of the KSS gates and disappeared from sight, the finality, irreversibility, and tragedy of the moment struck her. Hee Ae felt a yawning chasm open inside her and stretch a hollowness that had no bounds, and it started to suck her sanity into its lightless depths almost from the start.

Mr. Paik and the accompanying KSS staff attempted to comfort the weeping and sobbing mothers. Mr. Paik was an educated man, a graduate of Korea National University—the Harvard of Korea. He took on the KSS directorship because of his Christian beliefs and his administrative talents. Moments, such as this morning, were very bittersweet for him. He was convinced that each of the children who was put on that bus represented a miracle caused by God; that God gave strangers—thousands of miles away—the willingness to open their homes, their lives, and their hearts to a child that otherwise would have had no future with any opportunity or promise. But he could also feel the pain and inconsolable sorrow of the mothers who stood around him this day. He knew it would mean almost nothing and that his words would be little remembered or appreciated. But his faith and his own aching heart pushed him to express his fervent belief in the ultimate good that would come out of today.

"As you know, I am a Christian. I know that there is nothing I can say to diminish the pain you are feeling right now. But I do want to say 'thank you' to each one of you, for your sacrifice, strength, and love. I believe that God has given you the strength and the wisdom—and enough true love of your child—to do your duty as a mother. Each of you has put the life of your child ahead of your needs and wants, above your pain of loss. I believe, as much as I believe that there is a true heaven that awaits us all, that God will bless you and your son or daughter for the sacrifice that you have made."

Paik paused and looked around. The women, still crying in silence, were politely listening to him, their Korean culture so strongly ingrained in them to give deference to educated authority—especially when it was male authority—that they pretended to listen, despite their consuming internal agonies.

"Please, I invite each of you to join me and my staff to a breakfast that we have prepared for you. I know that many of you have long travels ahead of you and the breakfast will be needed."

Paik gestured with his arm outstretched, sweeping it from the group of women toward the building that had the staff dining room, and he bowed. Mrs. Young led the way, similarly gesturing with her arm as the other staff women joined her, each bowing, gesturing, and moving along the drive toward the dining room.

Hee Ae had followed too blank and void filled to resist or have any thought other than to follow where she was led. She ate robotically, and there was little conversation other than the staff making short, perfunctory comments about the food as it was served and passed. After the meal, KSS provided a van and took most of the women to Seoul Station, the main train terminal in Seoul. The train ride from Seoul to Munsan Village was one long blur of strangers' faces, too-frequent stops, and the press of embarking and debarking passengers. Once she got to a window seat, Hee Ae stared uncomprendingly out the train's window at the landscape gliding past.

You've done your duty . . . this is the best thing for his future . . .

She kept repeating these thoughts and smoking her cigarettes, one after another, through the long train ride and through her numb walk through the cold January day back to her little room.

And then she started drinking. And never stopped.

Now it was two weeks later and she knew, based on the hallucinations, her inability to focus on anything or care about anything, that her rationality and mind had slipped further into the void inside her, and that all she wanted to do was to go further into it and to stop her unbearable pain.

The weather had taken a turn and plunged below zero as a cold, high-pressure air mass had slid down from the Arctic Circle north of Siberia. The wind was gusting from the northwest and the temperature was twenty below. In her drunken and nearly psychotic state, Hee Ae waited until sunset and took her bottles with her and walked out into the gathering dark with only a single layer of thin clothing on. She stumbled and tripped up the same path that her son had followed when he had gone looking for food and found instead his murdered landlord. Hee Ae was headed to that very spot. She was drinking from an open bottle as she swayed and trudged through the closing darkness along the snowy path. She had decided that she would not live through the night. She had heard that freezing was not a bad way to die. With the sun's setting and the onset of night, the temperature dropped further. By the time Hee Ae had reached the weeds and shrubs that were off the side of the little-used path where her son had stumbled upon the fixed dead eyes of the old man, the temperature had dropped to minus thirty.

She sat down in the snow. She was shivering uncontrollably and could barely get the bottle to her lips and drain it. She shakingly opened the next bottle, her cold hands barely able to grasp the twist-off cap. As her core temperature fell, she became hypothermic and her body reached its maximum shivering response. She decided to lie down in the blowing snow and tried to lie still. Other than the wind, there was a dead silence in the darkening night. She could hear the beat of her heart in her eardrums. Her heat began to drain away more rapidly; fifty percent of Hee Ae's heat loss was through her head. The cold started to make its penetration felt through pain in her extremities. She drank more from the soju bottle and felt a sense of warmth.

Alcohol dilates the little blood vessels near one's skin, the capillaries, sending blood to the surface of one's skin and giving the sensation of warmth. But as the blood is brought to the surface by the alcohol, Hee Ae's body heat was actually being more rapidly dissipated. As her body temperature continued to fall, the cold rendered her brain much less efficient. In the current conditions, Hee Ae's core temperature would have been falling about one degree every thirty to forty minutes, but because of the alcohol, she lost heat much faster. Extreme apathy hit her at ninety-one degrees, and a pervasive stupor beyond her inebriation arrived and increased at ninety degrees and lower. Her final coherent thought:

The pain is gone . . . I'm sorry my Young Nam-ya . . . please still love me . . .

Hee Ae passed out and by the time her core temperature had fallen to eighty-eight degrees, her body had stopped its unconscious attempts to warm itself by shivering. Her blood had thickened due to the freezing of the water inside it, and her metabolism had fallen by more than thirty percent.

At around eighty-six degrees, her heart, its electrical impulses short-circuited by freezing nerve tissues, became arrhythmic, meaning it stopped beating regularly and started to jerk in random spasms.

She would be found in the morning by a pair of Buddhist monks out to visit the burial site further down the trail, empty soju bottles lying near her, the flesh of her limbs waxy and stiff as old taffy; her pulse would be nonexistent, her eyes open and staring and fixed, her pupils would be unresponsive to light.

But cold, as deadly as it is, can sometimes work miracles.

Noah had just cleared customs, getting his passport stamped by the stoic-faced Korean immigration officer. He was unsmilingly waved through, and the officer gestured to the person next in line. He was channeled through a set of exit doors that led into the international arrivals waiting area at the Busan ferry terminal. Noah was met by a sea of black hair and Asian faces, pressed against the ropes that were strung some twenty feet away from the doors. He turned to his right and followed others who had just exited from customs, toward the exit gap in the limiting ropes. He saw no one he recognized, and saw no one who seemed to be waiting for him.

As he walked into the waiting area beyond the ropes, with his duffle bag's strap slung over his shoulder, he stopped and scanned the crowd. His heart threatened to strangle him as it seemed to crowd into his Adam's apple.

Jesus . . . she's not here.

The disappointment was physical and raw. He had come all this way. Relived all those painful memories and wrung out the limits of his soul, only to be left standing blank and alone.

What did you expect, Noah? A brass band and ticker tape? You're an idiot . . .

He kept turning and wandering in circles, searching the uniform sea of black hair, dark eyes, and expressionless Asian features.

"Young Nam!"

A throaty female voice rang out, and people turned in the direction of the sound, including Noah. Pushing past a knot of people, a tiny old woman came trot-shuffling forward directly toward Noah. He immediately recognized her. Her face was much more weathered, wrinkled, and lined, but it definitely was her.

It was his mother.

The woman who had been his whole universe when he was a tiny, frightened, starving child. She had been his air, his water, his sun; and he had literally tried to die to make her happy. Before he could respond or react, she was on him and hugging him tightly.

"Young Nam! Young Nam! Young Nam!"

She kept repeating his name, and she was crying and gripping her arms around his waist in a tight hug. The first thought that popped into Noah's head was:

She's so small!

Noah's Korean mother barely reached four feet eight inches. In his memories, she had been a towering person, a shadowing figure who loomed larger than anything or anyone in his world. It was shocking to now see her as she really was. A simple, small, peasant woman. Human, real, madly hugging him. The intensity of her hugging and grasping of Noah and her repeated, unending shout-ing of his Korean name were drawing stares and attention from people around the two of them.

Noah hugged her back. He had the most indescribable mix of feelings. He would not have been able to articulate what he felt. There was relief that she had actually come. There was triumph in completing a long trail of clues and steps to actually find her. And there were the old feelings that he had crammed down for all those years, when he had forced himself to only feel in the pres-ent and never the past. He could feel a bond that only can come through birth and touch and smell and dependence between a newborn and his mother. His yearning for her when he was so small came roaring back. Noah threw his arms around her tiny shoulders and held her tight.

And the name, in Korean, that he had known her by, popped into his head and through his lips.

"Omma!"

Mommy!

An eighteen-year-old Korean normally would not use that word to refer to his mother, but it was the only word, the only name that he had known her by. The two of them held each other, swaying back and forth and calling each other's names. They were sur-rounded by a roiling sea of hurrying people, dragging luggage and small children. But mother and grown son were oblivious to the bustling mass of humanity that flowed around them, each lost in his or her thoughts, wonder, and indescribable emotions. Some of the nearby people gave curious stares before moving on with their lives and destinations. Noah wasn't sure how long he had held her when they finally released each other.

Noah's mother stepped back and took full stock of her son. It had been twelve years since that heart-tearing, pre-dawn morning when her son had left on a jet plane. Noah could see her smiling and looking approvingly up at him. And he looked at her. Noah realized that he was seeing her in two separate ways simultaneously.

There was a lens in his perception that still saw her through his six-year-old perspective; she was his mommy and the emotions that went with that were surging fully through his being. However, at the same time, he was seeing her as a total stranger and a foreigner, as an American would perceive a small, wrinkled, elderly Asian woman whom he had never truly met. There was a part of his mind that told him that he knew nothing of who this woman really was. He didn't know her favorite color, her preferred food, her friendships, her family, her work history, her humor, her beliefs—nothing.

Noah's "mommy" was not a full human being, but a memory of the prevailing, elemental force in his very young life. Little children do not perceive their parents as people, as having pet peeves and limited perspectives, jealousies, aspirations, hopes, failed dreams, and resigned acceptances. The desperate need and love he had felt for her as a small child still was within him, because that little boy's memories, dreams, hurts, and fears were still in him.

As he looked at Lee Hee Ae, Noah realized that Lee Young Nam would always love his mother with all his heart, and that heart would always burn with a desire to be her true, dutiful son. But in a shocking, utterly unexpected flash of revelation, Noah Lindquist understood with every part of his reasoning, heart, and eternal soul a simple truth.

Noah Lindquist was not Lee Young Nam.

The hurts and pains of Young Nam were not the hurts and pains of Noah and vice versa. The little boy who left on a jet plane twelve years ago never landed. The beginning of Noah Lindquist was when he had landed and was met by Noah's mother, Noah's father, and Noah's sisters and brother, and Noah's world.

"People only can know you and you are only real to them because of what they see. You are who you are because of what people see you do."

Noah remembered the words of his mother, Ellen. Noah and Young Nam were related, but like stepsiblings, with different mothers. Young Nam had spoken a different language, ate different food, thought different thoughts, and perceived the world very differently. And his actions had been the actions of a small foreign child perceived by a foreign society. Noah was American and spoke English, thought as an American, perceived the world through American filters, and was perceived by an American society. His Americanness was validated by the fact that in Japan, and now here in Korea, he was clearly perceived as an American. He knew, as never before, who he was and who he was not. And he no longer felt torn at all. He was Noah Lindquist: American.

It was a stunning revelation for Noah.

All the more so because it happened in a crowded ferry boat terminal arrivals lobby in Busan, South Korea, ten thousand miles away from American soil.

He was just starting to wonder if his Korean mother understood what he now understood—that he was not her little Young Nam; that the little boy would never come back—when she asked Noah, in fluent Japanese:

"Anata-no namae wa nan desuka? Anata wa moh Young Nam ja nain deshyoo, neh . . ."

What is your name? You're no longer Young Nam, it seems . . .

Lee Hee Ae had grown up under Japanese occupation. What little education she had received had been all in Japanese. If Noah had not applied for a Rotary International Exchange scholarship, been selected, and had not chosen Japan, he would never have learned to speak Japanese. And therefore, would not have been able to speak with his Korean mother. His Korean mother and he were able to communicate directly because she could still speak the language of her oppressors, and Noah could speak the language of the magical culture of his student exchange.

"Boku-no namae wa Noah Lindquist desu."

My name is Noah Lindquist.

"I am so very pleased and happy to meet you, Noah. You have grown into a fine, handsome young man. You look like a movie star!"

She laughed as she said the last, and Noah could see that his Korean mother was missing a few teeth. Noah laughed as well, and they departed the arrivals lobby, Noah carrying his duffle bag off one shoulder and Hee Ae gripping his other arm and staying close. They had a train to catch that would take them from Busan to Munsan-Ri, an eight-hour journey that would give them the time needed to catch up and start to learn about who each was. Noah would meet his cousin, whom Brad Jackman had met at the Munsan train station, and stay with his mother at his uncle's home in Munsan. Hee Ae would take him around and reintroduce him to many people who were still living in Munsan, who had known Young Nam and now marveled at meeting Noah Lindquist.

Lee Hee Ae would also share with Noah what had happened to her after he was sent off to America, who she was now and the profound transformation—a literal rebirth—that she had been through.

Chapter 39

Noah

A s the Citation V taxied to a stop near the GAT terminal at Mankato Regional Airport, Mike handed Noah his suit coat. "Here you go, Mr. Lindquist. I trust your flight was okay?"

"Thanks, Mike. Yes, great flight."

"Glad to hear it. I'll bring your roller bag around to you once you're down the steps outside. And . . . just confirming, we'll be back to pick you up at 1:30 p.m. tomorrow afternoon to take you back to Hartsfield."

"Sounds good, Mike. Thanks."

Noah put on his tailor-made suit coat and pulled his silk tie knot tight. When traveling on business, which he would be starting tomorrow, he found that by wearing one of his business suits, he was able to have one more change of business attire available than what he could pack in his Tumi roller bag, and the suit he wore usually stayed less wrinkled than the ones that were packed. He'd become an expert carry-on packer and could fit an amazing amount of clothing, shoes, socks, and toiletries in a roller bag that fit in any overhead compartment on any plane worldwide.

Plus, he wanted to look good for his mother.

This is the last time she'll see me . . . forever . . .

Noah picked up his briefcase. He walked down the plane's aisle, which was high enough that he could stand fully upright. Before turning to deplane, Noah stuck his head into the cockpit.

"Thanks, Captain. Great flight and baby-smooth landing."

"Thanks, Mr. Lindquist. I try to please."

"I'll see you tomorrow afternoon. Thanks again."

"Take care . . . and . . . our thoughts and prayers are with you, Mr. Lindquist. Debbie told us what's happening."

"Thank you, Captain Nelson."

Noah gave a nod of his head, turned and exited the plane's door on its port—left when facing forward—side and stepped into the pleasant Minnesota air that smelled of fields and freshly mown grass, and walked down the plane's steps.

The sky was hazy as the barometer continued to fall since its high of 29.98 inches, heading to its low of 29.74 inches later in the evening. The temperature was a slightly cool seventy degrees and would not get above seventy-three degrees today. There was a black Ford Explorer parked about twenty feet away toward the exit gate in the fencing that surrounded the airport. There was a woman in a pantsuit standing next to the vehicle, presumably the driver.

The plane's copilot brought Noah's Tumi bag to him as he descended the steps onto the tarmac.

"Here's your bag."

Mike pulled the handle up and locked it for Noah.

"Thanks, Mike."

"Mr. Lindquist, my father passed away from cancer last year. I know how hard it is. Know that my thoughts are with you . . . let me know if you'd like anything special for the flight back tomorrow . . . it would be our pleasure to get whatever you'd like."

The copilot looked directly into Noah's eyes, and Noah could see the genuine concern and outreach. He was grateful for the words and the sentiment, but his insides were wracked with tension and mounting anxiety.

"Thanks, Mike. I'll see you tomorrow."

Noah shook the man's hand and turned to walk to the SUV and found that the woman was standing next to him to take his bag and escort him to the SUV. Her name was Jackie and she made small talk, to which Noah politely listened, but he was too consumed with his thoughts to meaningfully participate in the conversation. It was only a short fifteen-minute drive until she dropped him off at his destination.

Elmore opened the door after Noah had rung the bell. His parents now lived in a two-bedroom condo in St. Peter at a building that was filled with retirees who needed minimal assistance. It was housing for independent-living elderly, but had a minimal staff on site, just in case anyone might need some assistance. His mother had made the decision some seven years earlier to downsize and sell the house in which Noah had grown up. She had said that she and Elmore wanted to make this decision on their terms and not when demanded by health or other circumstances, and that she wanted to redeploy their resources to allow her and Elmore to travel. And they did. They traveled seemingly nonstop all over the country and the world, until Ellen's cancer treatments brought the travel to a halt.

"Hi, Dad."

"Well! Hello, Son! Välkommen hem!"

"Thanks, Dad."

Noah stepped through the open door and shook his father's outstretched hand. Elmore's big hand swallowed Noah's and gave it a firm grip.

"I see you brought something for your mother," eyeing the huge bouquet of roses and lilies that Noah was carrying. "Ellen! Sweetheart! Noah is here! How was the flight, Son?"

"Fine, Dad. How's Mom?"

"She's feeling a little better today. She's not having to use as much of the morphine drip, so I think she'll be pretty clear when you talk to her."

Noah noticed that his father looked tired and had pronounced bags under his eyes. His whole face was sagging and drooping more than he'd ever seen.

God, he looks so sad . . . and worn . . .

"Here, put your bags over here, and I'll put those flowers on the table by the window. Your mother is going to like them. Why don't you go on back to the bedroom and visit with your mother."

Noah walked into his parents' bedroom and saw his mother lying in bed; there was an IV stand with two clear bags hanging next to the bed. He guessed that one was simple fluids for hydration and nutrients, the other was the morphine that she could control and direct into her veins to manage her unending pain. He was shocked at how gaunt, hollow, and emaciated she was. Her yellow, jaundiced coloring added to her alarming appearance. Her blue eyes were very sunken into their sockets as she looked toward Noah when he entered. He had never seen her like this. Ellen Lindquist had always been so put together, everything matched, coordinated, accessorized, and in its place. Always the picture of effortless perfection and efficiency in a feminine, coiffed sort of way.

But not now. It was very clear that she was dying. Noah felt his gut tighten and his heart compress.

But despite the jaundiced yellowing of the whites, his mother's eyes were still bright, intelligent, and earnest.

"Hi, Mom . . . it's great to see you."

"It's good to see you, too, Noah!"

She beamed at him and her smile transformed her face. As gaunt and jaundiced and sunken as it was, something of the pert, pretty, blonde all-American girl came through. Her smile shot a ray of warmth and love for his mother through Noah that never failed to succeed in making him stand a little straighter and feel the way he did when Ellen used to clap loudly and long at his piano recitals in grade school, because it was the smile she had given him so many times in his past when she had radiated her pride and joy in something he had done.

Noah saw that his parents had pictures of all their children and grandchildren on the walls of the bedroom. He saw the official photo of himself that was taken for his Navy commissioning, fourteen years earlier. His green eyes were looking directly into the camera, and he sat behind a polished desk in his Navy officer dress white uniform—choker whites—crisply starched and gleaming, with gold buttons and black with gold braid shoulder boards. His hands were crossed in front of him and on the desk next to his hands was his white, black, and gold-braided officer cap sitting on top of his white uniform gloves. His sword lay across the desk, gleaming in its gold and bone handle and gold braid.

Noah remembered her smile and sparkling blue eyes when he graduated from college and a day later, was commissioned an officer in the United States Navy by an act of Congress. He had stood in front of his Uncle Andy, who was dressed in his old, formal dress whites that still fit him perfectly—his chest filled with medals from WWII through Vietnam. Noah had stood and raised his hand along with Lt. Commander Andy Swenson, who administered the oath of office, and repeated the words of the oath.

"To support and defend the Constitution of the United States of America against all enemies, foreign and domestic; that I will bear true faith and allegiance to the same."

His mother had beamed and smiled, and her sparkling bright blue eyes radiated her energy, efficiency, and her pride, especially when she came up and removed his midshipman shoulder boards and replaced them with the epaulettes of a commissioned officer on the shoulders of his starched dress whites.

The essence of that smile shone warm and radiant from the now cancer-gaunt, emaciated face of his mother.

"I'm so glad that you came, Noah. I like that suit on you. It looks like you're taking good care of yourself . . . "

"Thanks . . . of course I'd come, Mom . . . as I told you and Dad, I have to fly to Brussels tomorrow, that's why I'm all suited up."

"And here I thought you'd dressed up for me!"

She managed to give a soft rendition of her signature laugh and ending decrescendo.

"Oohhhh deeaaaarrrrrr."

Just then, Noah's dad poked his head through the door.

"Can I get you anything, Sweetheart? Noah, how about a cup of coffee? I just made a fresh pot with the Mr. Coffee."

"I'm fine, Dear, maybe some chipped ice though."

Elmore had reluctantly given up his beloved instant Folgers crystals when everyone seemed to have shifted to drip coffee makers in the mid-1980s. Even though Mr. Coffee sold over a million units in 1974, it took Elmore a decade to give up his tried and true coffee crystals. The drip coffee maker did, however, let Elmore Lindquist expand upon his skills in boiling water.

"Sure, Dad. I'd love a cup. Black is fine. No cream or sugar. Thanks."

As Elmore strode toward the kitchen, Noah turned back to his mother.

"Mom, are you in much pain? Is there anything I can do for you?"

She didn't answer for a minute, searching Noah's face and her thoughts before answering.

"Noah, you know I don't like it when people go on about me . . . yes, the pain is pretty constant, but a little better today. Liver failure is a painful process, but the morphine helps . . . and your dad's attention is a great comfort . . . "

"Well, I'm glad that you're not doing any more clinical trials."

"Me too, but I would choose do it again if I could . . . no regrets on my part, but I think it was hard on your father. You know how I feel about making every day count, and I know that someday, at some point, someone will be cured of their disease in some small part because of what I did . . . that I will have added to the success of this new type of treatment.

"Noah, I know that you have been very successful in so many ways and that you have earned your MBA and worked hard for your positions . . . and . . . I'm glad to share with you how very proud of you I am."

She beamed her magic smile again at Noah.

"I know where you came from, better than anyone but you and your birth mother . . . but what matters ultimately is not where you came from or how far you go . . . what matters is what you do now . . .

"Only God can exist *throughout* all time and *at* all times. Noah, we can exist only now. Remember what I told you—you are what you do—but the *key* thing about this truth, Noah, is that you can only *do*—act—*now*, in the present. We cannot act in the past. It's forever fixed. We may not be around or able to act in the future. Only in the present, only now, can we make a choice and choose to do, to act."

Ellen shifted in the bed, a wince of pain contorting her face before it passed and she regained a position of relative comfort. As the liver fails, the body begins to retain toxins and fluids, causing the limbs to swell and making any position painful.

Jesus H. Christ! I know that everyone dies . . . and some will die of liver failure . . . but, God! Why her? Why assign such a painful death to her? If anyone deserves to pass peacefully in her sleep, isn't it Mom?

But he also knew that if God was the type to ask for volunteers—because somebody had to die a painful death—that his mother would be likely to raise her hand.

Can I ever live up to her example?

Noah was listening to what his mother was saying, because he knew that she was intentionally not taking much morphine so that she would be coherent. It made him ashamed and torn to think that he was in any way the reason that she was enduring more pain than she needed to.

The least I can do is listen fully.

"Mom, why don't you take some of the medicine?"

"I'm fine, Noah . . . I'm just worried that you may be losing sight of what really matters . . . don't take this the wrong way. I'm not criticizing you about your having to go do your business trip tomorrow. I don't want you to be putting your life on hold for me, and I appreciate your coming to visit.

"You need to work to make a living, and I am very proud of how well you're doing that . . . just remember that you work to live and not the other way around . . . okay?"

Noah nodded. He could tell that the morphine was in her system, although his mother was good about teaching things—the best way to fold a shirt or best cleaning technique to remove a certain stain—she usually was not an exhorting type, not really a "heart-to-heart" talk sort of person. It would have been too against the deep Swedish emotional reserve. So her opening up and talking in this way probably had something to do with the meds, or so Noah thought.

"Many will acknowledge that it's not what we get in life that matters, but what we are willing to give . . . but, *my* point is more basic . . . *willing* to give is not the same as *actually* giving . . . and only when we give *now*, in the present, does it matter. It's the only place we exist—the present.

"Make sure that you are doing the right thing in the present; to be proud of each 'now,' Noah, and you will have a past—which is just all of our prior 'nows'—that is truly worthy and the potential of a future that you won't fear . . . don't get too proud of things and achievements, Noah. Instead, be proud of your actions."

"I'll try, Mom . . . I know I owe so much to you and Dad."

"Oh, stop it, Noah! You owe your dad and me nothing! Like each of us, you owe only the Lord for the blessings he has given to all of us . . . besides, you came to us as a grown boy. I've read that by the time children are six, they have learned ninety percent of everything they will learn in life, so give the Lord the credit."

It was time for Noah to interrupt.

"Wait a minute, Mom. All the values that I have are because of you and Dad! Not only have both of you taught me so much, but you lived what you taught, you always set the example. Plus, your children—my brother and sisters—all taught me and demonstrated the values you and Dad set. I would be nothing like who I am, but for you and Dad! And I'm not talking about the physical and material environment you provided. But it was things like all the Christmases and everything else you provided, the moral and the spiritual—the intangible invisible —things that you provided by the fact of who you are.

"Yes, I have a birth mother, but you're the one that has taught me and molded me; the lessons you taught me are the ones I turn to every day, from how I put away my underwear to how I respond to my boss and my own fears and hopes! And Dad is the *only* man I have ever called "father." He is the only man who has shown me through his example what a real man is and does. The example of the two of you shows me what a husband and wife should be and do.

"Dad told me not to disagree with you, Mom, but on this point, I have to. It may be true that a human being learns ninety percent of everything by the age of six, but that ten percent was what truly made me; it was the crucial element."

Noah's emotions were taking sway of him and sweeping him along. He couldn't believe that he was saying all this. This was not the sort of conversation that ever went on in the Lindquist household. Swedes were too stifled to express emotions—certainly not openly vulnerable ones—to each other. Most things usually never went spoken. But his agony and sense of pending loss—starkly painted in the emaciation and waste that was in his mother's face and body—was driving the words stampeding out of his thoughts and heart.

"Human beings share ninety-seven percent of our DNA with chimpanzees, but I think you would agree that that three percent makes all the difference in the world. It's what makes us human . . . and what you and Dad gave me, taught me, and demonstrated daily to me is what makes me, me . . . and I adore you for giving me such a gift. I love you, Mom, for giving me "me" by giving so much of yourself to me."

Noah suddenly stopped talking, and his mother simply looked at him, oddly. An awkward silence hung between them unexpectedly.

Just then, Elmore returned to the bedroom with a cup of coffee for Noah and a plastic cup with crushed ice for his wife.

"Sorry, Sweetheart, it took me a bit to crush the ice the way you like it."

He set the cup down on the bedside stand, next to the IV pole. The awkward moment evaporated with the familiar boom and presence of Elmore in the room.

"Thanks, Dear."

As his father turned to hand him the coffee, Noah thought that his mother looked suddenly exhausted.

"Thanks, Dad. Mom, why don't I let you rest a little and we can visit more a bit later? I can catch up with Dad for a bit."

Ellen grimaced again and this time she pushed the button that would release some of the morphine drip and let some of the opiate into her vein to cushion the pain that clearly was draining her. She closed her eyes and nodded. And whispered.

"Sure, Noah . . . and . . . thank you . . . for . . . for what you said. Remember what I said . . . "

"I will, Mom."

And he would. Always.

Chapter 40

Hee Ae and Noah

Y ou're a *nun*?" Eighteen-year-old Noah Lindquist was sitting across from his Korean mother on the train headed to Munsan from Busan. There was a small foldout tray between them. On it were some snacks that Noah had purchased for them as the woman with the snack cart had passed: dried squid and dried persimmons. Each also had a glass of hot barley tea. Outside the window, the Korean winter landscape blurred past.

"Yes," Hee Ae made the simple reply.

"But how did this happen and why?"

Lee Hee Ae began by telling Noah about what happened after that cold winter morning, after she watched him taken away in a bus. She explained how the pain of that morning didn't lessen, but grew worse and eventually all consuming. She had never experienced such emotional pain—and she was no stranger to anguish, hurt, and loss. She shared with her son, now grown a foreigner and a young man, that she ended up unable to endure the pain and sought to end it by ending her life. She described the winter night where she went off to die on a mountain trail. When she finished telling Noah about freezing to death that night, Noah interrupted.

"What! You died? But you're obviously not dead!"

Maybe my Japanese—or hers—is not working here. I must have misunderstood! Noah was confused.

"Yes. I died that night. The next morning, I was found frozen to death by two Buddhist monks. Through them, the power of

Mahayana Buddha brought me back from the dead and breathed life into me."

The lowest recorded core temperature in a surviving adult human being is 60.8 degrees. It is even lower for children. In Canada in 1994, a two-year-old girl survived after being found frozen with a core body temperature of 57 degrees. Freezing slows the body's metabolism and can put it into a state of near suspended animation. Cardiologists and neurosurgeons use this knowledge when conducting certain heart and brain surgeries. When in this state, the heart rarely beats and the body can stay undamaged for hours. The key to survival for those who are in this suspended state is, first, being identified as not truly dead and, second, being skillfully revived.

The monks who had found Lee Hee Ae were familiar with metabolic slowing, both through meditation and through the fact that many monks often were nearly frozen in their meditations in frigid conditions. Therefore, they carefully listened—long and patiently—for any sounds of a heartbeat. And finally the monk with his ear pressed to Hee Ae's chest heard a slow, faint "thu-lump." And after waiting, again another, very faint.

One monk went to the nearest military camp, because he knew that there would be medical facilities and doctors. The other stayed with Hee Ae, having first wrapped her up in the long robes and coats they had been wearing and pressing his body next to the frozen woman. Military medicine is quite familiar with injuries and death from cold exposure, especially in Korea. The most famous battle during the Korean War was the battle of the "Frozen Chosin" where many men died from freezing. The monk who had left brought back emergency medical personnel who transported Hee Ae to a military hospital where she was successfully revived.

Hee Ae had only a grade school education. To her, she had been brought back from the dead, and only god—the Mahayana

Buddha—the all powerful, timeless spirit that brings enlightenment and freedom from suffering to all sentient creatures was responsible. Her reasoning was simple: She remembered dying and then she was found by Mahayana Buddhist monks. Therefore, the Great Buddha had sent his monks to find her and bring her back to life.

Hee Ae explained that after she recovered, she found that she felt reborn. She gave up alcohol and tobacco and offered herself in the service of the Buddhist temple from which the two monks had come. It turned out that their home temple was in Taegu. So she entered herself as a novice and worked at sweeping and other menial jobs. And she had stayed living and working at this temple since then. She was too uneducated to become a true nun, but she had found a spirituality that she had never been taught or possessed and committed her life to her god, to serving others as they sought enlightenment and release from suffering, because Buddha had given her a new life and had released her from her demons, her suffering.

"Unbelievable," Noah whispered, now staring out the train's window, trying to figure out what to believe. Certainly, the old woman who was his little-boyhood mother seemed to believe completely, and radiated an obvious sincerity and transparency about the truth of what she believed.

But he had to say what was now burning within him, the revelation that had struck him just after the explosion of emotions that occurred when they had been reunited at the ferry terminal, among a moving throng of strangers.

"But, Omma. You made me promise to come back for you and take you back to America . . . but, but I was just a little boy . . . and I'm still a student . . . so . . . and even if I could . . . I'm not sure how my parents—my American mother and father—would feel. I know that you told me it was my duty as your true son but . . . but, I'm not your Young Nam anymore . . . and . . ."

Noah's words hung there in the space between him and his birth mother. There was silence for a long time. Noah's Korean mother looked intently at her grown-up son. And Noah could not read the expression in her eyes or on her face. Then she spoke, very purposefully and with emphasis. And a warmth came through the chasm of nonfluent language that yawned between them.

"You are a man now, though still young. You still have your whole life in front of you; a life I dreamed of for you. You already are a scholar studying in a foreign country and also accepted at a university! You have no duty to me, Young Nam . . . I mean, Noah."

She said his American name awkwardly, like it didn't fit—in her mouth or on his face.

"I made you promise so that you would want to live . . . you were just a small child and you were understanding things wrongly . . . I wanted you to think that your duty was to take care of me so that you would live and succeed. I never meant for you to keep the promise I made you make. No real mother would force such a burden on her small son.

"You have a different mother now . . . and a father, who raised you and taught you. You are no longer my son who was my little Young Nam. You are now a young man named Noah Lindquist and your American mother and father are now your true parents. Your duty is to them, for they have given you a life that I never could and made you the man you are. My dream came true. I have lived to see that I did not make a mistake; that my pain and suffering were not for nothing! Just like my duty is now to my Buddha who has given me my life and freed me, your duty is to your parents. Be a good son—to them.

"And then my little boy, Young Nam, the boy you once were, will have been the true son to me, his mother. You became all that I had hoped and dreamed he—you—would be . . . I did what I did, all of it, for you, because I so dearly loved you. But sometimes love is not enough . . . and until I was reborn, you alone were the only thing that I loved more than myself . . ."

Hee Ae reached across the little table, and in the rattle and swaying of the train, she grasped Noah's deformed, scarred left hand in both of her rough, calloused ones. She leaned over and kissed his hand, held in hers.

Hee Ae would stay true to her words, making no demands of him, while she continued to work and serve her Buddha and her beliefs. She and Noah would only stay remotely connected through occasional letters and only three additional reunions: when Noah visited Korea once as a US Navy officer, once as a global business executive, and once when he flew her to Atlanta so that she might finally see America with her own eyes. Noah would learn through a cousin that Hee Ae passed away in the summer of 2011. He would remember her words and her sacrifice and the gifts he fully understood and appreciated them to be.

As his tiny Korean mother held his scarred hand in hers and kissed it, tears were streaking their trails down Noah's cheeks. All the anxiety that had been built up on his journey to meet her suddenly was released and flowing as tears, and the little boy that Noah could still feel inside himself radiated a singular thought that throbbed in Noah's mind and reflected in the farthest corners of his heart:

I love you, Omma . . . thank you.

Chapter 41

Ellen and Noah

Noah felt the Citation leveling off after its leap into the sky from the cornfields of Minnesota. He had said good-bye to his dad. And good-bye to his mother. They had had some more time to talk, but discussed only normal things, especially when his sister Carla and her family came over to have dinner together. There was no way to know exactly how long his mother would hang on. She was insistent that she would die as she had lived: being a force of hope and support for her children, not someone that would stop or put a hold on their lives.

But the final good-bye, as he hugged his mother as she sat in a wheelchair in her condo's living room, was as hard a task as he'd ever faced. He knew that he would most likely never see again this amazing woman, this force of faith and purpose and service, the woman who had most made him the man he was. And so it would be. This was the last time he saw his mother alive. She had held him tight and had felt so frail. As Noah had turned a last time to wave as he got to the front door, he saw his mother's eyes bright and blue and sparkling, just like when he had first met them, nine minutes past midnight on a cold and clear and unforgettable January night. Some of that sparkle was from tears today—just like that first time. But she shot him that smile that belonged only to Ellen Lindquist.

She had handed him an envelope that simply had "Noah" written in Ellen's perfect cursive.

"Read this on your flight."

"I will, Mom. Good-bye."

"Good-bye, Noah."

Noah opened the envelope and there was a short note in his mother's hand and a yellowed, small article from the May 1970 American Lutheran Church Women's periodical, *Scope*. He read the note from his mother.

Dear Noah,

I'm not very good at expressing my feelings to my children, especially about how much I love each of you. It is the only thing I regret, my inability to fully express my love in words. I have saved the article from the ALCWs *Scope* all these years, thinking that I would share it with you someday, because it says what I felt but could never have said and certainly not so well.

Know that I am at peace with what is coming. I know that I will see my Heavenly Father and my Savior, Jesus. I know this because I had lost faith many years ago, when I had lost a son. But, God answered my prayers—not just with the blessings of the children He'd already given me and the ones He gave me after, but in the way He called me that led to you, and back to faith and His love. I had many doubts and fears answering His call. And, at times, I vainly tried to make you into my lost son, but God had His plans.

Long ago I had dreamed of getting my lost son back, but God gave you to us. A God that can know my dreams better than I and fulfill them in ways that I could not have imagined is one that I am happy to go to when He calls me to His home.

Remember, I have loved each of my children and always will. And you are my son.

Love always,

Mom

What Noah now felt so clearly was the depth of Ellen's personal love for him. But he realized she had known—as had his Korean mother—that her love alone would not have been enough. Noah understood now as never before that there is a greater love that transcends personal love. What had allowed him to survive his past and pursue a boundless future had been the love embodied in his mother's faith, her world, and her dreams—that she had given him all that she was as a person.

Through the watery blurriness of his tears, Noah took out the small page from the periodical. There was a title. The author is cited as Julie Ann Stine:

To the Little Boy in Korea Who Will Be Our Son

We have only your picture before us. As we look into your face we wonder what you will be like, what you are feeling and hoping.

Maybe you're a little scared, just as we. It can't be easy for a little boy to leave his friends, his country, his language and to move into a brand new life. It can't be easy for you to leave your mother, whatever the ties have been between you, and to step off a plane into the midst of a new family and a new mother.

I'm a little scared too, because I will be that new mother, but I look forward to loving you as I do my other children. I hope that you will learn to love me. But we're not guaranteed love in this adventure, are we?

You have been told that you are coming to your father's country, and so you are. We trust and pray that America will be good to you . . .

I find myself thinking much about your Korean mother these days, hoping that she has been good to you and that she has loved you much. Perhaps her greatest gift to you is a love big enough to let you go. I am ashamed before such love. I don't think I could be that strong.

We are ready, waiting for you to make your long trip to your new country, your new home, to us. Don't be scared. We'll be there when you get off the plane and although we won't be able to speak your language, we'll put our arms around you to show you our joy, and if you think it's alright I'll give you a kiss.

Your new Mom

The sleek jet arched across a cloudless sky, leaving contrails that gleamed white and misty in the thin, high air as it carried Noah Lindquist toward an unrevealed future, contained in the dreams of his two remarkable mothers. . . . And known for certain only by God.

Joel L. A. Peterson

As a first-time book author, writing has not been Joel L. A. Peterson's primary profession. In his book *Dreams of My Mothers*, he brings his unique background as a biracial international adoptee and combines it with his personal insights into multiple cultures and his professional experiences to create an exceptionally enthralling and inspirational story that engages and touches the hearts and thoughts of readers.

Peterson is the founder and CEO of Student Planning Services, LLC, a leader and paradigm-changing provider of comprehensive supplemental educational support services. At the same time, he continues to be the managing partner and CEO of Pintoresco Advisors, LLC. Previously Peterson was a US Navy officer, an executive with global corporations, and an insider in the elite world of global mergers and acquisitions. Peterson is a PhD pre-doc in Education Policy at Claremont Graduate University and earned his MBA from Virginia Tech and BA from the University of Virginia. He lives in the Los Angeles area with his wife, Darleen.

Learn more about Joel L. A. Peterson and *Dreams of My Mothers* at www.dreamsofmymothers.com and connect on Facebook.